Coursebook

Iwonna Dubicka
Marjorie Rosenberg
Bob Dignen
Mike Hogan
Lizzie Wright

B2 >

Business Partner

FT Publishing
FINANCIAL TIMES

GSE
Global Scale of English

Contents

Introduction for learners

Why...
Business Partner?

Our research talking to teachers and learners proved a few very obvious points.

1   People study business English in order to communicate more effectively in their workplace or to find a job in an international environment.

2   To achieve these goals, you need to improve your knowledge of English language as it is used in the workplace, but also develop key skills for the international workplace.

3   People studying business English have different priorities and amounts of study time. You therefore need a flexible course which you can adapt to suit your needs.

Business Partner has been developed to meet these needs by offering a flexible course, focused on delivering a balance of language and skills training that you can immediately use to improve your performance in your workplace, studies or job search.

Why...
skills training?

Language is only one aspect of successful communication. Effective communication also requires an understanding of different business situations and an awareness of different communication styles, especially when working across cultures.

In *Business Partner* we refer to 'Communication skills' and 'Business skills'. Every unit has a lesson on these two areas.

*   'Communication skills' (Lesson 3) means the soft skills you need to work effectively with people whose personality and culture may be different from your own. These include building relationships, handling difficult communicators and managing challenging feedback.

*   'Business skills' (Lesson 4) means the practical skills you need in different business situations, such as skills for taking part in meetings, presentations and negotiations.

Why...
authentic content?

In order to reflect the real world as closely as possible, *Business Partner* content is based on authentic videos and articles from leading media organisations such as the BBC, the NIKKEI Asian Review and the Financial Times. These offer a wealth of international business information as well as real examples of British, U.S. and non-native speaker English.

Why...
video content?

We all use video more and more to communicate and to find out about the world. This is reflected in *Business Partner*, which has two videos in every unit:

*   an authentic video package in Lesson 1, based on real-life video clips and interviews suitable for your level of English.

*   a dramatised communication skills video in Lesson 3 (see p.6 for more information).

Why...
flexible content?

This course has been developed so that you can adapt it to your own needs. Each unit and lesson works independently, so you can focus on the topics, lessons or skills which are most relevant to you and skip those which don't feel relevant to your needs right now.

You can then use the extra activities and additional materials in MyEnglishLab to work in more depth on the aspects that are important to you.

What's in the units?

Lesson outcome and self-assessment

Each lesson starts with a lesson outcome and ends with a short self-assessment section. The aim is to encourage you to think about the progress that you have made in relation to the lesson outcomes. More detailed self-assessment tasks and suggestions for extra practice are available in MyEnglishLab.

Vocabulary

The main topic vocabulary set is presented and practised in Lesson 1 of each unit, building on vocabulary from the authentic video. You will get lots of opportunities to use the vocabulary in discussions and group tasks.

Functional language

Functional language (such as managing bad news, discussing priorities, facilitating a discussion) gives you the capability to operate in real workplace situations in English. Three functional language sets are presented and practised in every unit: in Lessons 3, 4 and 5. You will practise the language in group speaking and writing tasks.

 In MyEnglishLab you will also find a Functional language bank so that you can quickly refer to lists of useful language when preparing for a business situation, such as a meeting, presentation or interview.

Grammar

The approach to grammar is flexible depending on whether you want to devote a significant amount of time to grammar or to focus on the consolidation of grammar only when you need to.

- There is one main grammar point in each unit, presented and practised in Lesson 2.
- There is a link from Lesson 5 to an optional second grammar point in MyEnglishLab – with short video presentations and interactive practice.

Both grammar points are supported by the Grammar reference section at the back of the coursebook (p.118). This provides a summary of meaning and form, with notes on usage or exceptions, and business English examples.

Listening and video

The course offers a wide variety of listening activities (based on both video and audio recordings) to help you develop your comprehension skills and to hear target language in context. All of the video and audio material is available in MyEnglishLab and includes a range of British, U.S. and non-native speaker English. Lessons 1 and 3 are based on video (as described above). In four of the eight units, Lesson 2 is based on audio. In all units, you also work with significant audio recordings in Lesson 4 and the Business workshop.

Reading

You will read authentic texts and articles from a variety of sources, particularly the Financial Times. Every unit has a main reading text with comprehension tasks. This appears either in Lesson 2 or in the Business workshop.

 In MyEnglishLab, you will also find a Reading bank which offers a longer reading text for every unit with comprehension activities.

Speaking

Collaborative speaking tasks appear at the end of Lessons 1, 3, 4 and the Business workshop in every unit. These tasks encourage you to use the target language and, where relevant, the target skill of the lesson. There are lots of opportunities to personalise these tasks to suit your own situation.

Writing

- Lesson 5 in every unit provides a model text and practice in a business writing skill. The course covers a wide range of genres such as proposals, reviews, blogs and emails, and for different purposes, including internal and external company communications, summarising, making requests and giving reasons.
- There are also short writing tasks in Lesson 2 which provide controlled practice of the target grammar.
- In MyEnglishLab, you will find a Writing bank which provides models of different types of business writing and useful phrases appropriate to your level of English.

Pronunciation

Two pronunciation points are presented and practised in every unit. Pronunciation points are linked to the content of the unit – usually to a video/audio presentation or to a grammar point. The pronunciation presentations and activities are at the back of the coursebook (p.112), with signposts from the relevant lessons. This section also includes an introduction to pronunciation with British and U.S. phonetic charts.

Reviews

There is a one-page review for each unit at the back of the coursebook (p.104). The review recycles and revises the key vocabulary, grammar and functional language presented in the unit.

 ## Signposts, cross-references and MyEnglishLab

T **Signposts for teachers** in each lesson indicate that there are extra activities in MyEnglishLab which can be printed or displayed on-screen. These activities can be used to extend a lesson or to focus in more depth on a particular section.

L **Signposts for learners** indicate that there are additional interactive activities in MyEnglishLab.

 → page 000
Cross-references refer to the Pronunciation bank and Grammar reference pages.

MyEnglishLab

Access to *MyEnglishLab* is given through a code printed on the inside front cover of this book. Depending on the version of the course that you are using, you will have access to one of the following options:

Digital Resources powered by MyEnglishLab including: downloadable coursebook resources, all video clips, all audio recordings, Lesson 3 additional interactive video activities, Lesson 5 interactive grammar presentation and practice, Reading bank, Functional language bank, Writing bank and My Self-assessment.

Full content of MyEnglishLab: all of the above plus the full self-study interactive workbook with automatic gradebook. Teachers can assign workbook activities as homework.

The **Global Scale of English (GSE)** is a standardised, granular scale from 10 to 90 which measures English language proficiency. The GSE Learning Objectives for Professional English are aligned with the Common European Framework of Reference (CEFR). Unlike the CEFR, which describes proficiency in terms of broad levels, the Global Scale of English identifies what a learner can do at each point on a more granular scale – and within a CEFR level. The scale is designed to motivate learners by demonstrating incremental progress in their language ability. The Global Scale of English forms the backbone for Pearson English course material and assessment.

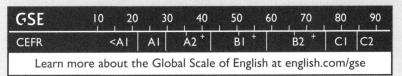

GSE	10	20	30	40	50	60	70	80	90
CEFR		<A1	A1	A2 +	B1 +	B2 +	C1	C2	

Learn more about the Global Scale of English at english.com/gse

COMMUNICATION SKILLS
Video introduction

Introduction

The Communication skills videos (in Lesson 3 of each unit) introduce you to the skills needed to interact successfully in international teams, with people who may have different communication styles due to culture or personality.

In each Communication skills lesson, you will:

1 watch a setup video which introduces the main characters and challenge of the lesson;

2 watch the main character approach the situation in two different ways (Options A and B);

3 answer questions about each approach before watching the conclusion.

There is a storyline running through the eight units, with the main characters appearing in different situations. Each clip, however, can be watched separately and each lesson done independently without the need to watch the preceding video clips.

Communication skills video storyline

- EN-Tek, which stands for Ethical Energy Technology, is a creative engineering start-up based in Cambridge, UK. EN-Tek develops cheap and innovative solar energy products that improve the lives of people in developing countries.
- Go Global is an investment capital organisation based in London which specialises in supporting innovative projects in developing countries.
- EN-Tek has been talking to Go Global because it needs a financial and business partner to help produce and sell its latest invention, a solar-powered water pump, in Bangladesh.
- The Go Global team suggest China as the production location as they are familiar with the manufacturers there, but EN-Tek want to produce the water pumps in Bangladesh in order to support the local community.
- Throughout the eight units of the book, we watch Go Global and EN-Tek negotiate their differences as they also face a range of challenges at different stages of the project.

Characters

Sanjit Singh (British Indian) En-Tek Lead Product Developer, (units: 1, 2, 4, 5, 6, 7, 8)
Claudio Lemos (Venezuelan) Go Global Key Account Manager (units: 1, 2, 3, 5, 6)
Katie Evans (Australian) EN-Tek Sales and Marketing Manager (units: 1, 3, 4, 5, 7, 8)
Emma Berg (Norwegian) Financial Analyst at Go Global (units: 1, 2, 6, 7)
Paweł Polkowski (Polish) Production Manager at EN-Tek (units: 2, 3, 4, 8)
Gary Roach (Canadian) Independent marketing consultant/expert (unit 4)
Claire James (Canadian) Go Global Marketing Specialist (units: 4, 5)

Video context by unit

1 Building relationships
Video synopsis: *Sanjit is unsure of the relationship with Go Global. Do they have the same values and goals?*

2 Team communication
Video synopsis: *EN-Tek and Go Global meet to discuss their differences of opinion regarding production location.*

3 Managing bad news
Video synopsis: *Katie receives some bad news. Paweł advises her on how to discuss this with Claudio.*

4 Handling difficult communicators
Video synopsis: *An independent marketing expert is brought in to offer advice on branding.*

5 Managing challenging feedback
Video synopsis: *Claudio and Sanjit have differences of opinion regarding sales figures.*

6 Transparency in business
Video synopsis: *Claudio has to decide how transparent to be regarding what might become a serious issue.*

7 Dealing with urgency
Video synopsis: *The teams need to communicate in order to address an urgent issue.*

8 Coaching and mentoring
Video synopsis: *Sanjit offers Katie a role in EN-Tek's next business venture.*

Corporate culture

1 >

'If the highest aim of a captain were to preserve his ship, he would keep it in port forever.'

Thomas Aquinas, Italian philosopher

Unit overview

1.1 ▶ Workplace culture

Lead-in

1 **Read the definition and discuss these questions.**

1 Can you think of attitudes and beliefs that are shared in your culture?
2 How would this affect the workplace? Discuss these points.
- how people feel about hierarchy in companies
- the way people behave and communicate
- what people wear
- how people work together
3 What other aspects of work might be affected by culture?

cul•ture /ˈkʌltʃə/ n [C,U] the attitudes or beliefs that are shared and accepted by a particular group of people or in a particular organisation

VIDEO

2A **You are going to watch a programme about a company which feels it is important to treat all employees fairly and equally. Think of all the things the company might do to carry this out.**

Well, they could give everyone free lunches or more time off.

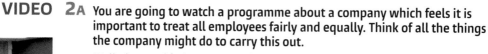

B ▶ 1.1.1   **Watch the video and find out what the company actually did.**

3 **Watch the video again and answer the questions.**

1 What exactly was the change that Gravity Payments made in their pay to employees?
2 How did this change help Korinne?
3 What was Alyssa able to do?
4 What did some senior staff do in response to the change and why?
5 How did this change directly affect the employees and the quality of their work?
6 What positive effect did the publicity about the increase in salaries have on the company?
7 What did one of their customers say about the change?
8 What did staff do to thank their boss?

4 **Work in pairs or small groups. Discuss these questions.**

1 What are some of the effects that corporate culture can have on the lives of employees?
2 How important is a high salary to you? Is it more important than a good working atmosphere?
3 What do you think motivates employees? What motivates you personally to work or study hard?
4 Do you think other companies should use Gravity Payments as a role model? Why / Why not?

 Teacher's resources: extra activities

 Teacher's resources: alternative video and extra activities

Vocabulary

Elements of corporate culture

5A **Match 1–4 with a–d to make sentences from the video.**

1 We talk about the 'culture' of a company – this might mean its dress code or
2 Dan Price announced the company's minimum salary would
3 We are going to have
4 They felt their skills and experience were not

   a go up to $70,000 a year.
   b recognised in the new more equal pay structure.
   c the way in which staff communicate with their managers.
   d a minimum $70,000 pay rate for everyone that works here.

B **Work in pairs. Look at the sentences in Exercise 5A again and underline the collocation* in each sentence which refers to corporate culture. What do the collocations mean?**

dress code – the type of clothes people are expected to wear

6 Decide if the definitions of the underlined words are correct. Correct the incorrect definitions.

1 <u>Company hierarchy</u> refers to staff organised on one level.
2 The <u>values</u> of a company are the amount of money the company is worth.
3 <u>Organisational behaviour</u> looks at how people in an organisation work together and how this affects the organisation as a whole.
4 A <u>good atmosphere</u> in a company means that employees can open the windows when they want to get fresh air.
5 A <u>strategy</u> is a plan for achieving an aim.
6 <u>Company structure</u> means that the company has a very strict hierarchy.
7 The <u>image</u> of a company refers to the TV commercials a company produces.
8 An <u>open-plan office</u> is one which does not have walls dividing it into separate rooms.
9 <u>Flexibility</u> refers to people or plans that can be changed easily to suit any new situation.

7 Complete the text using the words in the box.

atmosphere code flexibility image pay strategy structure values

Corporate culture is different from company to company but very often it is connected to the ¹_____ the company has. This affects the company ²_____ as well as the ³_____ rate. Some companies are more formal and have a specific dress ⁴_____ while others feel that it's important to have ⁵_____ in what people can wear. Asking employees for input when developing a(n) ⁶_____ for the future can make employees feel valued and can help to create a good ⁷_____ . Each company has to decide these issues for itself and they all go together to create the ⁸_____ the company has both internally and externally.

8A Work in pairs. How important is it to find out about the culture of a company before you begin to work there?

B Choose the elements of corporate culture in Exercises 5B and 6 that are most important for you and put them in order, starting with the most important. Then discuss your list with a partner.

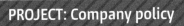
Teacher's resources: extra activities

➔ **page 114** See Pronunciation bank: Stress in compound nouns

---

▶ PROJECT: Company policy

9A Work in small groups. Discuss these questions.
- Which values and/or company practices do you think cause most problems in companies in your country? Explain why and give examples where possible.
- Have you had personal experience of this yourself? If so, give examples.

B Work in pairs and decide on a fictional company in which you work. Choose three of the problem areas in Exercise 9A and decide what your company policy is on each. Prepare a 'mini welcome' for new employees. Include explanations about why your company has these policies.

C Regroup with someone from another pair. Roleplay your two different 'mini welcomes'. Take turns to be the employee who explains company policy and the new employee who listens and asks questions.

Self-assessment
- How successfully have you achieved the lesson outcome? Give yourself a score from 0 (I need more practice) to 5 (I know this well).
- Go to My Self-assessment in MyEnglishLab to reflect on what you have learnt.

1.2 Employee retention

Lead-in **1** Match the words and phrases in the box with the definitions.

| diverse work   menial tasks   promotion   sabbatical   work–life balance |

1 work which needs little skill
2 a fixed period of time when someone takes an agreed break from their job
3 the fact of getting a better paid, more responsible job
4 a situation in which you are able to give the right amount of time and effort to your work and to your personal life outside work
5 jobs that are very different from each other

2 Work in pairs or small groups. Discuss the terms in Exercise 1 and what you think their effect might be on employee retention.

Reading **3** Read the article quickly. What details does it mention about the terms in Exercise 1? What other ideas for employee retention does the article mention?

The text says work–life balance efforts could make young employees' lives better.

4 Read the article again and decide if these sentences are *true* (T) or *false* (F).
1 All bankers at Morgan Stanley are given month-long paid sabbaticals.
2 JP Morgan expects its employees to dress formally for work.
3 People outside the banking world think that not working Friday nights or having two free hours every week are very important for employees.
4 Goldman Sachs has a specific strategy to keep their junior bankers.
5 Millennials do not put salary first when looking for a job.
6 Employees need to believe that they have a future at a company in order to support it.

 Teacher's resources: extra activities

FT

Investment banks' work-life balance schemes will pay off

Morgan Stanley has started extending its month-long paid sabbatical scheme to include some of its junior bankers. Credit Suisse is now
5 encouraging all European employees to take Friday night and Saturday morning off. Swiss rival UBS tells employees to keep two hours a week for personal business. And JP Morgan
10 has told employees to take every weekend off unless they are working on a 'live deal' and has relaxed its dress code to business casual. Non-bankers may think these work-life
15 balance efforts (Friday nights off? two hours a week?) are not important, but they may truly improve the lives of many young Wall Street and City employees.
20 The banks are also taking specific steps to improve retention at a time when other companies have been stealing some of their young stars. Goldman Sachs was the first to
25 implement a junior banker retention initiative that included quicker promotions, fewer menial tasks and more diverse work. Royal Bank of Scotland and Barclays soon followed.
30 By the time they have been there a few months, Morgan Stanley will have told top first-year analysts that they have a bright future at the bank.
35 These retention efforts make sense when looking at the recent survey of millennials in 25 countries by Manpower Group. It found that 21- to 36-year-olds prioritise job security above everything except money when
40 choosing their employers. Before the financial crisis, Wall Street could use huge bonuses to keep its young employees. Now the banks have to find other ways to do this. Humane
45 working environments and proper career development are a good way to start.

Hopefully, within a few years these new initiatives will have made
50 a real difference. The best way to get staff members to care whether their employer will be doing business in the future is to convince them that they will be working there when it
55 happens.

Grammar Future Continuous and Future Perfect Simple

5A **Look at the underlined verb forms in the article and match them with the definitions of the Future Continuous and Future Perfect Simple.**

---

1 We use the **Future Continuous** to talk about an event that will be taking place at a particular moment in the future.

action starts before and finishes after the point of reference

now   point of reference,   future
               e.g. next Friday at 5 p.m.

Next Friday I will be finishing the report.

2 We use the **Future Perfect Simple** to talk about events in the future which will be finished by a certain time.

action happens before the point of reference

now   point of reference,   future
               e.g. next Friday at 5 p.m.

By next Friday I will have finished the report.

B **What information can you find near the underlined verb forms in the article that tells you when each action will take place?**

By the time they have been there a few months, Morgan Stanley *will have told* top first-year analysts that they have a bright future at the bank.

C **How are the Future Continuous and the Future Perfect Simple formed?**
The Future Continuous is formed with ¹_____ + ²_____ + ³_____ participle.
The Future Perfect Simple is formed with ⁴_____ + ⁵_____ + ⁶_____ participle.

➡ **page 118** See Grammar reference: Future Continuous and Future Perfect Simple

6 **Complete the sentences with the Future Continuous or Future Perfect Simple forms of the verbs in the box. Consider if they will be in progress or will be finished.**

> change   do   improve   promote   rest   take

1 In April he _____ a month-long paid sabbatical.
2 My company has just announced that it _____ the office to an open-plan set-up over the weekend. It's a shame, I really liked my quiet office.
3 I'm glad the weekend is here. By next Monday I _____ and should have the energy for a very busy week.
4 By the middle of the next decade, investment banks _____ the working conditions of their employees a great deal and should see better rates of employee retention.
5 There is a lot of discussion about what companies _____ in the future to keep their employees motivated.
6 Our boss said that by the end of the year they _____ a number of junior staff to more senior positions.

T Teacher's resources: extra activities

➡ **page 114** See Pronunciation bank: Auxiliary verbs in the Future Continuous and Future Perfect Simple

Speaking **7A** **Complete the questions with the Future Continuous or Future Perfect Simple forms of the verbs in brackets.**

1 What kind of job _____ (you / look for) in the future? Do you think this is going to be an exciting field?
2 By the end of the year what _____ (you / finish)? Is there anything _____ (you / not finish)?
3 What do you think _____ (you / do) ten years from now?
4 By the time you have worked for five (more) years, what position _____ (you / reach)? And in ten years?

B **In pairs or small groups, ask and answer the questions in Exercise 7A.**

Self-assessment
- How successfully have you achieved the lesson outcome? Give yourself a score from 0 (I need more practice) to 5 (I know this well).
- Go to My Self-assessment in MyEnglishLab to reflect on what you have learnt.

COMMUNICATION SKILLS
Building relationships

Lesson outcome	Learners are aware of different ways to build relationships and can use a range of phrases for building trust.

Lead-in

1 **In pairs, read the comments from two professionals and discuss the questions.**

1 Think of one potential advantage and disadvantage of each style.

2 How important do you think building trust is at work? Why?

> 'I trust people fast. I like to be open with people from the beginning and share information. I think focusing on common objectives also helps to build trust quickly and makes a team more efficient.'

> 'I don't really focus on trust at the start. I focus on getting my own job done. Relationships and trust building comes later after people prove they're competent and can deliver what the team needs.'

VIDEO

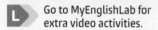

Go to MyEnglishLab for extra video activities.

2 ▶ 1.3.1 **EN-Tek and Go Global have entered into a partnership. Watch the video. What are Sanjit's three concerns about working with Go Global?**

3A **In small groups, discuss which is the best communication style (Option A or B) for Sanjit to use in the meeting with Go Global. Give reasons for your answers. As a class, decide which video to watch first.**

Option A – Focus on building trust and collaboration: Be open and ask questions to explore others' ideas. State clearly your respect for others' skills and commitment. Focus on positives and joint opportunity.

Option B – Focus on task completion and your own objectives: Explain your objectives. Ask questions to explore possible problems with completing the task.

B **Watch the videos in the sequence the class has decided, and answer the questions for each video.**

Option A ▶ 1.3.2
1 Which two topics does Claudio say are important to discuss?
2 Where do Go Global want to set up production?
3 According to Emma what are the major issues?
4 How does Sanjit remain open to others' ideas, stay positive about the working relationship and show respect for others' commitment?

Option B ▶ 1.3.3
1 At the beginning of the meeting, what does Sanjiit say he needs to know?
2 Why aren't the distribution partners good enough according to Emma?
3 How does Sanjit challenge Emma about her analysis of the situation?
4 How do we know Claudio understands and supports Sanjit's objective to go with local people?

4 **In pairs, discuss which approach you think was most effective in establishing a positive working relationship based on trust. Why?**

5 ▶ 1.3.4 **Watch the Conclusions section of the video and compare what is said with your answers in Exercise 4. Do you agree? Why / Why not?**

Reflection

6 **Think about the following questions. Then discuss your answers with a partner.**

1 Which of the two relationship building styles in Exercise 3 do you prefer? Why?

2 In which situations might you use your non-preferred style? Why?

Functional language

Building trust

7A Look at the strategies in the table for building trust with people you work with. Then complete the table with these phrases from the video.

a Could we help you [with that]?

b We both want to [go forward with this].

c I like your suggestion to [get more data].

d One way to solve this is [just] to [send our analyst].

e To be honest, I feel [a little] worried [about your proposal].

f I understand what you're saying about [distributors].

Focus on common objectives	Let's wait until we [have the detailed quality report] and decide together [next week]. 1 _____
Share ideas	Can I suggest that [I give an update on …]? 2 _____
Be open about thoughts and feelings	Frankly, I'm concerned that … 3 _____
Show empathy	I can see you're [concerned about …]. 4 _____
Offer support	Would it be [useful] for me to … ? 5 _____
Show trust in others	Based on [your experience], how do you think we can … ? 6 _____

B In your experience, what else can you say or do which can help to build trust with other people?

8 Complete the dialogue between an IT manager (Maria) and an external consultant (Ralf) using phrases a–f from Exercise 7A.

M: With these project delays, I don't see how we can possibly finish things on time.

R: I'm still very confident.

M: And, ¹_____ rising costs. We're currently 20 percent over budget.

R: ²_____ costs. This is a concern.

M: Exactly. And I really don't see what we can do about it.

R: OK, look. ³_____ reduce the time we're spending on testing.

M: Yes, ⁴_____ reduce your time. But you need to test as you develop things.

R: That's true. ⁵_____ develop software which works. But testing is expensive.

M: ⁶_____ with the testing? Some of our people could pick this up quickly.

R: That could work. We reduce costs, keep testing quality, and deliver on our promise.

M: OK, let's try this idea. Thanks, Ralf. I knew you'd come up with something.

Teacher's resources: extra activities

9A Work in pairs. You work at the same company and are meeting to decide which of two candidates (Alice Andrews or Mike Preston) will lead on a new project. Read your role cards and prepare for the meeting. Remember the strategies from Exercise 7A.

Student A: Read the role card on page 126.
Student B: Read the role card on page 128.

B Hold your meetings and try to arrive at a decision.

C At the end, discuss how you could improve the communication.

> TASK

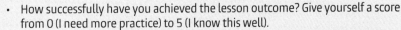

Self-assessment

- How successfully have you achieved the lesson outcome? Give yourself a score from 0 (I need more practice) to 5 (I know this well).
- Go to My Self-assessment in MyEnglishLab to reflect on what you have learnt.

1.4 > BUSINESS SKILLS
Presenting yourself

Lead-in   **1**   Work in pairs. Read the blog about presenting yourself. Which idea in each section do you think is the most important? Why? Add your own ideas to the list of things to do when presenting yourself.

8 TIPS for presenting yourself to make an impact

First meetings with international colleagues give you the opportunity to present yourself formally and informally. Presenting yourself effectively can help you build long-term positive relationships.

STEP 1: Be proactive during informal personal introductions before a team meeting

1 Approach people proactively and enthusiastically, and present useful information about yourself.

2 Ask questions to show you are open and curious.

3 Find common points to build the relationship between yourself and others.

STEP 2: Build trust during the formal round of personal presentations to the team

4 Volunteer to begin the round of personal introductions to create a positive mood in the room.

5 Build trust in yourself by giving details about your role, expertise and experience.

6 Show commitment and say something positive about working with the people in the room in the future.

STEP 3: Close positively after the team meeting

7 Clearly show interest in what people have said during your first meeting with them.

8 Say goodbye to everyone. Offer support and express positive feelings about meeting again in the future.

Listening   **2A**   🔊 1.01   Listen to Sue Jacobs as she introduces herself to two new colleagues, Angela and Martin, just before a meeting for their new project team. Answer the questions.

     1 Where does Sue say she works?

     2 Which questions does she ask?

     3 What does Sue discover that all three have in common?

     4 How does she end the conversation?

   B   🔊 1.02   Now listen as Sue and her two colleagues present themselves formally during the meeting. What does each speaker say about the three topics below? Which personal presentation do you prefer, and why?

     • responsibility and experience

     • main area of expertise

     • thoughts about the project

   C   🔊 1.03   Listen as Sue says goodbye to her new colleagues and answer the questions.

     1 What does Sue want Angela to send her?

     2 What does she offer to do for Martin?

     3 How does Sue end the conversation?

   D   Work in pairs and discuss the questions.

     1 How well do you think Sue presented herself across the whole event? Why?

     2 Which of the blog tips do you think she used?

     3 In your experience, how effective will her presentation style be in different cultural contexts? Why?

Functional language **Self-presentation**

3A Look at these phrases used by Sue in Exercise 2. Match each phrase (a–j) with one of the tips in Exercise 1.

a I really liked what you said about [your approach to projects in Portugal].

b I'm happy to start [the introductions].

c I'm [Sue], from the [London] office.

d Oh really? Me, too.

e My current job is [Head of Financial Controlling in the UK].

f If you need any help with [tickets for the theatre …], just let me know.

g So do you [both] work [in local finance teams]?

h I know what you mean!

i I joined [Hansens at the beginning of last year].

j I'm really delighted to [be part of this team].

B Use phrases a–h to complete the personal presentation below.

a the job is quite stressful

b if you need my help in any way

c the main task was

d I'm proud to be involved

e I'm based in

f I used to work on

g it's going to be great working with you again

h I'm now responsible for implementing

So, my name's Mike Foley and ¹_____ the New York office. I've been with the company now for around five years. I've always worked in IT. In the past, ²_____ the service desk, that was my first job, mainly just for our U.S. operations. ³_____ troubleshooting some of the more complex issues. Since last year, I've been working far more internationally, mainly on projects, as ⁴_____ new software solutions at Group level. What else? OK, I have to travel quite a bit; probably 30 percent of my time is on the road to the USA, Canada and Latin American locations. I really enjoy it, but ⁵_____ at times. I have to say, I'm really excited to be working on this project. I know a couple of you, and ⁶_____ . I guess we all understand that this is a really important project for the company, and ⁷_____ . Just finally, ⁸_____ , don't hesitate to ask. I'm here to collaborate. Thank you.

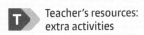
Teacher's resources: extra activities

C Prepare a similar introduction about yourself to a new project team using the phrases in Exercises 3A and B.

4A Work in small groups and read the information. Then choose an industry for your company.

> **TASK**

Professional context

You work for a leading company in your industry. You are at the company headquarters for a meeting to kick off a large innovation project. The project aims to bring staff from different levels and countries of the organisation together to brainstorm new product ideas.

B Prepare a professional identity for yourself using the template on page 126 and think about how you will present yourself to your group.

C Go back to your groups and roleplay the three stages of presenting yourself.

Step 1: Meet and present yourself informally to the people in your project team before the meeting.

Step 2: Present yourself formally to the team during the meeting.

Step 3: Say goodbye to your team members at the end of the meeting.

D At the end, vote for who gave the most inspirational personal presentation.

Self-assessment

- How successfully have you achieved the lesson outcome? Give yourself a score from 0 (I need more practice) to 5 (I know this well).
- Go to My Self-assessment in MyEnglishLab to reflect on what you have learnt.

Lesson outcome	Learners can plan and write an informative company news blog.

Lead-in

1 Read the blog about a company sabbatical policy. Find the extra word in each line.

Two months in the Caribbean?

by Sarah Deeks,
HR manager

1　Want time off from the work? Then you are sure to be delighted by our new initiative. We are

2　offering you the chance to have a 2-month sabbatical, returning back to your current position,

3　if you have worked with us for more than five years. Full salary is to be paid during which

4　the sabbatical providing for you do volunteer work or visit a country you have not been to

5　before. Staff who want to participate are expected to return to work and stay for at the least

6　six months. The HR team can talk to you through your sabbatical plan by offering advice,

7　answering your questions and preparing with a structured, pre-planned re-entry process

8　for your return. Although that it is exciting to be offered a sabbatical, you are likely to

9　have concerns about time away from work so don't be hesitate to contact us or click on

10　the link to find out if more about this exciting new programme.

Functional language

2A Complete the table using words from the blog.

Title/Introducing	Informing	Concluding
Two months in the Caribbean?	We are offering you the 3_____ to …	Although this is exciting, you are likely to have concerns …
Want time 1_____ from work?	Full 4_____ is to be paid if you …	Don't 6_____ to contact us …
Staff are sure to be 2_____ to learn that …	The HR team can help by 5_____ a structured re-entry process.	Click on the 7_____ to find out more about …

B Write these phrases in the correct place in the table in Exercise 2A.

> Great news!　We would welcome any comments you might have about …
> New opportunity for all staff!　Let us know if you wish to participate.
> The changes come into place next month.　The company is happy to announce that …
> If you are interested, please contact …　We are opening our new office in Ecuador.
> Why not take advantage of an exciting new scheme?

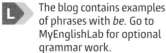

Teacher's resources: extra activities

The blog contains examples of phrases with *be*. Go to MyEnglishLab for optional grammar work.

➡ **page 118** See Grammar reference: Phrases with *be*

▶ TASK

3A Work in pairs. Turn to page 126, look at the spidergram and decide where the information should go in a blog. Think about how to introduce, inform and conclude effectively.

B Now write the blog in about 200 words.

C Exchange blogs with your partner. How different were they? Having read your partner's blog, how could you improve yours?

Self-assessment

- How successfully have you achieved the lesson outcome? Give yourself a score from 0 (I need more practice) to 5 (I know this well).
- Go to My Self-assessment in MyEnglishLab to reflect on what you have learnt.

Training and development

> 'The only thing worse than training your employees and having them leave is not training them and having them stay.'
>
> Henry Ford, founder
> Ford Motor Company

Unit overview

2.1 ▶ Learning on the job

Lesson outcome Learners can use vocabulary related to training and development.

Lead-in **1** **Discuss these questions.**

1 Read the definitions. Which do you think matches 'training' and which 'development'?

a the teaching or learning of a range of skills employees can use in a variety of positions and/or for future careers

b the process of teaching or being taught the skills for a particular job or activity

2 When do you think that on-the-job training for a particular position is necessary? Are there times it is not very important?

3 Does development of general business skills benefit the employees, the company or both? Why?

VIDEO **2** ▶ 2.1.1 **Watch the video. What type(s) of training and development does each trainee talk about?**

 ▶ Lucrece  ▶ Kina  ▶ Ashley

3 **Watch the video again and complete the notes about the three types of training mentioned.**

INDUCTION TRAINING
- To know the ¹_____ and its systems, policies, other colleagues
- To understand and feel a ²_____ of company culture
- Learning about company ³_____ and procedures

MENTORING
- Mentor should be an experienced ⁴_____
- Mentor offers support, usually on a ⁵_____ basis
- Mentors advise which skills to learn and which ⁶_____ to work in

ONLINE TRAINING
- Staff members can ⁷_____ it anytime and anywhere
- Can do it on any ⁸_____ – home computer or mobile phone.
- Some programs use both online and ⁹_____ sessions – blended learning

4 **Work in pairs or small groups. Are induction training, mentoring and online courses common in your country? Why / Why not?**

T Teacher's resources: extra activities

➔ **page 114** See Pronunciation bank: Stressing key words in sentences

Vocabulary **Training and development**

5 **Complete the sentences with words from the video.**

1 Training courses can help to drive c _ _ _ _ _ d _ _ _ _ _ _ _ _ _ _ .

2 A key part of the i _ _ _ _ _ _ _ _ p _ _ _ _ _ _ _ _ is to help new team members feel a part of the company's culture.

3 Mentoring can be used for specific j _ _ - r _ _ _ _ _ _ t _ _ _ _ _ _ _ or more general career development.

4 One of the really useful things about being a m _ _ _ _ _ is that my mentor introduces me to very important people in the industry.

5 An advantage of o _ _ _ _ _ c _ _ _ _ _ _ is that you can do them whenever, wherever.

6 Whatever type or d _ _ _ _ _ _ _ m _ _ _ _ _ a company uses, training and development opportunities are important for both staff and the company itself.

6A Match the sentence halves.

1 When a company needs to check the **standards** reached in training sessions

2 Employers are finding that making e-learning training available to employees

3 A person with **emotional intelligence** can

4 **Practical courses** are used to teach

5 A **skills set** comprises

6 **Competency** at a job can be learned

7 When there is **rapport** between people,

8 We generally begin with a

a adds to their **motivation** as they can access the courses when and where they like.

b skills for the workplace.

c it means that there is **understanding** and friendly agreement in a conversation.

d through both training and experience.

e **needs analysis** so that we know which training programmes to offer to which employee.

f what a person can or can't do.

g it can use **benchmarking** to do this.

h control their emotions and show empathy.

Teacher's resources: extra activities

B Work in pairs and discuss the meaning of the words in bold in Exercise 6A.

7 Complete the pairs of questions with the correct form of the word in capitals. Then discuss the questions with a partner.

MENTOR
1 Do you think that _____ programmes help junior staff to develop?
2 What do you think a _____ can learn from a more experienced staff member?

TRAIN
3 Is it better to have an external _____ for courses or can someone from the company take on this role?
4 What kinds of things do people learn in job-related _____ ?

ANALYSE
5 Should training programmes be based on what people said in a needs _____ questionnaire, or defined by their managers?
6 Should a mentor encourage a mentee to solve problems using _____ thinking or tell them what to do based on their own experience?

MOTIVATE
7 Why can it be difficult to find the _____ to learn while on the job?
8 What helps you to be _____ ?

> **PROJECT: Induction to a new job**

8A Work in pairs. You have been asked to prepare an induction programme for a company you know. Consider these points.

- what information new employees need
- how long the induction should last
- if the induction should be individual or in groups
- where the induction should be held
- if employees need an overview of the whole company or just their department
- how exactly the new recruit(s) should be taught about their new role

B Try out your ideas on another pair.

If you thought of the <u>same</u> institution, note down any interesting ideas the other pair had that you didn't think of.

If you thought of <u>different</u> institutions, make suggestions about what you would want to know if you began to work there.

C Go back into your original pairs and plan a short written programme for the induction day. Give a general idea of the sessions, their timing, where the different parts of the induction will take place and who will lead them.

Self-assessment

- How successfully have you achieved the lesson outcome? Give yourself a score from 0 (I need more practice) to 5 (I know this well).
- Go to My Self-assessment in MyEnglishLab to reflect on what you have learnt.

Lesson outcome	Learners can use modal verbs in the passive voice to talk about ability, (lack of) obligation, necessity, permission, possibility, prohibition and recommendation.

Lead-in

1 Look at the words and phrases in the Venn diagram. Work in pairs and discuss:
- how each word/phrase relates to training and development.
- why each word/phrase was put where it was.

  'Functional approach' is in 'training' because it would be used in one job or department.

TRAINING   EITHER TRAINING OR DEVELOPMENT   DEVELOPMENT

- functional approach
- job-orientated
- task-orientated
- _____
- _____

- blended learning
- in-house training
- _____

- cross-functional approach
- general business skills
- preparation for future challenges
- _____
- _____

2 Complete the Venn diagram using the words and phrases in the box. Can you think of any other terms or concepts that might fit into this diagram?

| external training   long-term goals   mentoring   preparation for career |
| short-term goals   skills specific to a job |

Listening

3A ◀)) 2.01   **Listen to a conversation between Mike, from the European Head Office of a large automotive manufacturer, and Teresa, the Brazilian HR Director. Why is Mike in Brazil and what does he speak with Teresa about?**

B Listen again. What do Mike and Teresa say about a) what 'training' is, b) what 'development' is and c) the methods used to deliver them?

4 Choose the correct option. Listen to the conversation again if necessary.

1 Mike wants to base the global strategy on
  a the training and development strategy in Brazil.
  b the approach at the company's biggest site.
  c best practices that are already in place in different countries.

2 Teresa thinks it is necessary to
  a have one person in charge of all HR Departments.
  b have one strategy for long-term and short-term goals.
  c tell Mike about the difference between training and development.

3 Teresa says that when delivering training they always have to
  a rent space outside the building.
  b prepare materials to hand out.
  c decide where the training should be held.

4 Development is best used when
  a it is necessary across departments.
  b employees are interested in business theory.
  c an employee is ready to grow.

5 Teresa points out that development
  a is always necessary for future careers.
  b is cross-functional.
  c is necessary before moving people from one department to another.

5 Work in pairs. Do you think companies should work more on developing new employees instead of those who have been with the company for a long time? Why / Why not?

Teacher's resources:
extra activities

Grammar Modals in the passive voice

6A 🔊 2.02 **Listen to these extracts from the conversation between Teresa and Mike and complete the sentences. Contractions count as one word.**

1 These training sessions _____ _____ to make sure …

2 The supplier might ask how a part _____ _____ _____ , so …

3 This _____ _____ _____ carefully …

4 And what other factors _____ _____ _____ _____ into account?

5 … specific skill training _____ always _____ as worthwhile.

6 It _____ _____ _____ without thinking carefully …

B Compare the six extracts in Exercise 6A. What do they all have in common? How are extracts 1 and 5 different from the others?

C Modals can be used to express ability, obligation, lack of obligation, necessity, permission, possibility, prohibition and recommendation. What is the function of the modal in each of the phrases in the box?

> can be used   could be improved   do not have to be trained   ought to be done
> have to be taken into account   might be moved   mustn't be decided
> needs to be developed   should be held   would be considered

'Can' in 'can be used' expresses ability or permission in the present.

➔ **page 118** See Grammar reference: Modals in the passive voice

7 Complete the text using the correct form of the words in brackets.

Training and development strategies [1]_____ (must / decide) by looking at both short- and long-term goals. The courses are often run by the HR Department and [2]_____ (need / budget) for. The overall strategies, however, [3]_____ (should / discuss) with the managing board as well. New recruits [4]_____ (may / expect) to take part in induction training which can last for several days in order to learn the skills they need for their jobs. Development is different as it is part of long-term goals and [5]_____ (would / consider) necessary for the future plans of the company. Those seen as future executives of the company [6]_____ (could / train) in leadership or communication skills. These would not be job-specific but [7]_____ (should / look at) as an investment in the future of both the employee and the company. In any case, all the options regarding both training and development [8]_____ (have / think) out carefully in line with the goals and long-term strategy of the company.

T Teacher's resources: extra activities

Speaking and writing **8A You have just taken over as one of the Managing Partners of a company. Everything seems to be a disaster. Make a list of things that need to be changed as soon as possible. Use the ideas in the box or your own ideas and passive modals where possible.**

> business clothes   coffee breaks   communication skills   computer systems
> IT skills   desks   food/meals   reports   tasks   telephone calls   workplace culture

Suitable business clothes need to be worn.

B Work in pairs and compare your lists. Prioritise the actions and discuss the specific steps that need to be taken.
A: Well, I think that suitable business clothes need to be worn by all staff at all times.
B: OK, I agree, but I think we should prioritise customer-facing staff.

C Write a short memo to staff outlining the key action points you discussed in Exercise 8B. Write 50–70 words.

Self-assessment • How successfully have you achieved the lesson outcome? Give yourself a score from 0 (I need more practice) to 5 (I know this well).
• Go to My Self-assessment in MyEnglishLab to reflect on what you have learnt.

Lesson outcome	Learners are aware of different ways to work in teams and can use a range of phrases for exchanging ideas.

Lead-in

1A In pairs, look at the diagrams which show two ways, or cultures, of working in teams. What do you think are the main features and advantages of each culture?

Team culture A   Team culture B

B ◀ 2.03 Listen to a team development consultant discussing team cultures. Compare what she says with your ideas from Exercise 1A.

C Overall, which team culture do you prefer? Why?

VIDEO

2 ▶ 2.3.1 Emma has received a report about quality at EN-Tek's preferred production site in Bangladesh. Watch as she discusses the findings with Claudio.

1 What is the main finding of the report from the auditor?
2 Who does Emma think should take the final decision on the location of production, and why?
3 Why does Claudio suggest a consultative approach?
4 What does Emma believe might happen if the wrong decision is made on location?
5 What does Claudio advise Emma to do?

L Go to MyEnglishLab for extra video activities.

3A In small groups, discuss which is the best approach (Option A or B) for Emma to use when she discusses the report findings with Sanjit and Paweł from EN-Tek. Give reasons for your answers. As a class, decide which video to watch first.

Option A – Individual expert role approach: Advise as an expert what the team should do. Focus on your own goals and make recommendations based on your own expertise; be convincing and persuade the team to accept your ideas.

Option B – Collective responsibility approach: Help the team to discuss and agree what to do. Focus on delivering shared goals; offer ideas and make suggestions; show openness and encourage people to discuss their ideas openly.

B Watch the videos in the sequence the class has decided, and answer the questions for each video.

Option A ▶ 2.3.2
1 What does Emma say is her role on the project?
2 What suggestion does the EN-Tek team make?
3 Is Emma open to their suggestion? How do we know?
4 How does Emma feel at the end of the meeting?

Option B ▶ 2.3.3
1 What does Sanjit say about the producers in Bangladesh?
2 Emma reminds everyone that they share the same objectives. What are they?
3 What suggestion does the EN-Tek team make?
4 Is Emma open to their suggestion? How do we know?
5 How does Emma feel at the end of the meeting?

4 In pairs, discuss the questions and agree what you can learn from Emma's experiences.
1 In what ways did Emma behave differently in the two videos? What happened as a result?
2 Which approach do you think will have the best outcome for the project and for the team?

5 ▶ 2.3.4 Watch the Conclusions section of the video and compare what is said with your answers in Exercise 4. Do you agree? Why / Why not?

Reflection

6 Think about the following questions. Then discuss your answers with a partner.
1 Look back at your answer to Exercise 1C. After watching the videos, would you still answer this question in the same way? Why / Why not?
2 What would help to make you feel comfortable working with your non-preferred style?

Functional language

Exchanging ideas

7A Match the phrases from the video (1–13) with the categories (a–e).

1. If I can add to that, [I think …].
2. Any thoughts [on that / on the matter]?
3. I think the best option [here] is [to be consultative …].
4. There are pros and cons of both [production locations / approaches].
5. What do you think we should do?
6. Why don't we [let my local guys try …]?
7. So shall we try [that]?
8. If we do that, then it will [lead to higher standards / make the decision easier].
9. Just picking up on what [Paweł] said, [why don't we …]?
10. Do we all agree with the idea to [run two pilots …]?
11. One option could be [to create a clearer and more detailed set of requirements].
12. What's the best way to [handle this]?
13. I (don't) think it makes sense [to look at the requirements again].

a Requesting ideas
b Contributing ideas
c Responding to ideas
d Developing ideas
e Moving from idea to decision

B Complete the extract from a sales team meeting using phrases from Exercise 7A.

Manuela: Tom, how are sales?

Tom: Not good. We're around 25 percent down on target.

Manuela: So, we need to increase sales. ¹_____ do? Jack?

Jack: ²_____ organise a special promotion? Customers like discounts.

Tom: I'm not sure. ³_____ we'll damage our margin. I prefer to cut staff.

Hugo: ⁴_____ Tom said about margins, why not talk to our suppliers and ask for a special discount? That could pay for the promotion.

Manuela: Good idea. OK, ⁵_____ that first? Jack, could you look into it more and report back?

8A Work in pairs. What would you suggest to the speaker in these situations? Use two or three phrases from Exercise 7A to contribute an idea and respond.

> 1 'The new guy in my team keeps missing deadlines. I'm the only one who's noticed.'

> 2 'I've been asked to go on a research trip. It's a great opportunity, but it's when I'm supposed to be visiting my parents in Australia.'

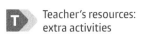

Teacher's resources: extra activities

B Choose one situation in Exercise 8A and continue the dialogue until you reach a decision. Use phrases from Exercise 7A.

❯**TASK**

9A Work in small groups and read the information.

> You and your colleagues have been asked to organise a team-building event at your place of work or study. You are going to discuss what type of event will be most successful in your department. Turn to page 126 for ideas.

B Individually, prepare your arguments for the ideas you agree and disagree with. Try to add your own ideas.

C Hold your discussions. One person should lead the discussion by requesting ideas at the beginning and trying to reach a decision at the end.

D Work with another group and compare your decisions. Did you use phrases from all five categories in Exercise 7A? What did you find difficult about the discussion?

Self-assessment

- How successfully have you achieved the lesson outcome? Give yourself a score from 0 (I need more practice) to 5 (I know this well).
- Go to My Self-assessment in MyEnglishLab to reflect on what you have learnt.

Facilitating a meeting

Lesson outcome	Learners are aware of ways to facilitate a discussion and can use a range of phrases to manage meetings.

Lead-in

1 Work in pairs. Read the definition of facilitation skills and answer the questions.

1 Which of the ideas in the text do you agree or disagree with? Why?

2 How far do you agree that everyone should share responsibility for facilitation? Why?

> 'Facilitation in a professional context is the art of leading discussions and meetings. It is a set of skills which guides people to discuss matters openly and productively. In practice, it means making sure everyone understands the objective of a discussion, helping people feel confident to express their ideas, helping people to listen to each other, ensuring all ideas are considered, and supporting people to come to the best decision. Without effective facilitation, meetings can become a waste of time. Most meetings have a facilitator but are often more effective if all the people at the meeting share responsibility and help to facilitate the discussion.'

Listening

2A ◆ 2.04 Listen to Takeshi Sakamoto as he facilitates the start of a meeting of learning and development experts in his company. The meeting is about possible changes to learning management in their organisation.

1 What does Takeshi define as the objective of the meeting?

2 What is his proposal for structuring the discussion?

3 What is Sam's suggestion and how does Takeshi handle this interruption?

4 What does Takeshi insist on at the end of the introduction? Why?

B ◆ 2.05 Listen as Takeshi and his colleagues discuss their options in more detail.

1 How does Takeshi respond to Sam's proposal to reduce spending on soft skills training?

2 Steve disagrees strongly with Sam. How does Takeshi handle this situation?

3 How does Takeshi involve Paula?

4 When Paula gives her opinion, how does Takeshi respond?

C ◆ 2.06 Listen as Takeshi moves the meeting to a decision.

1 Why does Takeshi interrupt Sam?

2 Which proposal does Takeshi make and why?

3 What feedback does he give the group as he closes the meeting?

D How well do you think Takeshi facilitated the discussion? Why? In your experience, would this style be effective to manage discussions in your own organisation? Why?

→ page 114 See Pronunciation bank: Linking between words

Functional language

Facilitating a discussion

3A At the beginning of the meeting, Takeshi worked hard to ensure that everyone participated in the conversation. Complete the phrases with the words in the box.

around	ensure	experience	hear	looking	off

Stating the objective	What we're ¹_____ to do [here] today is [to decide how to digitalise training].
Encouraging participation from all	As we discuss things, it's important for [everyone to speak up]. [Just] to ²_____ everyone can say something, [can we / let's …]. Can we go ³_____ the table first? Let's ⁴_____ everyone one by one, and then discuss.
Encouraging input from a specific person	Let's begin with you then, [Steve]. Can you kick us ⁵_____ ? [Paula] you have some ⁶_____ of [developing e-learning leadership training]. What do you think?

B Match the beginnings and endings of these sentences Takeshi used. Then decide which category in the table they belong to.

1 I agree [budget] is really important, but I want to
2 I think we actually agree that [there are good options for change here],
3 I realise that we (still) have different
4 Can I stop you there? [Buy-in] is definitely important, but I'm
5 It seems that there's a consensus

a afraid [time is pressing and we need to come to a decision ...].
b views on [some points].
c [to reduce spending on soft skills training].
d but [there are still a lot of details to work out ...].
e come to that [a little later / in a separate meeting].

Referring to agreement/ disagreement	
Managing how long people speak	

C Complete the phrases for the closing stages of a meeting using the words in the box.

proposal   progress   recap   round   step

Referring to follow-up actions	Perhaps the next [1]_____ would be to [look carefully at some of the risks].
	My [2]_____ would be that [you two work together on this].
	I'll email [3]_____ [some possible timings for the next meeting].
Summarising and closing	So, just to [4]_____ everything, ...
	I think we have made really good [5]_____ .

T Teacher's resources: extra activities

4A Work in groups of three. Read the scenario.

> **TASK**

You work for AIRCON, a Texas-based company which makes air conditioning units for sales in the USA. Following recent market research, the company has decided to expand into Europe – France and Germany – where there are big potential markets for your products.

The Managing Director of AIRCON has asked your team to evaluate some people management ideas created by the company's board to support internationalisation. Your task is to discuss some ideas, and decide which are most effective and cost-efficient.

B Read your role cards. Student A go to page 126 and Student B to page 129. Student C will be the meeting facilitator.

C When you are ready, roleplay the meeting to decide which ideas you agreed on.

Self-assessment

- How successfully have you achieved the lesson outcome? Give yourself a score from 0 (I need more practice) to 5 (I know this well).
- Go to My Self-assessment in MyEnglishLab to reflect on what you have learnt.

2.5 › WRITING
A training request

Lead-in

1 Read the email requesting a training course. Choose the correct option in italics. Then compare in pairs.

To: Walter Hernandez, HR Director
From: Anna Gayo, Design Project Team Leader
Subject: Training request

Dear Walter,

I am writing to request some more professional training. As I have just been ¹*employed / made* a project leader of a large team for the first time, I ²*believe / hope* that it is important to attend a project leadership training course. I have found an excellent course ³*offered / accessed* by Greyhouse University. It is a four-day course and offers a professional qualification upon successful ⁴*learning / completion*.

I realise that it is vital to develop my skills so that I can effectively ⁵*motivate / activate* my team and develop the most productive and efficient team ⁶*likely / possible*. ⁷*Furthermore / Further to*, I am interested in developing skills in order to ⁸*deal / handle* with conflict and the course provides training in this.

I would therefore like to attend this course in two weeks' time, if possible. My assistant is happy to cover for me during the course.

Please could you let me ⁹*know / see* if I can do it by tomorrow afternoon because registration for the course closes tomorrow evening. I attach full course details for your ¹⁰*knowledge / information*.

Kind regards,

Anna Gayo

Functional language

2A Complete the table using words from the email.

Requests
I am writing to ¹_____ some more professional training.
I would ²_____ like to attend …
Please ³_____ you let me know if …

Reasons
As I have just become project leader, it is ⁴_____ to attend a leadership course.
It is ⁵_____ to develop my skills, so that I can manage the team effectively.
Because registration closes soon …
I am ⁶_____ in developing my skills for dealing with conflict.

B In which part of the table in Exercise 2A would you put the following phrases?

Would it be possible for me to do a course?
I would appreciate it if I could …
I start work in Spain soon so I need to study Spanish.
I have just been promoted to manager so …
I do not have enough experience in this area.
It would be very helpful if I could attend a course.

➔ **page 119** See Grammar reference: Linking words for reason and purpose

T Teacher's resources: extra activities

L The email contains examples of linking words for reason and purpose. Go to MyEnglishLab for optional grammar work.

›TASK

3A Work in pairs. Turn to page 127 and look at the advertisement for a training course. You need to explain to your boss why you should do this course. Discuss the reasons you could give.

B Write an email of about 200 words to your boss requesting the course and explaining why you think you should do it.

C Exchange emails with your partner. Did you both use appropriate language to make your request? And did you use the same expressions to give your reasons? Having read your partner's email, how do you think you could improve your own email?

Self-assessment

- How successfully have you achieved the lesson outcome? Give yourself a score from 0 (I need more practice) to 5 (I know this well).
- Go to My Self-assessment in MyEnglishLab to reflect on what you have learnt.

Finance

> 'The quickest way to double your money is to fold it and put it back in your pocket.'
>
> Will Rogers, US actor, cowboy and newspaper columnist

Unit overview

3.1 > Recessions and depressions
Lesson outcome: Learners can use vocabulary related to finance and the economy.

Video: Past crashes and crises
Vocabulary: Finance and economic crises
Project: Research the history of a bank or financial institution

3.2 > Catching up with rivals
Lesson outcome: Learners can use expressions with future forms to express degrees of certainty and probability.

Reading: Adidas raises targets
Grammar: Expressing certainty and probability; Position of adverbs and adverbial phrases
Speaking: Discussing future changes

3.3 > Communication skills: Managing bad news
Lesson outcome: Learners are aware of different ways to manage bad news and can use a range of techniques and phrases for responding to bad news.

Video: Managing bad news
Functional language: Responding to bad news
Task: Balancing positives with negatives when giving bad news

3.4 > Business skills: Telephoning to clarify
Lesson outcome: Learners can use a range of phrases for clarifying complex or technical information on the phone.

Listening: A phone conversation to check details
Functional language: Asking for clarification and paraphrasing
Task: Making a call to clarify information in a financial document

3.5 > Writing: Annual report summary
Lesson outcome: Learners can organise and write a summary of a company annual report.

Model text: Summary of an annual report
Functional language: Useful phrases for annual report summaries
Grammar: Articles – *a/an*, *the*, no article
Task: Write an annual report summary for shareholders

Business workshop 3: p.92 | **Review 3:** p.106 | **Pronunciation:** 3.3 The letter 't' 3.4 Strong and weak forms of *that* p.115 | **Grammar reference:** p.119

3.1 ▶ Recessions and depressions

Lesson outcome	Learners can use vocabulary related to finance and the economy.

Lead-in

1 Discuss these questions.

1 How good are you at managing your money?
2 Which banks or financial institutions do you bank with?
3 Do you have any tips for saving money?
4 Have you ever invested in the stock market? What happened?
5 How is the economy doing in your country at the moment?

VIDEO

2 ▶ 3.1.1 Watch the video and put these events in order of severity (1 = the worst type of financial crisis).

> crash   economic depression   recession

3 Watch the video again and answer the questions.

1 On what date did the Wall Street Crash of 1929 happen?
2 What had been happening in the period just before the Wall Street Crash?
3 What was the total drop in the value of shares by the time the New York stock market stopped falling?
4 Was the Great Depression only in the USA?
5 Where was the origin of Black Monday in 1987?
6 Did the markets take a long time to recover?
7 Apart from the USA, which other countries were badly hit by the economic crisis that started in 2008?
8 What is meant by 'real economy'?

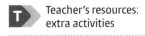

Teacher's resources:
extra activities

4 Work in pairs or small groups. Who do you think was responsible for the economic recession which began in 2008: governments, banks and financial institutions, business leaders, or people over-spending?

Vocabulary

Finance and economic crises

5 Complete the sentences related to finance with these nouns from the video.

> bankruptcy   credit crunch   depression   investment   loan
> losses   mortgage   recession   savings   stock market

1 A(n) _____ is something you buy, such as shares, bonds or profit, to make a long-term profit.
2 All the money that you have saved, especially in a bank or financial institution is called _____ .
3 _____ describes the situation when a company has less money than it did before, for example because sales have gone down.
4 The business of buying and selling stocks and shares is called the _____ .
5 When you are not able to pay your debts, this is called _____ .
6 A(n) _____ is an amount of money that you borrow from a bank, financial institution, etc.
7 A(n) _____ happens when borrowing money becomes difficult because banks reduce the amount they lend and charge high interest rates.
8 A legal arrangement by which you borrow money from a bank in order to buy a house, and pay back the money over a period of years is called a(n) _____ .
9 A(n) _____ is a difficult time when there is less trade or business activity in a country than usual.
10 A long period during which there is very little business activity is the worst type of financial crisis and is known as an economic _____ .

6 Choose the correct verb related to finance to complete the definitions.

1 To _____ means to fall to a much lower level or amount, or decline.

   a rise   **b** drop   **c** recover

2 To _____ is to become insolvent, or without enough money to pay what you owe.

   a lend   **b** go down   **c** go bankrupt

3 To _____ is to let someone borrow money or something that belongs to you for a short time.

   a bail someone out   **b** lend   **c** owe

4 To _____ is to return to a normal condition after a period of trouble or difficulty.

   a recover   **b** boom   **c** be insolvent

5 To _____ means to grow rapidly, or be very successful as a business or trade.

   a improve   **b** recover   **c** boom

6 To _____ means to help a person or a company that is in financial difficulty.

   a bail someone out   **b** borrow   **c** go bankrupt

7 Complete the summary about economic crises with the correct form of the words in brackets.

The Great Depression came after a period when the markets had been [1]_____ (boom) and shares had been steadily increasing in value. In the Wall Street Crash of 1929, the markets crashed because as more and more people sold their shares, the markets [2]_____ (drop) further, leading to many [3]_____ (bankrupt) and individuals losing their life [4]_____ (save).

On Black Monday in 1987, there was a rapid fall in the Hong Kong stock market and the panic spread quickly to Europe and the USA. The financial [5]_____ (lose) were great, although the markets [6]_____ (recover) quickly and there was no [7]_____ (depress).

In 2008, the economic [8]_____ (recede) was severe because the banking crisis affected the world's stock markets and the global economy suffered.

8 Work in pairs. Discuss these questions.

1 When there is a financial crisis, what are the effects on lending, growth, investment and employment?

2 Has your country suffered from an economic recession or downturn in recent years? What have been the effects?

T Teacher's resources: extra activities

PROJECT: Research the history of a bank or financial institution

9A Work in pairs or small groups. Research what happened to a bank or financial institution during a recent recession. Consider these questions.

- Did it survive the financial crisis? How? Was it bailed out by the government? How much did the bailout cost? Was the money paid back?
- Did it restructure or merge? Were there job losses? Did top executives stay on?
- How is the bank or financial institution performing now? Have company profits grown or declined? Do you think the bailout was worth it? Why / Why not?

B Present your findings to the class. Include some facts and figures and use graphs if possible. While you listen to your classmates, take notes and ask a question at the end of their presentation.

Self-assessment

- How successfully have you achieved the lesson outcome? Give yourself a score from 0 (I need more practice) to 5 (I know this well).
- Go to My Self-assessment in MyEnglishLab to reflect on what you have learnt.

3.2 ▶ Catching up with rivals

Lead-in **1** Work in pairs. Which sportswear brands are most popular with the people in your place of work/study?

2 Match the words and phrases in the box with the definitions.

> boost   bottom-line   make up ground   make your mark   profitability

1 the amount of profit a company makes
2 have an important or permanent effect on something
3 improve something and make it more successful
4 the amount of money that a business makes or loses
5 replace something that has been lost; become successful again

Reading **3** Read the article quickly and put the words in the correct order to make a sub-heading for the article.

catch up / German / to / with / rival Nike / races / sportswear company

4 Read the article again and complete the sentences using figures.

1 The previous CEO at Adidas had forecast profit growth of _____ each year.
2 The new CEO says it is likely profits will go up between _____ and _____ for the next _____ years.
3 Last year net profit increased by _____ to _____ .
4 The higher revenue and earnings targets raised shares by more than _____ .
5 The Adidas group reported digital sales of _____ last year.
6 Over the next _____ years they are hoping to reach digital sales of _____ .

Teacher's resources: extra activities

FT

New Adidas® chief raises group's sales and earnings targets

Adidas on Wednesday sharply increased its long-term sales and profit targets, as new chief executive Kasper Rorsted aims to make his mark on the German sportswear group.

Adidas's profitability falls behind that of rival Nike, and investors are hoping that Mr Rorsted will be able to boost the German groups' margins considerably.

Mr Rorsted, who took charge of the world's second largest sportswear company in October, has kept the previous CEO's strategy, which forecast high sales increases and 15 percent profit growth each year.

The Danish manager – who caught Adidas's attention after he boosted profitability at Henkel, the German consumer goods company – said that the group is certain to expand faster.

Mr Rorsted is targeting sales increases of 10 to 12 percent for the next three years, and profit growth of 20 to 22 percent. 'We will become better and more efficient,' he said. 'This, in turn, will help us to grow even faster than originally planned and to achieve ... bottom-line improvements for our shareholders.'

Alongside strong results last year – Adidas sales rose 14 percent to €19.3bn, while net profit increased by 59 percent to €1bn – the higher revenue and earnings targets helped push the group's shares up more than 6 percent in Wednesday morning trading in Frankfurt.

Part of the reason for Nike's better profitability compared to Adidas is the group's strong position in the North American market. Adidas made up ground last year, regaining its second position in the region, although it is thought that it probably won't gain first position in the U.S. market in the next quarter.

However, Mr Rorsted admitted that Adidas was still 'under represented' in North America, and says the group will probably continue to invest more than in other areas.

Adidas is also likely to sell off unwanted businesses. The group put its golf brands up for sale last year.

Adidas's online sales are also due to rise. The group reported it had €1bn of digital sales last year. Mr Rorsted has also said they are aiming to boost sales to €4bn over the next three years.

Grammar Expressing certainty and probability

5A **Look at the sentences. Are they *certain, planned, probable* or *improbable*?**

1 **a** It is certain that Adidas will boost profitability in the next quarter.

    b Adidas is unlikely to boost profitabilitab in the next quarter.

    c Adidas is definitely going to boost profitability in the next quarter.

    d Adidas probably won't boost profitability in the next quarter.

2 **a** Adidas is due to open new stores in the USA next month.

    b Adidas will probably open new stores in the USA next month.

    c It is likely that Adidas will open new stores in the USA next month.

    d Adidas is going to open new stores in the USA next month.

B **Which of the sentences have the same meaning?**

➡ **page 119** See Grammar reference: Expressing certainty and probability

6 **Choose the correct option in italics to complete the sentences.**

1 It has been confirmed that they *are going to / will probably* provide all the clothing for over 200 players in the next FIFA World Cup.

2 The U.S. sports brand currently has a 38 percent share in the branded footwear market, which is *definitely / certain* to rise over the next three years.

3 Sales are so bad that it is *unlikely to / unlikely that* the brand will increase its revenue this year.

4 Sports TV companies *will probably / are due to* make their programmes available on mobile phones next year, but the details haven't been confirmed.

5 Sports drink sales are up this year, although the increase in marketing spending means we *are due to / probably won't* boost profitability.

Teacher's resources: extra activities

Position of adverbs and adverbial phrases

7 **Look at the underlined phrases in the article. Complete the rules with *before* and *after*.**

1 We put *probably* _____ *will*, but _____ *won't*.

2 We put the adverb *also* _____ the verb *be*, but _____ the main verb with other verbs.

➡ **page 119** See Grammar reference: Position of adverbs and adverbial phrases

8 **Put the words in the correct order.**

1 next will the rise sharply Our online in quarter probably sales

2 probably by achieve end targets They month won't sales their the of the

3 is It year up unlikely price that will share the this go also

4 presentation is week at due to a also She make the of end the

Teacher's resources: extra activities

Speaking

9A **Write five sentences about future changes in your organisation or place of study using *(un)likely / certain / due to* or *probably / also* and suitable future forms.**

The organisation is due to move location next spring.

There probably won't be a new head of department next year.

B **Compare your sentences with a partner. Discuss whether you have the same level of certainty.**

A: We are likely to expand faster by taking on more overseas students.

B: Do you think so? I'm not sure I agree. I think we will probably grow faster if …

Self-assessment

- How successfully have you achieved the lesson outcome? Give yourself a score from 0 (I need more practice) to 5 (I know this well).
- Go to My Self-assessment in MyEnglishLab to reflect on what you have learnt.

❯ 31 ❮

Managing bad news

Lesson outcome	Learners are aware of different ways to manage bad news and can use a range of techniques and phrases for responding to bad news.

Lead-in 1A Work in pairs. Some people see the glass as half full and some see the glass as half empty. What do you think is the difference between these two types of people?

B Which category do you identify with most? Are you like this all the time or only in some situations? Why?

VIDEO 2 ▶ 3.3.1 **EN-Tek has received some bad news from the producer in Bangladesh. Watch as Katie discusses the news with Paweł.**

Go to MyEnglishLab for extra video activities.

1 What bad news does Katie receive by text from Bangladesh?
2 What does Katie say to Paweł about the bad news? Why?
3 What will Claudio think about the numbers, according to Paweł?
4 What does Paweł think might happen as a result of reporting poor budget numbers?
5 What advice does Paweł give Katie about how to approach her meeting with Claudio?

3A In small groups, discuss which is the best approach (Option A or B) for Katie to use in her meeting with Claudio. Give reasons for your answers. As a class, decide which video to watch first.

Option A – Focus on the positives – be optimistic and confident of success: Explain outcomes in positive terms, minimise any negatives, show confidence that success will come, show continued support for decisions that have already been agreed.

Option B – Focus on the negatives – be realistic and cautious because of risks: Explain outcomes in negative terms, acknowledge the negative aspects of the current situation and accept that changes need to be made to the strategy to achieve success.

B Watch the videos in the sequence the class has decided, and answer the questions for each video.

Option A ▶ 3.3.2
1 What is Claudio's initial recommendation as a result of the poor budget numbers?
2 Does Katie agree that costs are a significant problem?
3 What positive aspect of the project does Katie mention?
4 What is the outcome of the meeting?

Option B ▶ 3.3.3
1 Does Katie agree that costs are a significant problem?
2 Why is she against shutting down production in Bangladesh?
3 What kind of support does Katie suggest?
4 What is the outcome of the meeting?

4 In pairs, discuss the questions.
1 In what ways did Katie behave differently in the two videos? How did Claudio respond each time?
2 Having watched the two videos, what benefits do you think 'glass half full' and 'glass half empty' people can bring to a discussion?

5 ▶ 3.3.4 **Watch the Conclusions section of the video and compare what is said with your answers in Exercise 4. Do you agree? Why / Why not?**

Reflection 6 Think about the following questions. Then discuss your answers with a partner.
1 Think of a time, in a work or social situation, when you had to reach a decision with someone who had a significantly more optimistic/pessimistic view than you. How successfully did you each manage the situation?
2 Following this lesson, think of one thing you could do differently to manage such situations in future.

Functional language

Responding to bad news

7A Match the phrases in bold from the video with the categories a–h. Two phrases match one category.

a highlight positives
b minimise negatives
c emphasise negatives
d show confidence
e express doubt
f support current strategy
g propose changes

1 **I think we should continue to** help the guys locally / invest in new technology / focus on training.

2 **This is simply too** high / expensive / labour intensive.

3 **I'm really happy with the progress we've made** in a number of areas / with the advertising campaign / in expanding our market share.

4 **I'm not sure that we'll be able to** continue with local production / meet our targets / achieve what we wanted.

5 **I'm very disappointed with** the first quarter numbers / our lack of progress / the customer feedback.

6 **We have to find a new approach to** this / dealing with disagreements / marketing going forwards.

7 **To be fair, we're only a little** over budget / behind schedule / below target.

8 **I'm sure that we can turn this around and** get production up to standard / hit our targets / get back on track.

B Match the sentence beginnings (1–8) with the endings (a–h). Then match them to the correct category in Exercise 7A. Two sentences match one category.

1 Overall, I think things have gone
2 We just haven't made enough
3 But I'm extremely confident that we
4 I don't see how this
5 I think we simply need to keep
6 The market response was
7 Of course, there will be a few
8 I really think it's time to

a can work.
b will achieve our targets.
c setbacks and challenges.
d really well.
e look at alternative solutions.
f not what we were hoping for.
g doing what we're doing.
h progress in growth areas.

T Teacher's resources: extra activities

→ **page 115** See Pronunciation bank: The letter 't'

8A Work in pairs and read your role cards.

> **TASK**

Student A: Tell your employee that you plan to give them a more important role in an international project which will mean a lot more work for them and irregular hours. However, it will increase their profile in the company and give them the opportunity to travel.

Student B: Tell your employee that all staff have to take a 10 percent pay cut as your organisation is facing economic problems. Doing this will avoid the need to make compulsory redundancies and should help the company to start making profits again within two years. However, you know such measures can demotivate staff.

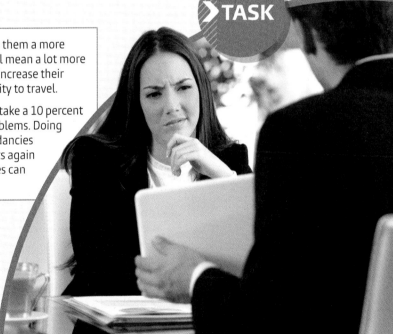

B Think about how you are going to communicate the news. Remember to balance the positive and negative.

C Hold your discussions. When you have finished, discuss how you each handled the situation.

Self-assessment

- How successfully have you achieved the lesson outcome? Give yourself a score from 0 (I need more practice) to 5 (I know this well).
- Go to My Self-assessment in MyEnglishLab to reflect on what you have learnt.

Lesson outcome	Learners can use a range of phrases for clarifying complex or technical information on the phone.

Lead-in

1A **Work in pairs. Discuss which action you take (a or b) in these situations.**

1 If I don't understand something when I'm having a call, I ...

    a interrupt and ask for clarification.

    b remain quiet and wait for an email summary to arrive after the call.

2 When communicating complex information during calls, I ...

    a regularly summarise the important information.

    b don't summarise often. It's better to keep moving and people can interrupt if they don't understand.

3 If someone says they don't understand me on a call, I ...

    a repeat myself slowly and clearly.

    b ask them what they didn't understand.

B **What might be the advantages and disadvantages of your actions in each situation?**

Listening

2 ◀) 3.01 **Listen to the beginning of a phone call and answer the questions.**

1 Why is Sam calling Pat?

2 What does he specifically want to clarify?

3 How does Pat offer to help?

3A ◀) 3.02 **Listen to the main part of the call between Sam and Pat. Which of these topics do they mention?**

1 gross or net figures   **6** the bottom line

2 targets   **7** product categories

3 the stock market   **8** profitability

4 margins   **9** return on investment (ROI)

5 average amounts

B **Match these words from the phone call with their meanings (1–7).**

average   column   gross   margin   net   quarter   row

1 a total amount before any tax or costs have been taken away

2 a period of three months in a financial year

3 a line of numbers or words in which each one is above or below another down a page, as in a spreadsheet like Excel

4 the amount of profit a business makes when selling something, after taking away what it costs to produce it

5 the amount you get when you add together several amounts and then divide by the number of amounts

6 a line of numbers or words in which each one is before or after another across the page, as in a spreadsheet like Excel

7 the final amount that remains after any tax and costs have been taken away

C ◀) 3.03 **Listen to the end of the call. What does Pat say about the glossary? Tick (✓) the correct option.**

a Sam can find it in any book.

b It can only be accessed with a link.

c One of her colleagues wrote it.

➡ **page 115** See Pronunciation bank: Strong and weak forms of *that*

Functional language

Asking for clarification and paraphrasing

4A Look at the categories in the table. Then complete the phrases from the phone call in Exercises 2 and 3 with the words in the box.

> clarify   correctly   follow   understanding   go over   refer   right   unsure

You would like clarification	There are a couple of things I'd like to ¹_____ . Just to confirm, [what's the target amount]? I'd like to double-check [something / that].
You didn't understand or didn't follow the logic of what was said	I'm having a little difficulty ²_____ [the concept of 'overall strategy']. Sorry, I don't ³_____ . [What are 'margins'?] Can I talk you through the points I'm ⁴_____ of? I don't know if my notes are ⁵_____ . I wrote down … . Is that correct? Can you ⁶_____ that again for me?
You can't remember the information	If I remember ⁷_____ , [I think we use …]. Is that right? Could you remind me [what you said about …]?
You didn't hear or there were technical problems on the call	Sorry, I didn't catch that. Could you say it again? I lost you for a second. Could you [repeat that, please]? The sound went for a moment. Would you mind [saying that last bit again]?
You would like specific details	Tell me, what exactly do the figures in column L ⁸_____ to? More specifically, [what's the margin on this]?

B Paraphrasing means expressing what somebody has said using different words. Match each sentence with its paraphrased equivalent.

1 The meeting is going to last all morning.

2 The EBIT is too low at the moment. We have to change that.

3 The timeline is across the top of the spreadsheet and the products are down the side.

4 We simply don't have enough staff at the moment and need more support.

5 This first half year will see our product line increasing by 50 percent.

a **What you're saying is** the columns are for weeks and the rows are for product lines.

b **OK, so that means** we won't be finished before 11 a.m.

c **In other words,** we're going to launch four new products before the summer.

d **If I understood you correctly,** you want to hire another salesperson.

e **Putting it differently,** we need to increase our margins, right?

T Teacher's resources: extra activities

5A Work in pairs. Prepare to roleplay two calls to clarify information in financial documents you sent or received. Read your role cards and prepare: Student A turn to page 127, Student B turn to page 129.

>TASK

B Roleplay the two calls. When making the call, remember to:

• say that there is information you want to clarify.

• use appropriate phrases to ask for clarification.

• paraphrase to check what you have understood.

C After each call, write a short email to your partner. Summarise what you discussed and what you now understand. Ask for confirmation.

6 In your pairs, compare the emails you wrote in Exercise 5C. Did you reach a common understanding at the end of each call?

Lesson outcome	Learners can organise and write a summary of a company annual report.

Lead-in

1 Read the extract from a summary of a company annual report. Choose the correct option in italics. Then compare in pairs.

To our shareholders

2018 was a year ¹*from / of* mixed results and challenges which were caused by the slow-down in the global ²*economy / economics* and the strength of the dollar, which affected our gross profit ³*lines / margins*. However, lower operating costs in Asia and Australia meant that we finished ⁴*more / much* strongly than expected in the fourth quarter, with growth of 3.5% on the previous quarter.

Sales revenues fell by 5% in the second quarter but after a ⁵*stable / steady* recovery over the next two quarters, we achieved an overall sales volume of $92 million, up 2% on 2017. Cash flow from operations ⁶*were / was* $43 million and we invested $20 million ⁷*in / on* capital expenditure including our internet infrastructure to enable customers to do business with us more easily. We also ⁸*repaid / refunded* $1 million of debt which we had borrowed to build the new factory. In addition, ⁹*despite / in spite* the challenges, we were able to raise our annual dividend by 2%. Last year we launched ten new product ¹⁰*marks / lines* in eight markets and these are doing very well, which gives us cause to be optimistic about 2019.

Functional language

2 Complete the table using the words in the box.

> cause   caused   coming   down   fell   making
> mixed   raise   recovery   result

Overview/Introduction
2018 was a year of ¹_____ results and challenges. The last year has seen the company ²_____ many tough decisions.
Reasons
The problems were ³_____ by the strength of the dollar. This was largely as a ⁴_____ of our entry into the Asian market.
Positive aspects
After a steady ⁵_____ over two quarters, we achieved good results. We were able to ⁶_____ our annual dividend by 2%.
Negative aspects
Sales ⁷_____ by 5% in the second quarter. We posted sales of $128 million, ⁸_____ 5% on the previous year.
Future outlook
This gives us ⁹_____ to be optimistic. The forecast for the ¹⁰_____ year looks promising.

➡ **page 120** See Grammar reference: Articles – *a/an, the, no article*

T Teacher's resources: extra activities

L The annual report summary contains examples of articles. Go to MyEnglishLab for optional grammar work.

› TASK

3A Work in pairs. Turn to page 128 and look at the summary of an annual report. What is the general problem with it? Discuss ways in which you could improve it using phrases from Exercise 2.

B Look at the key notes on page 127. Individually, write an annual report summary for your shareholders in around 200 words.

C Exchange summaries with your partner. Did your partner include all the information from the notes and use phrases from Exercise 2? Did your partner add any extra information? What do you think your partner did well?

Self-assessment	• How successfully have you achieved the lesson outcome? Give yourself a score from 0 (I need more practice) to 5 (I know this well). • Go to My Self-assessment in MyEnglishLab to reflect on what you have learnt.

Digital business

> 'There's no such thing as a digital strategy, just a strategy in a digital world.'
>
> Scott Gibson, Group Executive of Digital Practice, Dimension Data

Unit overview

4.1 > Digital disruptors

Lesson outcome: Learners can use vocabulary related to digital business and technology.

Video: A disruptive marketing start-up
Vocabulary: Digital business and technology
Project: Disruptive technology

4.2 > Talking technology

Lesson outcome: Learners can use zero, first and second conditionals and a range of complex linkers, e.g. *as long as, on condition that, providing/provided that, unless.*

Listening: Product presentations at a trade show
Grammar: Zero, first and second conditionals; Linkers
Speaking and writing: Trade show demonstration of an app

4.3 > Communication skills: Handling difficult communicators

Lesson outcome: Learners are aware of different ways to deal with challenging communication styles and can use a range of phrases for keeping meetings on track.

Video: Handling difficult communicators
Functional language: Keeping a meeting on track
Task: Managing a difficult meeting successfully

4.4 > Business skills: Negotiating strategies

Lesson outcome: Learners are aware of different negotiating strategies and can use a range of phrases for reaching agreement in a negotiation.

Listening: Positional and principled negotiation
Functional language: Reaching agreement in a negotiation
Task: Negotiating an agreement at work

4.5 > Writing: Short business proposal

Lesson outcome: Learners can plan, organise and write a short business proposal.

Model text: Short business proposal
Functional language: Useful phrases for business proposals
Grammar: Noun phrases to replace verb phrases
Task: Write a short proposal

Business workshop 4: p.94 | **Review 4:** p.107 | **Pronunciation:** 4.1 Stress in word building 4.4 Stress in phrases p.115 | **Grammar reference:** p.120

4.1 ▶ Digital disruptors

| Lesson outcome | Learners can use vocabulary related to digital business and technology. |

Lead-in

1 Complete the definition with the words in the box. Then work with a partner and think of examples of disruptive technology that have dramatically changed the way we do things.

> disrupts   disruptive   innovation

Being ¹_____ usually refers to causing problems and preventing something from continuing in its usual way. In technology, it refers to a(n) ²_____ that creates a new market and ³_____ existing ones, displacing established companies and products, for example the mobile phone replacing fixed phones.

BBC VIDEO

2A ▶ 4.1.1   Watch the video and choose the best summary.

Sentiance is a company that

a has made a digital platform which allows companies to create customer profiles based on daily routines and thereby improve targeting of marketing messages to mobile devices.

b helps Belgian companies to attract more customers so that they can target their digital products and services on people's way to work in the morning.

c is based in Belgium and has made a digital platform for different coffee shops and their connected customers so they can meet people with similar profiles.

B In the video, Frank Verbist from Sentiance gives an example of 'semantic' time. Put the words in the correct order.

different   different   morning   times   A   everybody   routine   is   for   at

3 Watch the video again and decide if these sentences are *true* (T) or *false* (F). Correct the incorrect sentences.

1 Sentiance can use the data about a person to find out where they are, how they travel and how fast they are going.

2 CEO Toon Vanparys says choosing the right moment is essential if the customer is going to respond positively.

3 Analyst Ian Maude says disruptive marketing is a completely new field so there's very little competition.

4 Eileen Burbridge says it would be very useful for companies if the data collected could be used to increase sales.

5 Toon Vanparys says it's all about participation, anticipation and disruption.

T ▶ Teacher's resources: extra activities

T ▶ Teacher's resources: alternative video and extra activities

4 Discuss in pairs. Are you afraid of companies collecting and using your data? What kind of personal data would you <u>not</u> want companies to access? Why?

Vocabulary

Digital business and technology

5 Complete the sentences with the words from the video.

> cloud   conversion   dump   mining   platform   tool

1 'In the _____' refers to having software or space for storing information on the internet, rather than on your own computer.

2 A data _____ is the act of copying information from one computer to another.

3 Data _____ uses a computer to examine large amounts of data, for example about customers and collect information that is not easily seen.

4 _____ in digital marketing is the number of sales generated in relation to the number of visits to a website.

5 In computing, a _____ refers to a piece of software designed to do a particular task. It can also be a piece of equipment, or a device, or a skill for doing your job.

6 In marketing, DMP stands for Digital Marketing _____ .

Word building – verbs, nouns and adjectives

6 Complete the table with the correct word forms.

Verb	Noun	Adjective
1 _____	analysis, analytics, analyst (person)	analytical
anticipate	2 _____	anticipated
convert	3 _____	converted
disrupt	4 _____ , disruptor	5 _____
6 _____	7 _____ (thing), innovator (person)	innovative
8 _____	9 _____	irritable, irritated, irritating
personalise	person, 10 _____ , personality	personal, 11 _____
12 _____	13 _____	predictable, predictive
visualise	14 _____	15 _____

7 Complete the sentences with the correct form of the word in brackets.

1 It's a start-up with many _____ (innovate) products.
2 We will create a program that is _____ (personal) for your company's needs.
3 He runs a business that specialises in the _____ (analyse) of consumer data.
4 _____ (predict) technology analyses past behaviour to predict possible future behaviour.
5 Contacting customers at the wrong time of day can be an _____ (irritate) which will not result in a sale.
6 Even businesses that are seen as market _____ (disrupt) today could be out of date in a short period of time.
7 If your advertisements target the right kind of people for your product, you will get a much higher _____ (convert) rate.
8 The data collected through your smartphone regarding your everyday movements, gives a better _____ (visual) of who you are as a person.

8 Discuss these questions with a partner.

1 How does digital technology help you every day in your place of work/study?
2 Are you a digital native, a digital immigrant or a digital nomad? Give reasons for your answers. Check the meaning of the terms online if necessary.

T Teacher's resources: extra activities

→ **page 115** See Pronunciation bank: Stress in word building

---

> ## PROJECT: Disruptive technology

9A Work in pairs or small groups. If you could invent a digital application, e.g. a mobile app, to make your life easier, what would it do? Think about how this 'digital disruptor' would offer a service or product at a specific time of day and how it would disrupt other businesses. Consider people's daily routines.

- how and when they commute to and from work
- where and when they have breakfast, lunch or a snack
- their domestic chores, e.g. doing the shopping, washing or cleaning
- the activities they like doing after working/studying
- the importance of 'semantic time', i.e. how people's routines might differ at certain times of the day

B Present your ideas to the class.

Self-assessment

- How successfully have you achieved the lesson outcome? Give yourself a score from 0 (I need more practice) to 5 (I know this well).
- Go to My Self-assessment in MyEnglishLab to reflect on what you have learnt.

4.2 ❯ Talking technology

| Lesson outcome | Learners can use zero, first and second conditionals and a range of complex linkers, e.g. *as long as, on condition that, providing/provided that, unless*. |

Lead-in

1 Work in pairs. Imagine you were networking with a potential international client at a trade fair but you didn't speak their language. How would you communicate?

2 How do you need to move each dial to make collocations using all the words? Look at the example to help you.

Example: Turn dial anti-clockwise once.

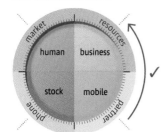  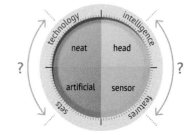

Listening

3 You are going to hear a demonstration of a new app and device called Multi-Babel. All of the collocations in Exercise 2 will be mentioned. What do you think it does?

| Arabic   Cantonese Chinese |
| Mandarin Chinese   English |
| French   German   Hindi |
| Indonesian   Italian   Japanese |
| Korean   Polish   Portuguese |
| Russian   Spanish |

4 🔊 4.01 **Listen to the demonstration at a trade show and answer the questions. Was your guess in Exercise 3 correct?**
1 What does the Multi-Babel app do?
2 Which of the languages in the box does Multi-Babel translate now?
3 What does the presenter predict will happen when you've tried it?
4 What is the reaction of the volunteer from the audience?

5 🔊 4.02 **Listen to another product presentation and complete the fact sheet.**

Telecom Company:
Dawnbreakers

Combining AI, voice recognition and a digital personal assistant

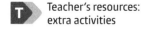
Teacher's resources: extra activities

Smartphone upgrades include:
- improved connectivity
- 1 _____
- increased pixel count
- 2 _____ screen resolution

Future improvements:
- 3 _____ function for interconnected home devices
- virtual reality content with 'wearables'
- improved 4 _____ function to manage work schedule

Upgrade for digital personal assistant:
- 5 _____ for voice recognition

Name of digital assistant: 6 _____
Example tasks include:
- 7 _____
- control your home devices remotely
- remind you of 8 _____
- book appointments

Grammar — Zero, first and second conditionals; Linkers

6 🔊 4.03 **Complete these conditional sentences from the product demonstrations. Contractions count as one word. Then listen to the extracts and check.**

Zero conditional
1 The Multi-Babel app _____ great if you _____ to network at conferences.

First conditional
2 Unless you _____ it through the earphones, everyone else _____ _____ _____ to hear your conversation!

Second conditional
3 If it _____ _____ high definition screen resolution, we _____ _____ video images so clearly.

7 A **Eamon from Dawnbreakers is talking to a potential client. Match the sentence halves.**

1 Chris will also be able to pay for items online for you providing
2 I'd like to add that the device is completely water-resistant
3 Discounts? We offer corporate clients a 10 percent discount on condition
4 Of course we can personalise their names as long

a unless it is under water for longer than an hour.
b that they buy more than 20 units.
c that your smartphone is set up correctly.
d as the client buys more than one model.

B **Look at the sentences in Exercise 7A again. Which four words/expressions are used to link the clauses in these conditional sentences?**

→ **page 120** See Grammar reference: Zero, first and second conditionals; Linkers

8 **Put the verbs in brackets in the correct form and choose the correct linker in italics.**

1 *If / Unless* a company _____ (develop) its digital business, it loses its competitive edge.
2 Our digital consumers might enjoy more personalised services *if / unless* we _____ (manage) technologies more effectively. But we don't.
3 We _____ (never be) an innovative organisation *if / unless* we don't change the way we work and digitalise everything.
4 This device adapts to the user's preferences *as long as / unless* it _____ (receive) data from a smartphone.
5 *Provided / Condition* that their product demonstrations _____ (be) successful, digital personal assistants would sell worldwide.
6 *If / On condition that* I _____ (be) you, I'd develop voice recognition technology further to reduce our dependence on touchscreens.
7 Smartphones will soon be replaced by robots *on condition / as long as* that artificial intelligence _____ (improve).
8 We will become one of the world's most revolutionary companies *as long as / unless* we _____ (not stop) innovating.

Teacher's resources: extra activities

Speaking and writing

9 A **Work in pairs. You are going to act out a trade show demonstration. Think of an imaginary or real app or device, or some tasks that a digital personal assistant could do. Use the ideas below if you wish. Then prepare some conditional sentences describing how it works.**

> a tablet that writes for you   a portable gadget that recycles energy
> a remote control for the home   an app for organising special events

You'll impress all your friends if you use this device!
Providing that it's fully charged, it'll last 24 hours.
Unless you click here, it won't …

B **Work with another pair. Take turns to present your products.**

C **When you have finished your demonstration, ask and answer questions critically. Are you interested in the idea? Why / Why not? What are the disadvantages?**
So, if I dictate the title and input some key words, this tablet automatically writes a report. But what will happen if my classmate also has the app and writes a similar report?

D **Write up the instructions for your device or app. Use conditional sentences and suitable linkers where possible. Write 175–200 words.**

4.3 COMMUNICATION SKILLS
Handling difficult communicators

Lesson outcome

Learners are aware of different ways to deal with challenging communication styles and can use a range of phrases for keeping meetings on track.

Lead-in **1A** Work in pairs. Which of these challenging communication styles have you experienced in your work or studies? Which styles do you find easy/difficult to deal with? Why?

Dominator: talks and never listens

Non-responder: Never says a word

Contradictor: Disagrees with everything you say

Joker: Constantly tells jokes

Analyser: Goes into too much boring detail

Technology user: Always on the phone

B What can a meeting leader do to deal with these behaviours during a meeting?

VIDEO **2A** ▶ 4.3.1 Watch as Sanjit receives a call from Claire (Go Global's Marketing Specialist) and discusses it with Paweł (Production Manager at EN-TEK).

1 What is Gary's role?
2 Why has Claudio asked him to meet with EN-Tek?
3 What is Gary going to bring to the project?
4 What does Paweł say about Gary?

L Go to MyEnglishLab for extra video activities.

B Do you think Claire and Paweł are right to warn Sanjit about Gary's communication style? Why / Why not?

3A In small groups, discuss which is the best approach (Option A or B) for Sanjit to use in the meeting with Gary. Give reasons for your answers. As a class, decide which video to watch first.

Option A – Accept and adapt – allow others to communicate in the way they prefer: Don't try to change how others communicate; adapt your own behaviour by talking more or less; be open to discussing ideas which are not on the agenda.

Option B – Intervene and control – manage the way others communicate: Interrupt to stop the other person talking; introduce and insist on following the agenda; focus the discussion on relevant topics; propose your own solutions for discussion.

B Watch the videos in the sequence the class has decided, and answer the questions for each video.

Option A ▶ 4.3.2
1 What does Gary say is 'really important' for Sanjit to think about?
2 What does Gary describe as 'one key thing' which he has done?
3 When Gary says 'It simply has to be changed', what does he mean by 'it'?
4 What does Gary say is unrealistic?
5 What did Sanjit learn and achieve in this meeting?

Option B ▶ 4.3.3
1 What does Sanjit propose as the first topic for the meeting?
2 What does Gary describe as a disaster?
3 What does Sanjit say to stop Gary interrupting Claire?
4 Which of Gary's ideas does Sanjit like?
5 What did Sanjit learn and achieve in this meeting?

4 Work in pairs. Which approach – accepting-adapting or intervening-controlling – do you think was most effective? Why?

5 ▶ 4.3.4 Watch the Conclusions section of the video and compare what is said with your answers in Exercise 4. Do you agree? Why / Why not?

Reflection **6** Think about the following questions. Then discuss your answers with a partner.

1 Which of the two styles do you prefer to use when dealing with challenging communicators? Why?
2 What is one advantage and one possible disadvantage of your own personal style? Why?

Functional language

Keeping a meeting on track

7A Complete the table with these phrases from the video.

a Let [her] finish [what she is saying / the point she is trying to make], please.
b [I think] that's really outside the scope of the [meeting / agenda / brief] …
c Can we slow down a little?
d Can I stop you [for a second / just there / for a moment]?
e We can come back to [the brand topic / the issue of dates] later.
f I'd like to stick to the agenda [and look at advertising first].

Reminding of the agenda	1 _____ 2 _____
Managing dominant speakers	Sorry, can I just add something here? 3 _____
Managing interruptions	[Simon,] we'll come to [you/that] in a moment. [Peter,] do go on. 4 _____
Postponing discussion	We do need to deal with [the budget issue], but let's finish [talking about dates] first. 5 _____
Reducing speed	Could you just go over that idea again? 6 _____
Pushing for a clear proposal	But what do you actually suggest we do about [this]? [Jan,] so is your idea that we [delay the launch]?

Teacher's resources: extra activities

B In your experience, what else can you do and say to keep meetings on track?

TASK

8A Work in groups of three. You are co-owners of a chain of restaurants. Decide on the profile of your restaurant and your customer base, e.g. a Spanish tapas bar for young professionals.

B Work individually. Look at the agenda for a meeting of the co-owners and write down some ideas for each point.

> 1 a new logo
> 2 the dessert menu which hasn't been popular with customers
> 3 where to advertise

C Read your role cards and prepare for the meeting.
Student A: Lead the meeting and ensure it is kept on track.
Student B: Read the role card on page 128.
Student C: Read the role card on page 130.

D Hold your meeting. When you have finished, discuss which phrases Student A used to keep the meeting on track and whether they were effective.

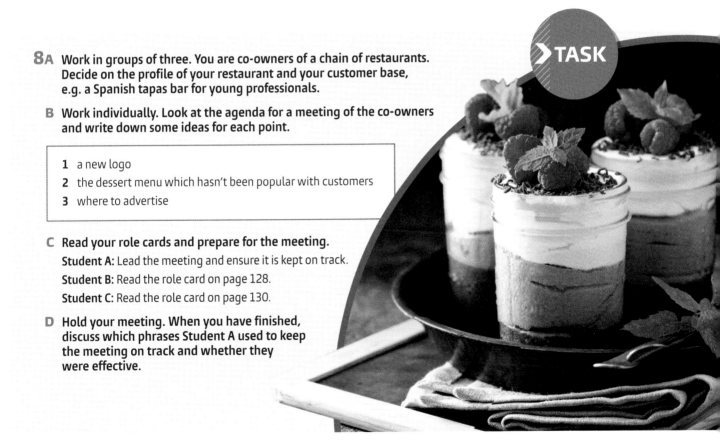

Self-assessment

• How successfully have you achieved the lesson outcome? Give yourself a score from 0 (I need more practice) to 5 (I know this well).
• Go to My Self-assessment in MyEnglishLab to reflect on what you have learnt.

Lesson outcome	Learners are aware of different negotiating strategies and can use a range of phrases for reaching agreement in a negotiation.

Lead-in

1 Work in pairs and discuss the questions.

1 Think about a time you were a) successful and b) unsuccessful in reaching an agreement with someone else. What happened? Why were you successful/unsuccessful?

2 Is it better to begin a negotiation with a specific position/goal in mind or to have a range of possible options?

3 Is it better to find out the other person's view in advance and prepare accordingly, or to just find it out during the negotiation?

4 Is it better to plan everything in advance or to just listen and react depending on what they say?

Listening

2 ◀) 4.04   ◀) 4.05   **Listen to two different versions of a negotiation about email access needs at work and answer the questions.**

Version A

1 What is Isabella unhappy about?

2 Who is the new company policy for?

3 What is the new policy trying to prevent?

Version B

1 Why does Daniel need to communicate with clients in the evenings?

2 What is a priority for the company?

3 What is a priority for Daniel?

3A Now listen again and decide if someone does the following in version A, B or both.

	A	B
1 Explains why the system was introduced.	☐	☐
2 Focuses more on the new company policy.	☐	☐
3 Focuses more on the individual's needs.	☐	☐
4 Gives examples of how the new company policy doesn't work for them.	☐	☐
5 Tells the other person what to do to adapt to the new policy.	☐	☐
6 Suggests working together on a solution.	☐	☐
7 Suggests reviewing their agreement on a regular basis.	☐	☐

B Work in pairs and discuss which approach was more successful, and why.

C Read the definitions and decide which approach was 'positional' and which was 'principled'.

Positional negotiation – a strategy in which you have a particular idea, interest or position, and look for ways in which you and the other person can agree, with each of you getting some of the things you want. You focus on what is best for you, and try to achieve the result you want.

Principled negotiation – a strategy in which you look for common interests, consider the needs and values of others, and focus on getting a result that is good for both of you and on keeping and improving your relationship with the other person.

➡ **page 115** See Pronunciation bank: Stress in phrases

Functional language

Reaching agreement in a negotiation

4A Complete the table with these extracts from the dialogues in Exercise 2.

a How about [if we lift the blockage until 10 p.m.]? Would that work?

b Yes, I think I can make that happen.

c How would you feel about [having an extension]?

d Yes, [I suppose] I can agree to that.

e Firstly, tell me about how this situation affects you.

f What are your priorities?

g Let me make sure I fully understand your perspective.

Establish the situation	First, let's look at the facts. We need to accept the fact that [some job losses are inevitable]. _____ _____
Explore the other's values and needs	How could you imagine this working? _____ _____
Offer suggestions	I think the best thing would be to [introduce the changes gradually]. Maybe this suggestion would work. [What about sharing the costs?] _____
Reach agreement	That sounds reasonable. _____ _____

B Put the words in the correct order to make sentences for finding solutions whilst negotiating.

1 if we think / a decision / of some / how about / before making / other options / ?

2 from / this / try and look / another / at / perspective / let's / .

3 this situation / to approach / there / is / another way / ?

4 we / that works / solution / how / might / for us / find a / all / ?

5 how / mutually / can / outcome / we / identify / satisfactory / a / ?

6 of / aren't / thinking / what / we / ?

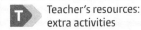
Teacher's resources: extra activities

> TASK

5A Work in pairs. Choose a scenario, decide your roles and prepare your negotiating positions.

Scenario 1: You are colleagues in a marketing department. The team is very busy because a new website is being launched at the end of the month. Role A: You want to take three days off to go to a friend's wedding abroad, but it will mean that your colleague (Role B) will have to do overtime.

Scenario 2: Role A: You want to buy ten interactive projection screens for your company meeting rooms. They cost $2,000 each but your budget is only $15,000.

Role B: You are the interactive projection screen salesperson. You can usually only give a maximum 12 percent discount on orders between five and ten units.

B Roleplay the negotiation. Continue to make suggestions until you reach an agreement.

• Make notes during the negotiation and give each other feedback so that you can improve each time you practise.

C Change partners and roleplay the negotiation again, changing some details if you wish.

D In your pairs, discuss what went well and what you could improve next time. Share your ideas with another pair.

Lesson outcome — Learners can plan, organise and write a short business proposal.

Lead-in

1 Read the business proposal. Proofread the proposal and find nine more language mistakes. Think about spelling and grammar. Then compare in pairs.

Automated dispensing system proposal

have

I propose that we purchase an automated dispensing system for all our pharmacies. Recently, there ~~has~~ been complaints about an increase in waiting times and errors with the measurement of medication when dispensing prescriptions. The use of an automated system would help to ease this issues.

The best solution is the *Disp+Medi* system. The medication are stored in special drawers with robotic arms to select the items which have been order by the pharmacist using a touch screen at the counter. The arm then selects the items used barcode recognition and drops them onto a conveyor belt headed for the counter. While we had this machine, waiting times would be dramatic reduced and there would be no errors, as long than the pharmacist has ordered the correct item.

Despite the high cost, my research indicate that we would be able to recover our investment within six months. In additional, increased efficiency would greatly increase customer numbers. I therefore recommend that we purchase the *Disp+Medi* system.

Functional language

2A Complete the table using words from the proposal.

Format	Examples
Introduction or Purpose statement	I ¹_____ that we purchase an automated dispensing system …
Brief summary of problem	Recently, there have been ²_____ about an increase in waiting times …
Solution to problem	The best ³_____ is the *Disp+Medi* system.
Plan, costs and schedule	Despite the high cost, … we would be able to ⁴_____ our investment within six months.
Conclusion	I therefore ⁵_____ that we purchase the *Disp+Medi* system.

B Where in the table in Exercise 2A would you place the following phrases?

> The new technology would enable us to … In order to solve this problem we need to …
> This proposal evaluates the use of … Deliveries have failed to arrive on time.
> It is expected that the initial costs would be … In conclusion, we feel that …
> The proposal aims to assess … The equipment could be installed immediately.
> To sum up, it is recommended that … The most efficient option would be …

 Teacher's resources: extra activities

 The business proposal contains examples of noun phrases to replace verb phrases. Go to MyEnglishLab for optional grammar work.

➜ **page 121** See Grammar reference: Noun phrases to replace verb phrases

›TASK

3A Work in pairs. Look at the proposal on page 127 and put the sentences in order.

B Turn to page 128 and look at some meeting notes about how to solve traffic congestion and pollution in Willow City. Write the proposal in around 200 words.

C Exchange proposals with your partner. How different is your partner's proposal from yours? Did your partner include all the information? What do you think your partner did well?

Self-assessment

- How successfully have you achieved the lesson outcome? Give yourself a score from 0 (I need more practice) to 5 (I know this well).
- Go to My Self-assessment in MyEnglishLab to reflect on what you have learnt.

Performance

5 >

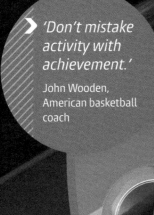

> '*Don't mistake activity with achievement.*'

John Wooden,
American basketball
coach

Unit overview

5.1 >	**Performance and rewards** **Lesson outcome:** Learners can use vocabulary which describes performance and rewards.	**Video:** The cyber manager **Vocabulary:** Rewarding performance **Project:** Moving up in the company
5.2 >	**A culture of rewards** **Lesson outcome:** Learners can use language of concession and can contrast ideas and information using linking words.	**Reading:** How to develop a rewarding culture **Grammar:** Linking words and concessive clauses **Speaking:** Concessions and compromises in your own life
5.3 >	**Communication skills:** Managing challenging feedback **Lesson outcome:** Learners are aware of different ways to deal with challenging feedback and can use a range of phrases for responding to feedback.	**Video:** Managing challenging feedback **Functional language:** Responding to challenging feedback **Task:** Responding to feedback from your manager
5.4 >	**Business skills:** Reviewing projects **Lesson outcome:** Learners can use a range of phrases to lead and participate in discussions around team and project performance.	**Listening:** A project review meeting **Functional language:** Leading and participating in review meetings **Task:** A performance development workshop
5.5 >	**Writing:** Performance review summary **Lesson outcome:** Learners can write a performance review summary.	**Model text:** Performance review summary **Functional language:** Positive comments and constructive criticism **Grammar:** Phrasal verbs **Task:** Write a performance review summary

Business workshop 5: p.96 | **Review 5:** p.108 | **Pronunciation:** 5.2 Intonation and linking words
5.3 Intonation when handling challenging feedback p.116 | **Grammar reference:** p.121

5.1 ▶ Performance and rewards

Lesson outcome	Learners can use vocabulary which describes performance and rewards.

Lead-in **1** **Discuss these questions.**

1 Would you like to start your own business? Why / Why not?

2 What might be the advantages of being your own boss?

3 Do you think that people should be rewarded when they do something well? Or is doing the job well just part of what employees are expected to do?

2 **You are going to watch a programme about a company called CyberAgent and how younger and older workers feel about working there. What complaints do you think young people might make about their employer? What about the older workers? Use ideas from the box or your own ideas.**

become a manager   corporate world   highly qualified and innovative
keep raising salaries   new recruits   new salary model   oldest got the biggest salary
recent university graduates   rewards its workers based on performance

Young people often complain that older employees always get the biggest salaries.

3 ▶ 5.1.1 **Watch the video. Were your ideas in Exercise 2 correct? Tell your partner one thing that someone said which surprised you.**

4 **Watch the video again and answer the questions.**

1 Why was Takato Oku frustrated when he began his career in business?

2 What did he do about it?

3 What surprised him about the ages of people he worked with?

4 What did HR Director Tetsuhito Soyama feel was unfair at many companies?

5 What came as a shock to older workers when the economy began to slow down after the economic boom of the 80s and 90s?

6 Why have some companies had problems when revising policies regarding rewards?

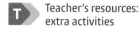

Teacher's resources: extra activities

5 **Work in pairs or small groups. Think of ways in which companies can reward employees. How would you feel about receiving these types of rewards?**

Vocabulary **Rewarding performance**

6 **Choose the option (a or b) which has the same meaning as the phrase in bold from the video.**

1 [Takato Oku] knew that his turn for **promotion and pay rise** was decades away.

a a better job and more money

b a management job and a bonus

2 Within two years he **rose through the ranks** to become a manager.

a moved up to a higher position soon after starting as an ordinary worker

b had a series of jobs, each with more responsibility than the last, and worked his way up in the company

3 CyberAgent rewards its workers based on our **performance**, not our age.

a how well they do their jobs

b how much profit they make for the company

4 ... companies could raise salaries for workers as a **reward for their loyalty**.

a a thank you for continuing to work for the company over many years

b financial compensation when someone works very hard during a specific time period

5 ... workers who were expecting **the guarantee of lifelong employment**.

a the same job for many years

b the certainty they would always have a job

7 Work in pairs. Match definitions 1–9 with the verbs in the 'magic table'. Write the correct number in each box. If your answers are correct, the columns and rows will all add up to 15.

☐ promote	☐ appraise	☐ recognise	= 15
☐ reward	☐ evaluate	☐ fail	= 15
☐ achieve	☐ advance	☐ succeed	= 15
= 15	= 15	= 15	

1 give someone something because they have done a good job
2 say publicly that someone has done a very good job
3 move up to a higher position in a company
4 successfully do what you tried or wanted to do
5 judge how good, useful or successful something is
6 give someone a better and more responsible job in a company
7 decide how well an employee is doing his or her work, usually after discussing with the employee how well he or she has performed during the past year
8 complete something or get a good result, especially by working hard
9 not be able to achieve something

8 Make nouns from the verbs in Exercise 7. Use the correct endings from the box. Some do not change their form. You may need to change other letters in the verb to make the noun.

-al	-ess	-ion	-ment	-ure

succeed → success

Teacher's resources: extra activities

9 Complete the sentences with suitable verbs and nouns from Exercises 7 and 8.

1 Workers hope to have their _____ recognised by management.
2 One of the goals of an employee _____ is to set targets for the future.
3 No one received a pay rise due to the _____ of one of our major product lines.
4 When staff members receive _____ for doing a good job, their motivation increases.
5 The company is finding new ways to _____ employees in order to retain staff.
6 She received a(n) _____ to a management position due to excellent performance.

10 Discuss these questions with a partner.

> *I don't have much work experience yet.*
> 1 What role do you think the reward system would play in your motivation?
> 2 What type of benefits would you ask about at a job interview?

> *I have experience of performance reviews and rewards at work.*
> 1 What types of rewards do you find personally to be motivating?
> 2 What kind of reward or benefit would you like to have that you currently don't have?

PROJECT: Moving up in the company

11A Work in small groups. Think about the company where you work or a company in a field you know well. You've been told you have some excellent business ideas and you want the chance to develop them. Prepare to convince your boss that you should be promoted. Consider:

- how your ideas will benefit the company, e.g. by addressing problems with competitors or creating new markets.
- why you feel people with innovative ideas should be promoted.
- whether a promotion in your case would be:
  A: a reward for a job well done.   **B:** good for the company.   **C:** both.
- whether a pay rise would encourage you to do even more than you do now.

B Work in pairs with someone from another group. Roleplay the conversation with your boss and explain your reasons for requesting a promotion. Then swap roles.

C Write an email of 100–120 words to the employee you spoke to in Exercise 11B. Acknowledge the key points that he/she made and explain your decision.

Self-assessment
- How successfully have you achieved the lesson outcome? Give yourself a score from 0 (I need more practice) to 5 (I know this well).
- Go to My Self-assessment in MyEnglishLab to reflect on what you have learnt.

5.2 ▶ A culture of rewards

Lesson outcome	Learners can use language of concession and can contrast ideas and information using linking words.

Lead-in

1 Work in pairs. What motivates you / would motivate you to work hard? Use ideas from the spidergram or your own ideas.

2 Choose the correct option in italics to complete the definitions of the phrases in bold.

1 **Performance incentives** are given to employees to *encourage them to work harder / pay them for work they have done.*

2 **Executives** are *people who carry out orders / managers in an organisation who help make important decisions.*

3 When workers are paid using **a piece-rate scheme**, they are paid *for the time they need to produce each item / per item they produce.*

4 If you receive **a six-figure salary** in the UK, you earn at least *£100,000 / £1,000,000.*

5 Someone who has **hit** his or her **targets** *has / has not* reached a particular goal.

Reading

3 Read the article. What types of rewards are mentioned, apart from bonuses?

4 Read the article again and decide if these sentences are *true* (T) or *false* (F).

1 The work of top managers and executives is easy to evaluate.

2 Productivity increased on fruit farms by using piece-rate schemes, bonuses for the managers and putting the workers in teams to compete against each other.

3 Recognising hair stylists in public was found to be a successful type of reward.

4 The main differences between pilots, fruit pickers and hair stylists is that pilots enjoy status, large salaries and belong to powerful unions.

5 Pilots were not satisfied with their jobs when their company acknowledged their success regarding fuel consumption, if they were not also given bonuses.

6 People generally do their best even if they don't have a clear picture of what the company considers success.

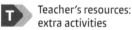

Teacher's resources: extra activities

FT

How to develop a rewarding culture

Here's a difficult management problem: who should be rewarded for high performance, and how? Routine and easily monitored jobs, such as flipping burgers, are natural candidates for performance incentives. However,
5 it's usually executives who tend to get bonuses in spite of their complex, hard-to-measure jobs which are poorly suited to performance-related pay. Nevertheless, it is also possible to respond positively to non-financial rewards such as praise, status or the satisfaction of a job
10 well done.

Experiments over the years have given us some understanding of this. On fruit farms, a piece-rate scheme which paid workers based on how much fruit they picked boosted productivity by 50 percent. Bonuses
15 for the managers ensured that work was distributed fairly and productivity increased another 20 percent. Running a competition encouraged workers to sort themselves into productive teams, and productivity increased by a further 20 percent.
20 In another study, hair stylists in Zambia's capital Lusaka were recruited to sell products to help prevent certain diseases. When they were praised for their work

at a public ceremony it proved a far better approach than providing financial incentives.
25 But sometimes neither a public ceremony nor a financial incentive is appropriate. Consider the case of long-haul airline captains. Unlike part-time sales people or fruit pickers, pilots have high status, six-figure salaries and powerful unions. Nevertheless, a recent
30 experiment discovered that it was effective to simply make pilots aware of saving fuel, although those who also hit specific targets on fuel consumption were even more satisfied with their jobs.

'I just couldn't believe the impact we had on job
35 satisfaction,' says a researcher. Although salaries were not increased for captains, the fact that the company was taking an interest in fuel saving, and acknowledging success, seemed to delight them.

Even though no performance scheme will fit every
40 occasion, the fuel-saving study does suggest an approach worth trying more broadly. If you want people to do a good job, tell them what success looks like to you – and that you've noticed when they've achieved it.

Grammar   Linking words and concessive clauses

5 Look at the underlined words and phrases in the article. They all serve the same function. What is it?

a to give further information

b to link and contrast two pieces of information

c to negate or change information which has come before

6 Underline the word or phrase in each sentence that links the clauses.

1 The employees were very motivated though they were only given recognition rather than a pay rise.

2 They continued to use performance-related pay, in spite of the fact that several experiments had shown that it was less effective than other schemes.

3 Despite experiencing a number of problems, they have not changed their strategies.

4 On the one hand, the union has fought for annual pay rises, but on the other hand, they understand that this may not always be possible.

5 Senior management awarded themselves bonuses, despite the fact that profits had fallen significantly.

→ **page 121** See Grammar reference: Linking words and concessive clauses

7 Choose the correct option in italics to complete the sentences.

1 *Despite / However* finding that rewards could lead to employee motivation, management decided to stop the rewards system completely.

2 On the one hand, employees have to work more hours, *in spite of, / on the other hand,* they receive overtime pay or extra time off.

3 Productivity has been declining for months *although / in spite of* employee motivation remaining the same.

4 *Even though / However* some work can be done from home, many companies prefer to have the workers in the factory.

5 Executives are often those who receive performance-related pay. *Nevertheless, / In spite of*, it is often difficult to evaluate how well they have performed.

6 We have announced a public ceremony to acknowledge the excellent work done by staff, *despite / although* not all employees plan to attend.

7 *In spite of / Despite the fact that* the targets were agreed in discussion with department heads, they are proving to be unrealistic in some areas.

8 Everyone agrees that reward systems are important for motivation *in spite of / though* not everyone agrees how they should be carried out.

T Teacher's resources: extra activities

→ **page 116** See Pronunciation bank: Intonation and linking words

Speaking   **8A** Complete the sentences to make true statements about you.

1 My dream is to work in a business which _____ . Nevertheless, I would be happy to _____ as well.

2 On the one hand, I really enjoy _____ . On the other hand, _____ is very important for me.

3 In the next five years I hope I will be _____ . However, if _____ happens, that will not be a problem.

4 Despite _____ at university, I would be happy working _____ .

5 Although I think _____ has many opportunities, I may look for a job in _____ instead.

B In pairs or small groups, compare your sentences from Exercise 8A and ask each other questions about them. Use questions such as *Is this the same for you? Do you feel the same way? Do you have a different opinion? Why / Why not?*

Self-assessment

• How successfully have you achieved the lesson outcome? Give yourself a score from 0 (I need more practice) to 5 (I know this well).

• Go to My Self-assessment in MyEnglishLab to reflect on what you have learnt.

5.3 ▶ COMMUNICATION SKILLS
Managing challenging feedback

Lesson outcome	Learners are aware of different ways to deal with challenging feedback and can use a range of phrases for responding to feedback.

Lead-in **1** Think of a time someone gave you negative or challenging feedback, for example about something you didn't do well. Look at the questions and discuss your answers with a partner.

1 What was it about?

2 How did you react?

3 What happened next and would you react differently next time?

VIDEO **2** ▶ 5.3.1 Watch the video and answer the questions.

1 What does Claire blame for the poor sales figures?

2 Why is Katie upset?

3 In your opinion, how appropriate were Claire's comments to Katie?

4 Do you think Sanjit should speak to Claudio about Claire's behaviour towards Katie?

L Go to MyEnglishLab for extra video activities.

3A In small groups, discuss which is the best way (Option A or B) for Sanjit to deal with the feedback on poor sales. Give reasons for your answers. As a class, decide which video to watch first.

Option A – Focus on protecting yourself

Give reasons for your position and defend yourself against challenging feedback.

Option B – Focus on the opportunity to learn and improve

Listen to the critical feedback and ask questions.

B Watch the videos in the sequence the class has decided, and answer the questions for each video.

Option A ▶ 5.3.2
1 What does Sanjit explain as being the big picture?

2 What does Sanjit say to defend a) the forecast and b) Katie personally?

3 What is Sanjit referring to when he talks about respect?

4 Does Claudio agree to hold off on redesigning the marketing campaign? How do you think he feels about it?

Option B ▶ 5.3.3
1 What does Sanjit ask Claudio to acknowledge?

2 What does Sanjit mean when he says 'I appreciate the point you are making, but not necessarily <u>how</u> you are making it'?

3 What is Claudio worried about regarding Sanjit's team?

4 What does Sanjit say they could all benefit from?

4 Work in pairs and discuss the questions.

1 How did Sanjit respond differently to feedback in the two videos? What happened as a result?

2 What are the advantages and disadvantages of each approach for a) the project and b) relationships within the team?

5 ▶ 5.3.4 Watch the Conclusions section of the video and compare what is said with your answers in Exercise 4. Do you agree? Why / Why not?

Reflection **6** Think about the following questions. Then discuss your answers with a partner.

1 Are you aware of your own preferred style when receiving feedback? Think about the example you gave in Exercise 1.

2 Decide on one thing you can do to respond to challenging feedback more successfully in the future.

Functional language Responding to challenging feedback

7A Complete the sentences from the video using the words and phrases in the box.

> accurate   and why   appreciate   improvement   point   the big picture
> this before   this might happen   useful   you're saying

1 I'm afraid you're not seeing _____ here.
2 I take on board what _____ .
3 There's room for _____ . I agree.
4 I'm not sure what you're saying is necessarily [_____ / quite true].
5 You have to remember that [we predicted _____ / I warned you sales might fall].
6 I can see your _____ .
7 That's _____ to think about.
8 We've talked about _____.
9 I understand what you're saying, _____ .
10 I _____ the point you're making, but not necessarily *how* you're making it.

B Now match the phrases in Exercise 7A with the correct category in the table.

Defending your position	Accepting criticism

8 Look at the four examples of challenging feedback. Think about how you would respond in each case. Then work in pairs and take turns to deliver the feedback and respond.

1 'You need to improve your accuracy. There are a lot of mistakes in your work.'

2 'That's the second month in a row you're late with your update report.'

3 'Your results are disappointing.'

4 'This isn't good enough. You need to address the communication problems in your team.'

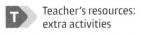 Teacher's resources: extra activities

➔ **page 116** See Pronunciation bank: Intonation when handling challenging feedback

9A Work in pairs and look at the graph. It shows information about the performance of two individuals: A and B.

- Decide on your roles: A or B. You will take turns to respond to feedback from your manager.
- Read some background information about your performance and prepare your responses. Student A turn to page 130, Student B turn to page 128.

B Follow the instructions and roleplay the situation.

- Student A: In roleplay 1, you are the team manager: Explain why you are disappointed with Student B's performance. Use the phrases on page 135 to help you.
- Student B: Use the arguments you have prepared to respond.

C Change roles and roleplay the situation again. In roleplay 2, Student B is the manager and Student A responds to the feedback.

D When you have finished, discuss how you each handled the challenging feedback and which phrases from Exercise 7A you found useful.

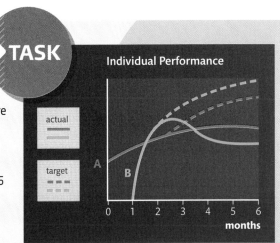

>**TASK**

Individual Performance

actual ━━

target ╍╍

Lesson outcome	Learners can use a range of phrases to lead and participate in discussions around team and project performance.

Lead-in **1** Work in pairs. Read about two approaches to 'failure' in business. Discuss which approach you agree with more, and why.

'If you want to be high performing, you need to avoid failure. I want 100 percent quality in my organisation and it can only be achieved when people understand that they are here to achieve high standards and mistakes are not accepted.'

'I want to develop an entrepreneurial and creative culture where people take risks to achieve more. We accept failure but encourage people to fail fast, to learn from mistakes and use the learning experience to innovate and deliver exceptional results.'

Listening **2A** 🔊 5.01 Listen to the beginning of a project review meeting. The aim of the meeting is to discuss what has and hasn't gone well so far, and what lessons can be learnt for the next phase of the project. The meeting is led by Carlota.

1 What does Hanna define as her main success so far?

2 What problems did she have?

3 What was the cause of the problem?

4 What does she see as the main learning point from her difficult experience?

B 🔊 5.02 Later in the meeting, listen to Carlota and her colleagues discussing what has been successful on the project so far.

1 What does Carlota thank Antoni for?

2 Carlota describes the production team as 'amazing'. Why?

3 What does Antoni give in terms of positive feedback?

4 Who does Carlota thank at the end of the meeting, and why?

C Carlota says that working face to face is always better than working remotely – using email, conference or video calls. Do you agree? Why / Why not?

Functional language **Leading and participating in review meetings**

3A Complete the phrases for leading a review meeting using the words in the box.

agenda   aspects   cause   comments   generally   plan   useful

State purpose of meeting	As you can see from the ¹_____ , what I want to do today is [take time to think about how we are doing things].
	I called this meeting because I feel we need to [have an in-depth discussion / review our strategy so far].
Invite ideas on what did/didn't go well	So just ²_____ speaking, what do you think about where things have gone well and where the problems were?
	I'd like to hear your ³_____ on [things that have gone well / any issues / the main challenges].
Explore what did/didn't go well	Which ⁴_____ of the project were the most [problematic / challenging / rewarding] exactly?
	What was the main ⁵_____ of this?
Focus on lessons learnt	So how do we ⁶_____ to do things differently [next time / from now on]?
	This has been ⁷_____ . We now know we need to [give ourselves realistic deadlines / prepare more thoroughly / plan better].

B Match the phrases for participating in a review meeting (1–8) with the categories (a–d).

1 Next time, we will insist on having [more time / clearer instructions / a bigger budget].

2 My big challenge was [in the early phases with production / finding reliable suppliers / meeting the tight deadlines].

3 Well, speaking openly, [the first designs I produced were not high quality / I underestimated the complexity].

4 If I'd planned more carefully at the beginning, [I could have produced a better design / I wouldn't have gone over budget].

5 On the whole, it turned out to be [a success / a great learning process / incredibly challenging].

6 In terms of my main/own success, I managed [to complete the first two phases on time / not to go over budget].

7 I think, overall, [it's been good / it could have been better planned].

8 I had to be very careful with [spending / scheduling / allocating different jobs] but managed it.

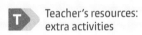

a Express an overall view
b Discuss what went well
c Discuss what didn't go well
d Identify lessons learnt

C Match the sentence halves.

1 Overall, it's great that we have …

2 I managed to do this …

3 This mistake was due to …

4 If I'd planned this more carefully, I could have …

5 Next time, I need to dedicate more time to …

6 It's important never to underestimate …

a preparing thoroughly before the project starts.

b the need for good communication.

c an oversight on my part.

d hit all of our most important targets.

e avoided these quality problems.

f by working very hard in the last few months.

T Teacher's resources: extra activities

4A Read the information.

▶ TASK

Professional context
You are attending a performance development workshop. The event offers individuals the opportunity to reflect and learn with others using their experiences of success and failure in the last twelve months. The process is designed to help individuals use their experiences to learn fast and achieve more in the future.

B Individually, think about your last twelve months and about a significant success and failure (real or invented). Use this template sent to workshop participants and prepare to talk about the experience.

Sharing stories to develop performance
- What was the success / failure?
- What happened? Why did it happen?
- What could / should have been done differently?
- What did you learn from the experience?
- What will you do the same / differently next time?
- How might this story help others to develop?

C In small groups, take turns to talk about your experiences: what went well / not so well; what learning experiences you gained, and which of these might be useful for the group. The group should feel free to ask questions during and after your explanation.

D When you have finished, as a class, reflect on your discussions. How useful was it to hear other people's stories? What did you learn? What might you do differently as a result?

Self-assessment
- How successfully have you achieved the lesson outcome? Give yourself a score from 0 (I need more practice) to 5 (I know this well).
- Go to My Self-assessment in MyEnglishLab to reflect on what you have learnt.

| **Lesson outcome** | Learners can write a performance review summary. |

Lead-in

1 **Read the performance review summary. Complete it with the words in the box. Then compare in pairs.**

adapt earn delegate demonstrate ensure give
keep manage meet recognise support take

I am pleased to report that you seem to have settled in well to your new job as team leader. You ¹_____ the ability to motivate your team with confidence, communicating effectively with them. You ²_____ clear instructions, listen actively and are quick to understand new ideas. You ³_____ work to match people's skills and ⁴_____ that they have the authority to go with that responsibility. You also ⁵_____ what your team needs, ⁶_____ them when necessary and ⁷_____ their trust and respect.

In addition you ⁸_____ well to changes and ⁹_____ the initiative to solve unexpected problems. More importantly, you consistently meet deadlines, and ¹⁰_____ your time effectively and have not fallen behind with work, despite the demands on your time.

I am encouraged by your work so far, despite occasional problems with defining your expectations clearly enough for the team. You have been able to ¹¹_____ all your deadlines, which has also been a great achievement, although sometimes this has affected accuracy. Nevertheless, I am confident that these areas can be improved with more professional training.

¹²_____ up the good work!

Functional language

2A **Complete the table using the words in the box.**

ability achievement although aptitude confident
consistently exhibit however impressed met

Positive comments
I am pleased to report that …
You demonstrate the ¹_____ to …
You display great ²_____ for solving problems …
You ³_____ good decision-making skills …
You adapt well to changes …
You ⁴_____ meet deadlines …

Constructive criticism
I am ⁵_____ with what you have done so far, despite …
⁶_____ you have done an excellent job, you …
Meeting all your deadlines has been a great ⁷_____ , although …
Nevertheless, I am ⁸_____ that …
You successfully ⁹_____ all the targets but …
¹⁰_____ , I feel that more training …

B **Are these phrases positive comments or constructive criticism?**

This can easily be resolved with more targeted training.
This can sometimes lead to delays.
Unfortunately, the results indicate that goals were not always reached.
You have empowered staff with authority.
Your work indicates a good knowledge of …

→ **page 121** See Grammar reference: Phrasal verbs

T Teacher's resources: extra activities

L The performance review summary contains examples of phrasal verbs. Go to MyEnglishLab for optional grammar work.

›TASK

3A **Work in pairs. Look at the performance review notes on page 128 and decide which are positive comments and which are criticism. Discuss ways to make the criticism constructive.**

B **Look at the notes on page 130. Write a performance review summary of about 200 words.**

C **Exchange reviews with your partner. Did your partner include all the information? Did your partner use phrases from Exercise 2 to make the criticism sound constructive?**

| **Self-assessment** | • How successfully have you achieved the lesson outcome? Give yourself a score from 0 (I need more practice) to 5 (I know this well).
• Go to My Self-assessment in MyEnglishLab to reflect on what you have learnt. |

Ethics

6

> *'Being good is good business.'*
>
> Dame Anita Roddick, founder of the Body Shop

Unit overview

6.1 ▶ Ethical choices

Lesson outcome	Learners can use language related to ethics in business.

Lead-in

1 Discuss these questions.

1 How interested are you in fashion?
2 Where do you usually buy your clothes and shoes?
3 Where were your clothes and shoes made? (Hint: check the labels!)
4 Are there any fast fashion brands that you never buy? Why?
5 How ethical are the brands that you are wearing?

VIDEO

2 ▶ 6.1.1 Watch the video on ethics in the fashion industry and answer the questions using the names of the speakers in the box.

> Alienor Taylor   Domenica Delfini Arroyo   Maxine Bédat   Mike Barry   Peter Ingwersen

1 Who is the co-founder of an ethical fashion brand?
2 Who is head of Corporate Responsibility for a UK retailer?
3 Which speaker finds the environmental and ethical impact of fashion unacceptable?
4 Who says there is tension regarding ethics between more expensive brands and fast fashion retailers?
5 Which designer is positive about the future of ethical fashion?

3 Watch the video again and complete the summary. Use one to four words in each gap.

According to Maxine Bédat, people are asking the question, [1]_____ ? This is because consumers are more aware of the ethical issues in the fashion industry. For example, in [2]_____ , a factory building collapsed and tragically [3]_____ . Domenica Delfini Arroyo at the Istituto Marangoni says the campaigns against unethical fashion started a movement where some labels and designers began to [4]_____ as ethical. As a result, clothing stores such as [5]_____ in the UK are trying to sell customers more [6]_____ by sourcing fair-trade cotton.

Meanwhile, at the London College of Fashion, [7]_____ are trying to use only ethically sourced materials. Domenica explains how the ethical debate has led to a(n) [8]_____ in the fashion business between top priced labels and the popular or [9]_____ brands. It seems the industry hasn't found an ethical [10]_____ yet. However, fashion designer Peter Ingwersen is more optimistic. Peter thinks fashion will become a(n) [11]_____ in the future and there won't be a difference between ethical and mainstream fashion.

 Teacher's resources: extra activities

4 Work in pairs. Why is it difficult for fast fashion to be ethical? Do you think it's any different for other industries? Why / Why not?

Vocabulary   **Business ethics**

5 Which word that is repeated in the video collocates with all these words?

> ... designer   ... industry   ... retailer   ... show

Example: Turn dial anti-clockwise once.

6 How do you need to move each dial to make collocations from the video using all the words? Look at the example to help you.

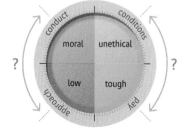

| be accused of |
| be aware of |
| be responsible for |
| campaign against |
| have an impact on |
| look across |
| take responsibility for |

7 Complete the questions using the correct form of the verbs with prepositions in the box.

1 If you _____ the whole fashion industry, is it more ethical today than it was?

2 An increasing number of clothing brands _____ unethical practices since people have become more informed about the issue.

3 Who do you think _____ the working conditions and sweatshops in Rana Plaza?

4 Who should _____ the health and safety of workers in the industry?

5 Do you think the public in your country _____ unethical fashion? Why / Why not?

6 If you were going to _____ unethical fashion in a way that would _____ the public, what would you do?

8 Choose the correct options in italics to complete the text from #lookgoodbegood.

Look good, be good

We all love clothes, but at what price? Looking ¹*across / for* the fashion industry, we see many manufacturers who are responsible for low pay and tough or even dangerous ²*conditions / condition*. Retailers are rarely transparent about the existence of sweat ³*stores / shops* or how they source their materials and garments.

Join us this week to campaign ⁴*of / against* unethical fashion! Make a difference by telling your family and friends to be ⁵*aware / beware* of ethical clothing brands and support our awareness campaign #lookgoodbegood.

Sign the petition in which we ask everyone in the fashion ⁶*industry / show*, not only those who are accused ⁷*for / of* unethical practices, to follow our five-point plan.

- Improve working conditions in factories and pay clothing workers a fair wage.
- Take responsibility ⁸*for / of* unethical conduct and end bad practices.
- Be transparent about supply chains and use ⁹*ethical / ethically* sourced materials.
- Promote and advertise ethical fashion ¹⁰*shopping / retailers*.
- Take care of our planet by taking ¹¹*responsibly / responsibility* for reducing carbon emissions and recycling.

Wear our 'Look good, be good' t-shirt, made of 100% organic, ¹²*fair-trade / fair* cotton and have an impact ¹³*for / on* the fashion industry. Show them we want to be responsible consumers and wear our clothes not in shame, but with pride!

 Teacher's resources: extra activities

PROJECT: Survey – How ethical are your clothes?

9A Work in pairs or small groups. You are going to survey your classmates to find out how ethical their clothes are. Prepare questions before you start. You want to find out:

1 who owns a garment made from organic or fair-trade cotton.

2 who sometimes wears vintage clothes.

3 who often gives their clothes away to charity.

4 who has bought clothes made of recycled materials.

5 who wears leather goods.

6 how often people buy fast fashion items, e.g. every two months / once a year.

7 where your classmates' clothes were made.

B Carry out your survey making careful notes of people's answers and the total number of people interviewed.

10 Write up your key findings as a report. You do not need to include all the data from your survey. Write 160–180 words.

Self-assessment

- How successfully have you achieved the lesson outcome? Give yourself a score from 0 (I need more practice) to 5 (I know this well).
- Go to My Self-assessment in MyEnglishLab to reflect on what you have learnt.

❯ 59 ❮

Lesson outcome	Learners can use the third conditional to talk about hypothetical past results of a previous action or situation.

Lead-in

1 How many different ways can you think of to measure how ethical a company or organisation is?

2 Complete the text using the words and phrases in the box.

> environment environmental financial framework measures
> people profits socially responsible

The Triple Bottom Line

The 'triple bottom line', also known as the TBL, is a(n) ¹_____ , or a structure for a set of ideas, that measures financial, social and ²_____ performance. The concept was first used in 1994 by John Elkington, founder of SustainAbility. It includes the three 'P's: ³_____ , people and planet. The first bottom line is ⁴_____ , evaluating income, profits and losses. The second bottom line refers to the ⁵_____ who are involved in a company's activities or affected by them, and how ⁶_____ the organisation is. The third bottom line ⁷_____ an organisation's impact on the ⁸_____ .

Listening

3 🔊 6.01 **Listen to an interview with Katrina Sands, an expert on ethics and the triple bottom line. Answer the questions.**

1 Which of the three 'P's is the easiest to measure?

2 What examples of the three 'P's does Katrina mention?

3 What example does she give of how the different bottom lines can be connected?

4 🔊 6.02 **Listen to Katrina talking about three businesses that are considered ethical for different reasons. Match the companies with the correct business sectors (a–c) and examples of ethical conduct (i–iii).**

Company	Business sector	Ethical conduct
1 Natura Cosméticos, Brazil	**a** Beauty products, healthcare, home care and chemicals	**i** social integration, diversity and sourcing
2 Kao Corporation, Japan	**b** Dairy products	**ii** sustainability, diversity and transparency
3 La Fageda cooperative, Catalonia, Spain	**c** Personal care products	**iii** integrity, preservation of the environment, diversity and social issues

5 🔊 6.03 **Listen to the final part of the interview. Which of these points does Katrina mention?**

1 environmental disasters such as oil spills

2 corruption in local government

3 use of palm oil

4 clearing forests in the Amazon

5 use of child labour

6 transparency of management salaries

7 the importance of making a profit

6 Work in pairs. Which of the three areas of the TBL is a) the most important for you? b) the most important in the place where you work/study? Why?

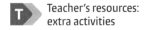

T > Teacher's resources: extra activities

Grammar **Third conditional**

7A 🔊 6.04 **Match the sentence halves. Then listen to the extracts from the interview to check your answers.**

1 They would have had inequality in the workplace
2 If they hadn't developed the Kao way, they
3 Kao could have had a good relationship with local people
4 If they had grown faster,

a if they had simply donated money to the community.
b would they still have been a responsible business?
c might not have been listed as one of the world's most ethical companies.
d if Natura hadn't taken on female managers.

B **Look at the sentences in Exercise 7A again and answer the questions.**

1 Do we use the third conditional for speculating about the past, the present or the future?
2 Which verb form is used with the *if*-clause?
3 Which modal verbs can we use instead of *would* in the main conditional clause?

➔ **page 122** See Grammar reference: Third conditional

8A **Complete the sentences using the third conditional.**

1 We _____ (not pay) such a high tax bill last year if we _____ (give) some of our profits to a charity for the homeless.
2 If they _____ (not take on) employees with disabilities, they _____ (not have) diversity in the workplace.
3 We _____ (could reduce) both our transport costs and carbon emissions if we _____ (source) all of our raw materials locally.
4 We _____ (might develop) a better relationship with the community if our staff _____ (do) voluntary work with local people.
5 If you _____ (take) care of employees better, _____ (you / retain) more staff last year?
6 _____ (we / save) more money if we _____ (recycle) all our waste?

B **Work in pairs. Do the situations in Exercise 8A involve profits, people or planet, or a combination of these?**

Teacher's resources: extra activities

➔ **page 116** See Pronunciation bank: Contractions and weak forms in third conditionals

Speaking **9** **Work in small groups. Choose an organisation or company you are familiar with and discuss these questions.**

1 How ethical is the organisation or company in terms of profits, people and planet? Consider some of these ways of measuring the triple bottom line.

Profits: costs, donations, income, profits, taxes
People: choosing partners and suppliers, health and safety of customers and staff, relationships with stakeholders, the recruitment process
Planet: carbon emissions and energy consumption, recycling, transport, use of natural resources, waste management

2 Think of specific decisions the organisation has taken in the last few years. How could the organisation or company have acted more or less ethically? Try to include third conditional sentences using some contractions in your answers.

If they'd been more transparent about profits, they wouldn't have had a problem with their reputation.

They could/might have been more ethical if they had considered their impact on the environment.

COMMUNICATION SKILLS
Transparency in business

Learners are aware of different ways to manage business relationships and can use a range of phrases for voicing concerns.

Lead-in

1 Work in pairs and read the text. Then discuss which statement (a or b) you agree with most. Why?

> **Relationships, trust and honesty**
>
> Business is built on relationships, and relationships are built on trust. And trust can be strongly influenced by culture. In some cultures the concept of honesty and the acceptability of not telling the complete truth may also be different.

a It is acceptable to not give information to a colleague or business partner if you feel it might worry them unnecessarily.

b It is always better to be open and transparent even if it causes problems.

VIDEO

Go to MyEnglishLab for extra video activities.

2A ▶ 6.3.1 **Watch as Emma (Go Global's Financial Analyst) gives Claudio (Key Account Manager) some information about the pan-Asian distributor they suggested to EN-Tek.**

1 What news does Emma have?

2 Has this news been confirmed?

3 What advice does she give to Claudio?

4 How does Claudio feel about Emma's idea?

B Do you agree with Emma's advice to Claudio? Why / Why not?

3A In small groups, discuss which is the best approach (Option A or B) for Claudio to use when talking to Sanjit. Give reasons for your answers. As a class, decide which video to watch first.

Option A – Be indirect and don't give all the information

Avoid sharing the information you have because it's not confirmed.

Option B – Be direct and share all the information

Be open and share the information you have even though it's not confirmed.

B Watch the videos in the sequence the class has decided, and answer the questions for each video.

Option A ▶ 6.3.2   **1** What does Sanjit feel they can benefit from?

2 How does Claudio deal with Sanjit's suggestion about SendAll?

3 How do you think Sanjit feels at the end?

Option B ▶ 6.3.3   **1** How does Sanjit describe working with SendAll?

2 How does Claudio deal with Sanjit's suggestion about SendAll?

3 Does Sanjit sound worried when he is talking about SendAll to Claudio?

4 Judging from the text Sanjit sends to Katie, how do you think he really feels?

4 Work in pairs. Discuss what lessons you have learnt about openness and how the two approaches can have different results. Think about how they can affect business decisions and the relationships.

5 ▶ 6.3.4 Watch the Conclusions section of the video and compare what is said with your answers in Exercise 4. Do you agree? Why / Why not?

Reflection

6 Think about the following questions. Then discuss your answers with a partner.

1 Think of a time, in a work or social situation, when you had to decide whether to be open or to manage the truth. Which approach did you take and what happened as a result?

2 Following this lesson, think of one thing you could do differently to manage such situations more effectively in future.

Functional language

Voicing and responding to concerns

7A Complete the phrases from the video using the words in the box.

| advocate confirmed entirely important light loud thought worry |

1 This information isn't _____ , but I think you should know.

2 Just thinking out _____ here, but maybe we can benefit [from going into partnership].

3 It's _____ to be open, so I want to let you know [what I've heard / about the latest developments / about the current situation].

4 I'm not _____ sure [at this stage / right now].

5 There might be [new issues / further difficulties / unexpected developments] that come to _____ .

6 I don't want to _____ you, but I feel I have to tell you this.

7 I'm playing devil's _____ here, but I'm not sure that [would be a good idea / is advisable / I would recommend that].

8 It's just a _____ . I could be wrong.

B **What other ways of voicing concerns can you think of?**

8 Match the questions (1–5) with the answers (a–e).

1 Can we have the report on the project results?

2 When will you have finished that task?

3 What do you think about the new suppliers?

4 Can you give me a straight answer?

5 Do you like my idea?

a To be honest, not really. I don't think it'll work.

b I'm concerned that they will not be able to keep up with demand.

c I'm afraid I might not be able to. It's complicated.

d I can't say for certain, but it will be soon.

e No, I'm sorry. It's not ready yet.

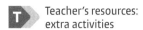
Teacher's resources: extra activities

9 **Work in pairs. What would you suggest to the speaker in these situations? Use two or three phrases from Exercise 7A.**

1 'I've heard that some of us are going to be made redundant next month.'

2 'I'm thinking of borrowing more money to keep the business running until it starts making a profit.'

3 'I'm going to leave my job and go travelling around the world.'

➤ TASK

10A **Work in pairs. You are colleagues and both have some concerns you want to raise. You also have some information that will be useful to your partner. Read your role cards and prepare for your discussions. Student A turn to page 128; Student B turn to page 132.**

B **Hold your informal conversations. Take turns to voice your concerns and respond to your partner's concerns, using phrases from Exercises 7 and 8.**

C **When you have finished, discuss which phrases you found useful and what you found difficult during the conversations.**

Self-assessment

- How successfully have you achieved the lesson outcome? Give yourself a score from 0 (I need more practice) to 5 (I know this well).
- Go to My Self-assessment in MyEnglishLab to reflect on what you have learnt.

| Lesson outcome | Learners can use a range of language to sell and promote products, services and ideas. |

Lead-in

1 Work in pairs and discuss the questions.

1 Do you think the ability to sell is important for all professionals, or only for specialist salespeople?

2 Do you think you are / would be good at selling? Why / Why not?

3 What do you see as the top three qualities of a good salesperson? Which is the most important? Why?

Listening

2A ◆ 6.05 **Luigi's company provides IT software services to small and medium-sized companies. He is at a local networking event and meets a potential new client, Caroline Macklin, who runs a tour business for English-speaking tourists.**

1 How does Luigi open the conversation?

2 What knowledge of the potential customer does he show?

3 What does Luigi explain as the specialism of his company?

4 What does he say his company's solutions offer?

B ◆ 6.06 **Listen to Luigi as he begins to promote and sell his services more strongly to Caroline.**

1 What does Caroline refer to as 'really useful'?

2 How flexible does Luigi claim the software is?

3 Caroline is worried about the complexity of the new software. How does Luigi deal with this concern?

4 What is the cost of the product?

C What are the advantages and disadvantages of Luigi's approach to discussing costs?

Functional language

Selling a product or service

3A Complete the phrases used by Luigi with the words in the box.

| benefit   certain   cost   enable   expertise   medium   price   solution |

Introduce what your company sells	We specialise in software solutions for small and ^{1}_____-sized companies.
	Our ^{2}_____ is in [providing the correct support / creating solutions / developing programs].
Explain how the product helps clients	Our solutions ^{3}_____ you to manage and communicate with clients more effectively.
	Your business will ^{4}_____ when you can [track sales / send follow-up emails].
Comment on costs	The final ^{5}_____ will depend on which solution you need.
	On the ^{6}_____ side, [I think we need to see what precise solution you need].
Show personal conviction in the product	I really believe this is the perfect ^{7}_____ for a small business like yours.
	I am absolutely ^{8}_____ that [we have exactly what you need / you will be totally satisfied].

B Luigi manages the conversation with Caroline by asking lots of sales questions. Match the questions (1–6) with the sales skills (a–f).

1 How does that sound?

2 So, what would be a useful next step?

3 Are there any other questions I can answer right now?

4 Is budget a major consideration for you?

5 So, how about if I come over, show you the product ...?

6 Could this software be useful for you?

a Check client needs

b Request feedback on what you said

c Explore possible blockers to a sale

d Invite further questions from client

e Focus on future action

f Propose next steps

C In pairs, take turns to sell these products and services to each other, using the phrases in Exercises 3A and 3B. Give each other feedback after each conversation.

- a technical product (e.g. smartphone, car, laptop)
- a must-see holiday destination
- a clothing brand
- a great place to eat
- an excellent training course
- a sports club

T Teacher's resources: extra activities

▶ TASK

4A Work in pairs and read the information. Then choose a product or service to promote – it could be something related to your current organisation or another product or service you know well.

> **Professional context**
>
> You are attending an industry networking event on behalf of your organisation. The objective is to meet people, discover their needs and promote your product or service. Ideally, you will set up further meetings with the people you meet to discuss needs and potential sales in more detail.

B In your pairs, use the template to prepare a short profile of the ideal customer for your product or service.

C Work with another pair. Explain your products and swap your customer profiles. Then take turns to be the salesperson and customer, and roleplay your sales conversations at the networking event. Try to achieve a positive response from the customer and an agreement to meet again.

D When you have finished both roleplays, discuss what went well and what you found difficult in each conversation. What would you do differently in future?

IDEAL CUSTOMER PROFILE

Professional background:

....

Potential needs for your product/service:

....

Benefits to them of your product/service:

....

Possible resistance to buying your product/service:

....

Availability for a future meeting:

....

Self-assessment

- How successfully have you achieved the lesson outcome? Give yourself a score from 0 (I need more practice) to 5 (I know this well).
- Go to My Self-assessment in MyEnglishLab to reflect on what you have learnt.

▶ 65 ◀

Lesson outcome	Learners can write an internal company newsletter giving news and describing future plans.

Lead-in

1 Complete the newsletter with one preposition in each gap.

Hero of the month

Salvador Fidalgo is our 'Hero of the month' [1]_____ his work on our local community programme. He has formed and coached a football team [2]_____ local teenagers and the youngsters have done so well that they have just won a regional football competition. Salvador says he has had a very rewarding time working [3]_____ these youngsters and, as a result, he is going to start a second team.

We encourage all staff [4]_____ participate in our programme, so you could become a community hero, too. We are currently establishing a project to turn unused public spaces [5]_____ useful community gardens where local residents can grow both vegetables and decorative plants. Therefore, if you are interested [6]_____ gardening or just enjoy working outside, please contact Human Resources immediately.

We are going to run a competition next month so staff can suggest ideas [7]_____ other projects we can be involved [8]_____ . A fabulous holiday is the prize [9]_____ the winning idea. What are you waiting [10]_____ ?

Functional language

2A Complete the sentences in the table with the correct form of the verbs in brackets. Refer back to the newsletter in Exercise 1 if necessary.

Recent news	Salvador [1]_____ (form) and _____ (coach) a football team ...
	The young people [2]_____ (won) a regional competition.
	He [3]_____ (have) a rewarding time ...
Current news	Salvador Fidalgo [4]_____ (be) our 'Hero of the month'.
	We [5]_____ (establish) a new garden-based project.
	Residents can [6]_____ (grow) vegetable and plants ...
Future plans	... he [7]_____ (start) a second team.
	We [8]_____ (run) a competition next month.

B Where in the table in Exercise 2A would you place the following phrases?

A school is being built in South Africa.   Employees can now take advantage of extra discounts.
One of our new projects has been filmed for television.   Only eco-friendly products will be sold.
Staff will have extra holiday for time spent on community work.
We introduced a new holiday strategy two months ago.

 T Teacher's resources: extra activities

 **L** The newsletter contains examples of linking words for causes and results. Go to MyEnglishLab for optional grammar work.

C Look at the table again and identify which tenses can be used for each category.

➡ **page 122** See Grammar reference: Linking words for causes and results

➡ **page 116** See Pronunciation bank: Chunking, pausing and stress when reading aloud

〉TASK

3A Work in pairs. Look at the notes for a newsletter on page 134. Classify them as recent news, current news or future plans. Think of a title for the newsletter.

B Use the notes from Exercise 3A to write a newsletter of about 200 words.

C Exchange newsletters with your partner. Did your partner include all the information? Did your partner use appropriate tenses for each type of news?

Self-assessment

- How successfully have you achieved the lesson outcome? Give yourself a score from 0 (I need more practice) to 5 (I know this well).
- Go to My Self-assessment in MyEnglishLab to reflect on what you have learnt.

Time management

> 'Until we can manage time, we can manage nothing else.'
>
> Peter F. Drucker, Austrian-American management consultant

Unit overview

7.1 > **Managing time**
Lesson outcome: Learners can use a range of vocabulary related to time management.

Video: Time management
Vocabulary: Managing time
Project: The working from home debate

7.2 > **Smart work**
Lesson outcome: Learners can use adverbials and time expressions correctly.

Reading: Cutting overtime in Japan
Grammar: Adverbials and time expressions
Speaking: Are you good at managing time?

7.3 > **Communication skills:** Dealing with urgency
Lesson outcome: Learners are aware of different ways to communicate urgency and can use a range of phrases for discussing priorities.

Video: Dealing with matters of urgency
Functional language: Discussing priorities
Task: Following up on emails

7.4 > **Business skills:** Difficult negotiations
Lesson outcome: Learners can use various strategies and phrases for dealing with difficulties in negotiations.

Listening: A difficult meeting
Functional language: Dealing with difficulties in negotiations
Task: Dealing with difficult people at work

7.5 > **Writing:** An email giving reasons
Lesson outcome: Learners can write an email to colleagues giving reasons for missing a deadline and outlining action required.

Model text: An email offering an explanation
Functional language: Problem, reasons and required action
Grammar: Prepositions of time
Task: Write an email to your boss about a problem

Business workshop 7: p.100 | **Review 7:** p.110 | **Pronunciation:** 7.2 Stress in adverbials and time expressions 7.4 Intonation when negotiating p.117 | **Grammar reference:** p.123

7.1 ➤ Managing time

Lead-in

1 **Discuss these questions.**

1 How do you keep track of what you need to do? Do you use an electronic or paper calendar, a list, etc.?

2 How do you plan what needs to be done when? Does this always work? Why / Why not?

3 How do you prioritise the tasks you have to do every day? How do you deal with deadlines?

4 Look at the four illustrations and answer these questions.
- How many of these time management methods have you tried?
- How useful were they to you?

VIDEO

2A **Work with a partner. You are going to watch a video about time management. What do you know about time management in these situations? What do you think is unique to each situation?**

a on traditional factory assembly lines

b in modern warehouses used by online retailers

c in international projects and teams

d for people who work freelance

B ▶ 7.1.1 **Watch the video and check your ideas.**

3 **Watch the video again and match the sentence halves.**

1 With production targets and project deadlines to meet,

2 Measuring and managing the time spent on tasks,

3 My main role in the team is to organise a schedule,

4 ... what really helps me is making a to-do list

5 Organising one's own time as a freelance

6 But whatever the role and whatever the industry,

a to allocate resources and set the goals for the team members.

b is worlds away from the experience of workers on Henry Ford's assembly lines.

c effective time management is a top concern.

d at the beginning of the week ...

e good time management will continue to be essential to business profitability and to an individual's career success.

f became part of a management approach known as Fordism.

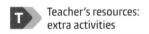

Teacher's resources: extra activities

4 **Work in pairs. What problems other than time can you imagine in planning projects with people located all over the world?**

Vocabulary

Managing time

5 **Complete the sentences to make verb + noun partnerships used in the video.**

| allocate   identify   maximise   measure   schedule   set   take   use |

1 Henry Ford was one of the first people to _____ **time**.

2 When managing time for a team, it is important to _____ **goals**.

3 Good time management is important in order to _____ **efficiency**.

4 Department heads may have to _____ **jobs** that need to be done by staff.

5 Team leaders are often the people who _____ **resources**.

6 Office workers today have to _____ **key priorities**.

7 Some people prefer to _____ **digital calendars.**

8 Freelancers need to stay focused and shouldn't _____ **a break** until they have finished a certain amount of work.

6 Read the definitions and complete the expressions with 'time' in the puzzle. When complete, you will reveal a common saying in the purple boxes.

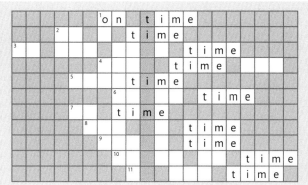

1. when you do things at the correct time or arranged time
2. when you deal with things separately (one after the other) or in separate groups of three, ten, etc.
3. when you do things so that they happen together
4. plan so that you have time available for something
5. time you spend on your job in addition to your normal working hours
6. spend time doing something that is not useful and has no result
7. when you do something before it is necessary
8. when you have no more time available to do something
9. use time doing a particular thing or pass time in a particular place
10. when you do something earlier than the time when it should be done
11. when you do something after something else has already happened

7 Match the sentence halves so that the words in bold are used correctly.

1. Team managers have to **allocate**
2. We had until the end of the month for the project but we were glad to finish **ahead**
3. An important part of time management is the ability to **identify**
4. Production managers organise the work on the assembly line in order to **maximise**
5. He is the type of person who needs to do one thing **at**

a. **of time** so that we could get started implementing the first steps.
b. **efficiency** so that the factory can produce as much as possible.
c. **a time** or he starts to feel stressed.
d. **resources** so that they will be used efficiently.
e. **key priorities** so that they can be dealt with first.

▶ Teacher's resources: extra activities

8 Decide with a partner if these statements are true or false for you.

I'm still studying and haven't started work yet.
1. Setting goals for yourself that need to be finished before you take a break is important when you study on your own.
2. It is not a good idea to waste time socialising at university because it is better to concentrate on getting your work done.

I have experience at work of managing my own time.
1. When you work from home, you need to maximise efficiency and manage your time.
2. Using internet access, a laptop or a smartphone and a digital calendar, you can work from anywhere.

▶ PROJECT: The working from home debate

9A Work in groups. You work in a centrally located office. The company needs to cut costs. Debate this management proposal, using the steps below.

'We propose moving to a smaller office further from the centre and having at least half our staff work from home.'

Group A: You are members of staff and are FOR THE MOVE. You like the idea of working from home and feel that you can make use of the time saved by not commuting.

Group B: You are team leaders and are AGAINST THE MOVE. You find it helpful when colleagues can collaborate and feel social aspects help team building.

• Prepare arguments for or against working at home. Give reasons and examples. Consider these points.

distractions   collaboration   commuting   flexibility
socialising   space for home office   the environment

• Prepare any counter arguments you anticipate the other team will make.

A: If I work at home, I can plan my day more easily. I can spend time with my family but also choose when I work. I will be able to save a lot of time as I won't have to travel.

B: People may save time by not commuting, but there could be more distractions at home.

B Debate in groups or as a class. Then vote individually for or against the proposal.

Self-assessment

• How successfully have you achieved the lesson outcome? Give yourself a score from 0 (I need more practice) to 5 (I know this well).
• Go to My Self-assessment in MyEnglishLab to reflect on what you have learnt.

7.2 ▶ Smart work

Lead-in

1 Work in pairs or small groups. Discuss these questions.

1 Do you find it difficult to complete what you need to do on time? Why / Why not?

2 How do you decide what to do first? Do you have or use a system?

3 Do you have any tips you can share?

2 Look at the phrases in the box and discuss them in your pairs or groups. What role do you think they play in time management?

> administrative work   excessive overtime   increased workloads
> work efficiently   lengthy meetings

Reading

3A Work in pairs. Read the title and subtitle of the article. What do you think the article will be about and what suggestions do you think might be made by the author?

B Read the article quickly and check your predictions in Exercise 3A.

4 Read the article again and complete the sentences.

1 Tatsuya Ito set his 'quitting marker' for _____ in the evening.

2 People decide what time their target for stopping work for the day should be by _____ .

3 Although quitting-time targets were not popular at first, staff find they work _____ .

4 Making staff aware of how long they need to do tasks, resulted in an _____ .

5 After the global financial crisis in 2008, management began to hold _____ .

6 The efforts made across the company have helped to _____ .

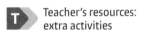 **Teacher's resources:** extra activities

5 Work with a partner. Discuss the ideas for managing time in the article. Which would be helpful to you? How would these work in your own situation?

NIKKEI ASIAN REVIEW

Cutting overtime in Japan – one company's efforts

Workers set quitting-time targets to encourage efficiency

Tokyo – Recruit Staffing is trying out methods to cut down on excessive overtime.

Stick to the plan

5 Tatsuya Ito, a 23-year-old salesman in Tokyo, placed a small green sign on his computer upon returning from a sales call, announcing to his colleagues that he was leaving **in**
10 **a few hours.** Such color-coded markers pop up across the office on a daily basis – in addition to the green 7 p.m. sign, there is blue for 6, yellow for 8 and red for 9 p.m. **at the latest**.
15 These are the work of Taisuke Shogetsu, the 49-year-old boss. The sales team almost never spends their day in the office but returns in the evening to take care of administrative
20 work. Each member sets his or her marker based on how much needs to be done.

Workers are not punished for missing their quitting-time targets.
25 **At first** though, people did not like the plan, saying that they could not finish by the target time. But the targets have helped employees to work more efficiently and staff hardly ever stay
30 past 6 or 7 p.m.

The team also limits the time each employee may speak at status update meetings and keeps company dinners short.
35 'It's important to reduce what needs to be done and be aware of the time work takes,' Shogetsu said. This philosophy has paid off: productivity at this Tokyo division climbed 4.5%
40 in 2015.

Testing solutions

These efforts are part of Recruit Staffing's 'smart work' program, begun in February 2013. After the 2008

45 global financial crisis, Recruit Staffing employees' workloads increased, encouraging management to find ways to use time more efficiently.

Information sessions were held for
50 staff and Recruit has **recently** begun changing how time is managed. Some of the ideas include requiring workers to report late-night hours, setting strict limits on number of hours
55 worked, and asking for ideas about how to cut lengthy meetings. These company-wide efforts have helped reduce the average length of the workday.
60 'Going forward, we aim to make the program about improving customer service, in addition to shortening working hours and improving efficiency,' an official said.

Grammar

Adverbials and time expressions

Different adverbs of frequency and time phrases appear in different places in sentences. For example:

Usually they finish their work by Friday afternoon. (beginning)

She **sometimes** works over lunch. (mid-position, i.e. between subject and verb or after *be* or auxiliary verb)

She does administrative work **from time to time**. (end)

Check the Grammar reference for more details about the position of these words and punctuation.

6 Look at the adverbials below. In which position (a–e) would you place the two underlined adverbials in the article?

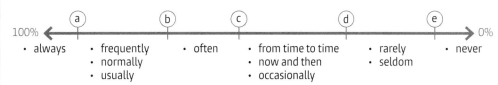

100% ← (a) ──── (b) ──── (c) ──── (d) ──── (e) → 0%

· always	· frequently	· often	· from time to time	· rarely	· never
	· normally		· now and then	· seldom	
	· usually		· occasionally		

7 Look at the time expressions in bold in the article and match them with their meanings. Which refer to the past and which to the future?

1 used to talk about the beginning of a situation, especially when it is different now
2 no later than the time mentioned
3 not long ago
4 at a particular time from now

8 Match the expressions using 'day' (1–3) with their meanings (a–c). Find an expression in the article to replace 'every day' in sentence 3. Where can these expressions come in sentences?

1 Many of us sit at our computers <u>all day</u>.
2 You can come by to see me <u>any day</u>.
3 Staff members put in many hours <u>every day</u>.

a on an unspecified day
b from Monday to Friday/Sunday
c from morning till evening

➜ **page 123** See Grammar reference: Adverbials and time expressions

9 Put the word or phrase in brackets into an appropriate position in the sentence. Where there are two, do not change the order.

1 They leave the office before 7 p.m. (almost never)
2 He goes to visit customers. (from time to time)
3 We take clients out for dinner. (occasionally)
4 They didn't like the idea, but now they think it is an excellent one. (at first)
5 You can find me at work from Monday to Thursday, but remember I don't work on Fridays. (any day, normally)
6 We should have more information. (in a few days)
7 Because meetings last about three hours, they have started to look into making them shorter. (usually, recently)

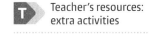

Teacher's resources: extra activities

➜ **page 117** See Pronunciation bank: Stress in adverbials and time expressions

Speaking

10 Work in pairs. Ask and answer these questions. Is your partner good at managing his/her time? Ask follow-up questions to get more information.

1 Do you usually say 'yes' to everything?
2 Do you often put tasks off until you feel like doing them?
3 Do you feel overwhelmed at first when you are given a deadline for a new project but then realise that you just need to work step-by-step?
4 Do you always make sure that everything you do is perfect no matter how long it takes?
5 Do you almost never deal with a task until it is a crisis?
6 Do you put off what you need to do on a daily basis because you work best under pressure?
7 Do you find that you rarely judge correctly how long a task will take?
8 Do you have a plan or routine that you follow every day?

How do you feel when you … ?
What would you need to manage your time better?

Self-assessment

- How successfully have you achieved the lesson outcome? Give yourself a score from 0 (I need more practice) to 5 (I know this well).
- Go to My Self-assessment in MyEnglishLab to reflect on what you have learnt.

Lesson outcome	Learners are aware of different ways to communicate urgency and can use a range of phrases for discussing priorities.

Lead-in **1A** Discuss in pairs. How quickly should you respond to an email that is asking for information? How might your usual response time cause you problems when working in teams?

B What would you say in each of these situations?

1 'Why haven't I heard back from you yet? I emailed you yesterday.'

2 'You responded at night last time, so I assumed you always check your emails then.'

3 'Don't just call me to follow up on an email without checking my availability first.'

VIDEO **2** ▶ 7.3.1 Watch as Sanjit shares some concerns with Katie.

1 What information has Sanjit found out about their distributor?

2 What is Sanjit surprised by?

3 What three options does Katie suggest to Sanjit?

L Go to MyEnglishLab for extra video activities.

3A In small groups, discuss which is the best approach (Option A or B) for Sanjit to use when following up with Emma. Give reasons for your answers. As a class, decide which video to watch first.

Option A – Low pressure: send a friendly email reminder to check when you might be able to get a response.

Option B – High pressure with urgency: call the other person to confirm that they got your email, ask why there hasn't been a response yet, and ask for the information you need.

B Watch the videos in the sequence the class has decided, and answer the questions for each video.

Option A ▶ 7.3.2

1 Why did Katie recommend an email rather than a call?

2 What does Katie mean by Go Global's different perspective?

3 How does Emma respond? What do you think of her response?

Option B ▶ 7.3.3

1 How quickly did Sanjit expect to hear back from Emma and why?

2 How does Emma feel when she hears this and how does she respond?

3 Does Sanjit get the information he wanted?

4 Why do you think Sanjit and Emma are frustrated with each other during the call?

4 Work in small groups. What tips can you think of for dealing with urgency and timeliness?

5 ▶ 7.3.4 Watch the Conclusions section of the video and compare what is said with your answers in Exercise 4. Do you agree? Why / Why not?

Reflection **6** Think about the following questions. Then discuss your answers with a partner.

1 How do you feel if you don't receive a response from someone when you expect to?

2 Are you aware of your own approach to response times and how that might affect others?

3 Decide on one thing you can do to deal more effectively with requesting urgent information and responding to urgent requests.

Functional language

Discussing priorities

7A Complete the phrases from the video using the words in the box.

information   overloaded   prioritise   respond   response   sorry

Defining priorities	Please ¹_____ this. [It's urgent / It can't be delayed any further.]
Requesting an update: high priority	I need a ²_____ [by tomorrow morning / by the end of the day / as soon as possible (ASAP) / by (the) close of business (COB) / by (the) end of play (EOP)].
Requesting an update: low priority	When do you think you'll be able to [get back to me / let me know / give me a definite answer]? Let me know when you'll get a chance to [send me the ³_____ / write up the report / give me your feedback].
Responding	I'm ⁴_____ for not [getting back to you earlier / returning your call sooner]. I'm ⁵_____ [at the moment / right now]. Can I get back to you [tonight / by the end of the day / by tomorrow afternoon]? I've [seen your mail / got your message] and will ⁶_____ by tomorrow morning.

B Where in the table in Exercise 7A would you place the following phrases?

1 That's a lower priority – the deadline is still a few weeks away.
2 I'm in meetings this morning, but I'll send you an update when I get back to my desk.
3 Can you update us [on progress] as soon as possible? We were expecting delivery yesterday.
4 We need to make this our top priority or we'll miss the deadline.

8 Work in pairs and read the scenarios. Decide if each one is high or low priority. Take turns to call your partner to follow up on the situations.

Scenario 1: You are waiting for a report which is due from a colleague tomorrow. You haven't heard from them since last week and have had no response to a reminder email you sent two days ago.

Scenario 2: You were expecting to have next week's schedule by this morning so that you could inform your team. You haven't received anything and it's now 2 p.m. on Friday.

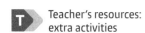
Teacher's resources: extra activities

❯TASK

9A Work in pairs. You are going to follow up on emails that your partner has not responded to. Read your role cards and prepare for your discussions: Student A turn to page 129, Student B turn to page 132.

B In your pairs, add any details you want to about the situations to make them more realistic for you. Then roleplay the two calls.

C At the end, discuss what you found easy and difficult about discussing your priorities. Which phrases from Exercise 7 did you find useful?

Self-assessment
• How successfully have you achieved the lesson outcome? Give yourself a score from 0 (I need more practice) to 5 (I know this well).
• Go to My Self-assessment in MyEnglishLab to reflect on what you have learnt.

❯ 73 ❮

Difficult negotiations

Lesson outcome	Learners can use various strategies and phrases for dealing with difficulties in negotiations.

Lead-in **1** **Work in pairs. Read the text about negotiating dimensions and discuss the questions.**

Dimensions for negotiating success

To be successful in negotiations that everyone feels committed to, negotiators must prepare for the following dimensions.

PEOPLE	➪	the people involved, who they are and how they want to be treated
CONTENT	➪	the things you are talking about, e.g. time, money, resources, etc.
PROCESS	➪	the procedure you use; the *way* it is done
STRATEGY	➪	the best approach to take in each specific negotiation stage, and in the overall negotiation

1 Why do we need to prepare all four dimensions? Talk about each one.
2 Why do we sometimes see people as difficult when negotiating?
3 Why might people sometimes see you as difficult when trying to reach agreement?

Listening **2A** 🔊 7.01 **Listen to a meeting in which Haruki, the team leader, tells one of his team members, Javier, that he needs to temporarily work in Japan.**

1 Why does Haruki need Javier to go to Japan?
2 Does Javier want to go?
3 In what way(s) do you think Javier's behaviour was 'difficult'?
4 How might Haruki have managed the conversation better?

B 🔊 7.02 **Later on, Haruki talks to Javier again. Listen and answer the questions.**

1 Why does Javier say there is no point in talking?
2 What usually causes delays?
3 Do they agree about Mia's and Julio's experience?
4 What plans has Javier already made?
5 What does Javier think will make things difficult for him?

C 🔊 7.03 **Listen to the final part of the conversation. Match the sentence halves to show how Haruki uses the negotiating dimensions to manage the situation.**

1	People: He asks for Javier's	**a**	understanding of some points.
2	Content: He tries to clarify his	**b**	open to suggestions for finding a solution.
3	Strategy: He shows himself to be	**c**	decision which works for both of them.
4	Process: He ends with a clear	**d**	overall opinion.

3 **Complete the four tips for managing difficulties in negotiations, using the words in the box. Which of these things did Haruki do?**

check   process   remain   set   take

1 _____ control
2 _____ your understanding
3 _____ a framework for communication / define the _____
4 _____ open

Functional language

Dealing with difficulties in negotiations

4A Match these phrases from the recordings in Exercise 2 with the categories a–e.

a Check your understanding ＿ ＿

b Refer to common understanding ＿ ＿

c Acknowledge the other person's perspective ＿ ＿

d Make suggestions / Be positive ＿ ＿

e State necessary action ＿ ＿

1 I know we're both on the same wavelength about their [experience / ability / skills / confidence].

2 In other words, you don't want to [send either of them / take the risk / give them too much responsibility].

3 I think we [can both agree / both have the opinion] that …

4 So what you're saying is [you definitely won't go / you don't like the idea].

5 How [about / would you feel if] we postpone your departure for a few days?

6 [From your point of view / In your opinion], it should take around a month of local support. Right?

7 We're going to have to go the extra mile to [get finished on time / meet the deadline / get the shipment out].

8 I understand your position, and reluctance, a bit more now.

9 This is a good thing that [can lead to more opportunities / we can all learn from / will open doors].

10 What that means exactly is that [I need you to go to Japan / we need to make this a priority / you have to take charge of the project / we are under-resourced / we need to develop new workflows].

B **How could you respond to these statements positively without seeming aggressive? Use phrases from Exercise 4A to help you.**

1 Why can't Mia or Julio go? (Refer to common understanding)

I think we can both agree that you're more experienced.

2 I can't go because I can't speak Japanese. (Acknowledge the other person's perspective and state necessary action)

3 I'm not going for two months. That's too long. (Acknowledge the other person's perspective and ask a question)

4 We've never done it that way before. (Make suggestions / Be positive)

5 I don't think it'll work like that. (Check your understanding)

6 That's a bad idea. (Check your understanding)

T Teacher's resources: extra activities

➔ **page 117** See Pronunciation bank: Intonation when negotiating

5A **Work in groups of three and read the scenarios. You are going to discuss each scenario to practise dealing with people you may feel are difficult. One person will be an observer for each discussion.**

❯**TASK**

Scenario 1 You (A and B) are colleagues working in the marketing department. It's very busy because the new website is launching at the end of the month.

Scenario 2 You (A and C) are in the same team meeting every Monday morning. These meetings are not usually very productive.

Scenario 3 You (B and C) are colleagues in the same department. B was recently promoted to become the team leader.

B Read your role cards and prepare: Student A turn to page 130, Student B turn to page 132, Student C turn to page 134. When you are the observer, make notes on how the discussion is managed and which phrases are used.

C Roleplay the three discussions. After each discussion, discuss what went well and what you can improve before rotating roles and moving on to the next scenario.

Self-assessment

- How successfully have you achieved the lesson outcome? Give yourself a score from 0 (I need more practice) to 5 (I know this well).
- Go to My Self-assessment in MyEnglishLab to reflect on what you have learnt.

Lesson outcome — Learners can write an email to colleagues giving reasons for missing a deadline and outlining action required.

Lead-in **1** Read the email and find the extra word in each line. Then compare in pairs.

Subject: Video for product launch

Hi Jake,

0   I'm really sorry to tell ~~to~~ you but, due to unforeseen circumstances, we've hit a
1   big problem completing the video which for your product launch.
2   At breakfast time this morning there was a major electrical failure in where we
3   are filming and some of equipment was damaged during the huge power surge.
4   Apparently, the electricity could be off for several more days so it's not highly
5   likely that we'll be at least for three days behind schedule even if we get back
6   to work on tomorrow, which is really worrying for everyone concerned. I therefore
7   propose that we travel to another location to complete the filming. If we will do
8   this, there'll only be a 3-day delay. The background scenery it won't be exactly
9   as planned, but this means that the video will be very ready for the launch.
10 I apologise for any inconvenience have caused, but assure you that the video will
11 be ready by next Friday at latest, providing you can accept the location change.

Functional language **2** Complete the table using the words in the box.

> arisen   because   caused   efforts   failure   hit   latest   main   re-assess
> solve   sorry   therefore   unforeseen   unfortunately

Introducing a problem	Explaining a reason	Outlining required action
I'm really ¹_____ to tell you that we've ²_____ a big problem.	There was a major electrical ⁷_____ in the town.	I ¹¹_____ propose that we travel ...
³_____ I won't be able to meet the deadline due to ⁴_____ circumstances ...	There is a delay ⁸_____ of a strike in the factory.	I'll have the job completed by Friday ¹²_____ .
Despite our best ⁵_____ , we are sorry to inform you that ...	The problem was ⁹_____ by late deliveries from suppliers.	We may need to ¹³_____ the schedule.
Unexpected problems have ⁶_____ with your order.	The ¹⁰_____ reason for the delay is ...	Extra staff are needed to ¹⁴_____ the problem.

 T Teacher's resources: extra activities

L The email contains examples of prepositions of time. Go to MyEnglishLab for optional grammar work.

➡ **page 124** See Grammar reference: Prepositions of time

 **›TASK**

3A Work in pairs. Look at the problems, reasons and actions on page 130. Match each problem with a reason and action and think about what phrases you could use to explain these.

B Look at the notes on page 129 and write an email of about 200 words to your boss about the situation.

C Exchange emails with your partner. Did your partner present the problems clearly, then give explanations and finally propose suitable action?

Self-assessment
- How successfully have you achieved the lesson outcome? Give yourself a score from 0 (I need more practice) to 5 (I know this well).
- Go to My Self-assessment in MyEnglishLab to reflect on what you have learnt.

Change

> 'The secret of change is to focus all your energy, not on fighting the old, but on building the new.'
>
> Socrates, Greek philosopher

Unit overview

8.1 **Change at Brompton Bikes**
Lesson outcome: Students can use a range of vocabulary related to change management.

Video: Brompton Bikes
Vocabulary: Change management
Project: Adaptability quiz

8.2 **Managing change**
Lesson outcome: Learners can understand and use reporting verbs and reported speech.

Listening: Difficult decisions and changes
Grammar: Reportin speech and reporting verbs
Speaking and writing: Telling and reporting a story

8.3 **Communication skills:** Coaching and mentoring
Lesson outcome: Learners are aware of different approaches to supporting colleagues and can use a range of phrases for coaching and mentoring.

Video: Discussing future options
Functional language: Coaching and mentoring
Task: The GROW model

8.4 **Business skills:** Brainstorming
Lesson outcome: Learners can use a range of strategies and phrases for leading brainstorming sessions.

Listening: A brainstorming meeting
Functional language: Leading a brainstorming session
Task: Brainstorming in small groups

8.5 **Writing:** Press release
Lesson outcome: Learners can organise information and use appropriate structures to write a press release.

Model text: A press release
Functional language: Useful phrases for a press release
Grammar: Passive voice with reporting verbs
Task: Write a press release

8.1 ▶ Change at Brompton Bikes

Lesson outcome	Students can use a range of vocabulary related to change management.

Lead-in

1 Discuss these questions.

1 What are / would be the risks and the benefits of cycling to your place of work or study?
2 If your company / organisation changed location, where would you like it to be? Think of a realistic location and give reasons for your answer.
3 How would this change in location affect members of staff and customers / visitors?

VIDEO

2A ▶ 8.1.1 **Look at the photo. Why do you think Brompton bikes might be unusual? Watch the video from 0:00 to 0:39 to check your answer.**

B Watch the rest of the video on managing change at Brompton and answer the questions.

1 Why did the company need to move location?
2 How successful was the move from the company's point of view?
3 How happy are the staff with the change?

3 Watch the video again from 0:00 to 0:26 and complete what the presenter says.

Change is a ¹_____ _____ _____ for everyone, whether it's starting school or college, ²_____ _____ or beginning a ³_____ _____ .

Companies also ⁴_____ _____ the need to change. It may be to ⁵_____ _____ , increase profits, or to ⁶_____ _____ new regulations. Whatever the reason, change can bring ⁷_____ and risk, so it needs very ⁸_____ _____ .

4 Watch the rest of the video again and decide if these sentences are *true* (T) or *false* (F). Correct the incorrect sentences.

1 Japan, East Asia and Europe are the main importers of Brompton bikes.
2 There are now almost 240 members of staff.
3 According to Greg Smith, the biggest risk was losing experienced staff.
4 Before the move, it took Tommy half an hour to get to work by underground or 45 minutes to cycle.
5 Management didn't consult staff before they moved.
6 The move happened in two stages: before Christmas 2015 and then in January 2016.
7 Tommy thinks the new site has more light and better views.

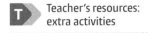

Teacher's resources: extra activities

5 Work in pairs. How easily would you adapt to a change in location of your usual place of work or study?

Vocabulary   Change management

6A Match the sentence halves from the video.

1 In order to **keep growing**, the company would
2 One of the main tasks was to **weigh up**
3 I was quite **apprehensive** at first, when the company first
4 We made sure we **consulted**
5 When the company actually moved
6 I am **coping** well now
7 People really have **adapted** well
8 The **morale** of the staff has improved

a informed us about **the move**.
b it was a very quick and **efficient** process.
c enormously as a result.
d with all our staff.
e have **to move** to a much larger site.
f the **risks** and **benefits** of different locations.
g to this new location.
h with the journey time.

B Work in pairs. Discuss the meaning of the words in bold in Exercise 6A. How do they relate to change management?

7 Look at the diagram about change management. Complete the words by adding the missing vowels.

1 pl __ n
2 c __ mm __ n __ c __ t __
3 t __ __ mw __ rk
4 eng __ g __

CHANGE
MANAGEMENT

5 impl __ m __ nt
6 impr __ v __
7 m __ __ s __ r __
8 s __ cc __ ss!

8 Complete the tips for dealing with change using the correct form of the words in capitals.

Why change?

1 Being flexible and knowing how to _____ to change is essential in order for organisations and people to keep growing and stay ahead of the competition. (ADAPTABLE)

2 Organisations often _____ change to improve _____ . (IMPLEMENTATION / EFFICIENT)

3 Whatever the reason, _____ change can bring about _____ and increase profits. (SUCCESS / IMPROVE)

4 However, if there is a lack of _____ and communication on the part of management, this may cause concern, _____ and uncertainty among staff. (PLAN / APPREHENSIVE)

5 It's important to _____ up all the _____ and benefits of any potential changes. (WEIGH / RISKY)

Teacher's resources: extra activities

9 Tell your partner about a time when you, or someone you know, resisted change. What happened? What should you/they have done differently?

PROJECT: Adaptability quiz

10 Do the quiz, 'How adaptable are you?' on page 135. Ask and answer the questions in pairs and discuss what you think your answers say about you.

11A Look at the 'A' answers in the quiz. What type of person would choose those? Why? Read the text 'Mostly As' on page 131. Do you agree with the description?

B Now work in a group of four which has two sub pairs. One pair writes a description for 'Mostly Bs' and the other writes a description for 'Mostly Cs'. Refer to the description for 'Mostly As' and write about 100 words.

Your answers suggest that you can sometimes be too …
You often feel you …
To change things in your life, start with …
It might be helpful to …

C In your group of four, compare your descriptions for personality types B and C. Do you think the other pair's description is accurate?

12A Work in pairs again. Write 2–3 more questions for the quiz, making sure that the answers correspond to the correct 'Mostly A/B/Cs' description.

B Test the questions from Exercise 10 and your questions from Exercise 12A on another partner. Do they agree with the personality type?

Self-assessment

- How successfully have you achieved the lesson outcome? Give yourself a score from 0 (I need more practice) to 5 (I know this well).
- Go to My Self-assessment in MyEnglishLab to reflect on what you have learnt.

| Lesson outcome | Learners can understand and use reporting verbs and reported speech. |

Lead-in

1 Work in pairs. How do you tend to respond to change? What sorts of changes would be the most and least disruptive for you? Use ideas from the box.

> buying a flat/house changing departments dropping out of university
> graduating last minute changes leaving home setting up a business

Listening

2A 🔊 8.01 Listen to Igor talking about making a tough decision about his choice of degree. What were his options?

B 🔊 8.02 Listen to Igor's decision. What did he do and was it a change for the better?

3 🔊 8.03 Listen to four more people talking about changes in their working lives. Make notes and answer the questions for each speaker.

1 What was the change?

2 How did he/she feel about or cope with the change?

3 Was it a change for the better, or did it make things worse?

4 Listen again and choose the correct option.

1 Ethan's boss wasn't replaced, although his company had said that it would be

  a a smooth transition.

  b a difficult time for a short period.

  c a period of uncertainty.

2 Pranali says she's quite good at adapting and is a(n)

  a anxious person.

  b flexible person.

  c courageous person.

3 Boon Tek says the new location is

  a far away on the other side of the city.

  b in a modern building but with few windows.

  c very remote, although there is more space.

4 Leticia's husband suggested going back to work because

  a she missed her colleagues.

  b her friends were still working.

  c it was difficult living with her.

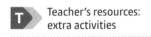
Teacher's resources: extra activities

5 Work in pairs. How would you feel about the changes if you were in the same position as the speakers?

Grammar

Reported speech and reporting verbs

6 Complete the sentences with the correct form of the words in brackets. There may be more than one possible answer.

1 Ethan said that he _____ (*not like*) changes because they _____ (*make*) him anxious.

2 Pranali told us that she _____ (*lose*) her job and that it _____ (*be*) a major change for her as it _____ (*come*) at a bad time.

3 Boon Tek said that once they were settled in the new laboratories, he _____ (*be able to*) appreciate they _____ (*be*) actually better off than before.

4 Leticia told us she _____ (*look*) forward to early retirement but that she _____ (*miss*) working, so she retrained. She told her colleagues she _____ (*give*) tai chi classes at her former company.

7A Identify the reporting verbs in these sentences about change.

  1 My parents advised me to follow my passion.
  2 Management insisted that the change of software was necessary.
  3 The client has just confirmed they won't be able to attend the meeting.
  4 The supplier informed us that they would put up their prices.
  5 Students complained that the new tables and chairs weren't comfortable.
  6 My colleague suggests that I change departments.
  7 My teacher suggested studying business administration.
  8 She promised to send me the relocation plan by next Monday.
  9 They'd promised us that the changes wouldn't take place until next year.
  10 He promised that he wouldn't make the same mistake again.

B Match the reporting verbs in Exercise 7A with the structures (a–e). Some verbs have more than one possible structure.

  a verb (*that*) + clause   **d** verb + someone (*that*) + clause
  b verb + *-ing*   **e** verb + someone + *to* + infinitive
  c verb + *to* + infinitive

➔ **page 124** See Grammar reference: Reported speech and reporting verbs
➔ **page 117** See Pronunciation bank: /s/, /z/, /ʃ/, /tʃ/ and /dʒ/

8A Work in pairs. Look at the sentences. Who do you think said these things?

> a brother or sister   a classmate   a lawyer   a new work colleague   a parent
> a technician   an administrator   an employee   management

  1 'I didn't touch your tablet! You always blame me for everything!'
  2 'How about helping me move these desks so that we can work in a group?'
  3 'Don't worry, I'll send you last month's figures next Monday, first thing.'
  4 'I'm sorry, but you need to send me a copy of your passport with your application. I can't process it without.'
  5 'We're phoning to let you know that we'll be installing the new equipment tomorrow at 8.30 a.m. Could you make sure that you will be in at that time?'
  6 'I'm really sorry I used your coffee cup. It won't happen again!'

B Rewrite the sentences in Exercise 8A using a suitable reporting verb from Exercise 7. Remember you don't have to report every single word and you will need to change some of the pronouns and time expressions.

  My brother complained that I always blamed him for everything.

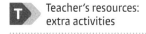
Teacher's resources: extra activities

Speaking and writing

9A You are going to describe a time when you experienced a major change at work, in your studies or in your personal life. Prepare what you are going to say before you start.

  1 Were you given any advice? What suggestions did your family and friends make?
  2 What helped you most/least with the change?
  3 How did you feel before and after?
  4 Thinking about it again, was the change a good thing? Why / Why not?

B Work in pairs and tell each other about the change. Take notes while you listen.

10A Work with a new partner. In your own words, retell the story your partner told you. Use reporting verbs and reported speech.

B Write up the story your partner told you in Exercise 9B, using at least six reporting verbs. Write 150–180 words.

Self-assessment

  • How successfully have you achieved the lesson outcome? Give yourself a score from 0 (I need more practice) to 5 (I know this well).
  • Go to My Self-assessment in MyEnglishLab to reflect on what you have learnt.

Lesson outcome	Learners are aware of different approaches to supporting colleagues and can use a range of phrases for coaching and mentoring.

Lead-in

1A **In pairs, read the definitions of coaching and mentoring and discuss the questions.**

> **Coaching**: partnering with clients in a process that makes them think creatively and inspires them to maximise their personal and professional potential. Coaching does not include advising or counselling, and focuses instead on individuals or groups setting and reaching their own objectives.

> **Mentoring**: providing wisdom and guidance based on personal expertise and experience.

1 In your own words, what is the difference between coaching and mentoring?
2 Have you ever been coached or had a mentor? How was the experience?
3 Have you ever coached or mentored others? How was the experience?

B **Do these situations refer to coaching or mentoring?**
1 Advising a friend on how they can solve a problem they have.
2 Asking questions about why someone feels they can't do something.
3 Telling someone how they can address an issue at work based on your experience.
4 Brainstorming options for someone's next professional development steps.

VIDEO

2 ▶ 8.3.1 **Watch as Sanjit prepares to discuss future projects with Katie.**
1 What does Sanjit want Katie to do next?
2 What are his concerns?
3 What does Katie think Sanjit wants to talk about?
4 How does she feel about this?

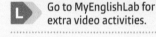

Go to MyEnglishLab for extra video activities.

3A **In small groups, discuss which is the best approach (Option A or B) for Sanjit to use in his conversation with Katie. Give reasons for your answers. As a class, decide which video to watch first.**

Option A – Be directive (a more mentoring style): Be direct and advise Katie on what to do.
Option B – Be non-directive (a more coaching style): Be less direct with the advice and ask questions.

Option A ▶ 8.3.2
Option B ▶ 8.3.3

B **Watch the videos in the sequence the class has decided, and answer the questions for Options A and B. In some cases both options are correct.**

In which option does:	A	B
1 Sanjit talk about the benefits of the new role?		
2 Sanjit express confidence Katie will do well in the new role?		
3 Katie voice concerns?		
4 Sanjit offer advice?		
5 Sanjit listen and take time for Katie's objections?		
6 Katie come up with solutions?		

4 **Think about the approaches Sanjit used in the videos and answer the questions.**
1 How does Katie feel at the end of each meeting about:
 a the new role? **b** communication with Sanjit?
2 What do you think might happen as a result of each meeting, both positive and negative?

5 ▶ 8.3.4 **Watch the Conclusions section of the video and compare what is said with your answers in Exercise 4. Do you agree? Why / Why not?**

Reflection

6 **Think about the following questions. Then discuss your answer with a partner.**
1 When supporting colleagues, do you ask questions or give opinions more?
2 How flexible are you with your style and are you aware of the impact that different approaches can have?

Functional language Coaching and mentoring

7A Complete the phrases from the video using the words in the box.

> approach   feel   make   should (x2)   tell   were

Coaching	What are your [options / goals / concerns]?
	How would you ¹_____ about the idea of [a fresh challenge / going abroad for a while / shadowing a colleague for a week]?
	How do you think you could best [²_____ / achieve] this?
	Do you think you ³_____ [get some further training / look at other options]?
	Have you considered [doing some research / applying for this role]?
	I can't ⁴_____ you what to do, but I can help you decide.
Mentoring	You ⁵_____ get [some further training / more details].
	You need to ⁶_____ [a decision / your mind up] about this soon.
	I think it would be best for you to [wait a while / think about it].
	If I ⁷_____ you, I'd [take this opportunity / ask for additional resources].

B Complete the dialogue using the words and phrases in the box.

> considered   good idea   mind up   opportunity   options   support

A: Thanks for your ¹_____ , Simone. What should I do next?

B: What ²_____ do you have as a next step?

A: Well, I'm not sure. What would you do if you were me?

B: If I were you, I'd take this ³_____ .

A: OK. So if I do that, what should I do first?

B: Have you ⁴_____ enrolling on a course?

A: That could be a ⁵_____ , I think.

B: I think you need to make your ⁶_____ about this soon.

T Teacher's resources: extra activities

8 Work in pairs. One of you is the coach and one is the coachee. The coachee wants to change departments at work but isn't sure how to do it, or if it's a good idea. The coach should ask questions and give advice using phrases from Exercise 7.

9A Individually, think of a problem or challenge you are currently facing and would be happy to discuss in a group.

▶TASK

B Now work in groups of three and discuss your challenges using the GROW model below. Rotate the roles three times so each person gets to play each role.

	Goal	Reality	Options/Obstacles	Way forward
GROW	After listing the problem/challenge, state your desired outcome or goal.	What is the current situation?	Which obstacles are standing in your way and which options do you have for overcoming them?	Thinking about the previous points, which next steps are you willing to commit to, however small?

Role A – Coachee: Let B guide you to a solution or next steps.

Role B – Coach/Mentor: Give support to A by giving advice and asking questions. Guide them through the GROW model.

Role C – Observer: Observe and take notes. Does B take more of a coach or mentor role? How successful does it seem?

C At the end of each roleplay, discuss the observer's feedback and what you can improve in the next roleplay.

8.4 ▶ BUSINESS SKILLS
Brainstorming

Lesson outcome	Learners can use a range of strategies and phrases for leading brainstorming sessions.

Lead-in **1A** 🔊 8.04 **Listen to a podcast about brainstorming and complete the flow chart.**

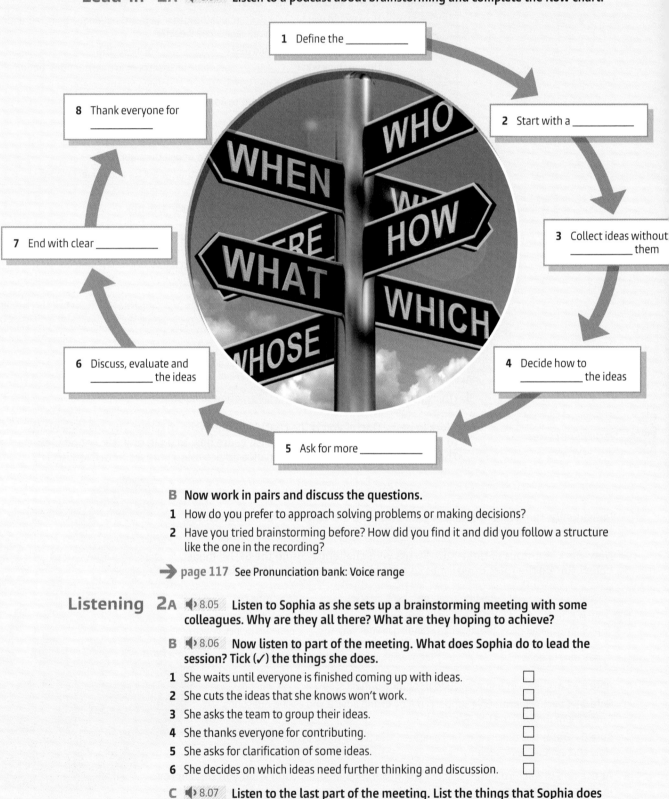

1 Define the _____

2 Start with a _____

3 Collect ideas without _____ them

4 Decide how to _____ the ideas

5 Ask for more _____

6 Discuss, evaluate and _____ the ideas

7 End with clear _____

8 Thank everyone for _____

B **Now work in pairs and discuss the questions.**

1 How do you prefer to approach solving problems or making decisions?

2 Have you tried brainstorming before? How did you find it and did you follow a structure like the one in the recording?

→ page 117   See Pronunciation bank: Voice range

Listening **2A** 🔊 8.05 **Listen to Sophia as she sets up a brainstorming meeting with some colleagues. Why are they all there? What are they hoping to achieve?**

B 🔊 8.06 **Now listen to part of the meeting. What does Sophia do to lead the session? Tick (✓) the things she does.**

1 She waits until everyone is finished coming up with ideas. ☐

2 She cuts the ideas that she knows won't work. ☐

3 She asks the team to group their ideas. ☐

4 She thanks everyone for contributing. ☐

5 She asks for clarification of some ideas. ☐

6 She decides on which ideas need further thinking and discussion. ☐

C 🔊 8.07 **Listen to the last part of the meeting. List the things that Sophia does to bring it to a close.**

D **Overall, how well do you think Sophia led the brainstorming session? Why? In your experience, would this creative process be successful in your national or corporate environment? Why / Why not?**

Functional language

Leading a brainstorming session

3A Complete the phrases from the recordings in Exercise 2 using the words in the box.

address   agreed   expand   go   idea   opening   session   statements

a _____	We're here today to ¹_____ the challenges presented by [the fast growth of our organisation / the threat from our competitors / the rapid changes in the market]. At the end of the ²_____ , [it would be great if we could have a clear idea of some steps we can take / it would be ideal if we have resolved this one particular issue].
b _____	These ³_____ highlight [the issues we're facing / some of the concerns we have to deal with]. These ⁴_____ questions will help us to [think about the main challenges ahead / identify where we need to focus first].
c _____	Feel free to [introduce any idea or make any suggestions you like]. There is no right or wrong, [all contributions are valid].
d _____	How would you like to [group / categorise] them?
e _____	Could you ⁵_____ [on this point for us]? Can you elaborate on that?
f _____	Adding to that ⁶_____ , [we could also update these tasks on the team status board].
g _____	What does everyone think about [that as an option / the idea that has been put forward]? Are we all ⁷_____ that [we're going to try the 'Daily stand-up' idea]?
h _____	Let's ⁸_____ with [that idea / what has been suggested / our agreed solution / that as a plan of action].

B Match these categories with the correct section (a–h) of the table in Exercise 3A.

1 Start with questions and statements about the issue   5 Make a decision
2 Build on the ideas of others   6 Collect as many ideas as possible
3 Ask for ideas about procedure   7 Discuss and evaluate
4 Define the goal   8 Ask people to give more details

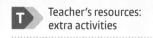
Teacher's resources: extra activities

4A Work in small groups and choose one of the scenarios below.

▶ TASK

Scenario 1
A reduced number of trains will stop in your town at peak times. Local officials are concerned it will discourage businesses from locating there. Local businesses are worried about recruitment and residents/commuters are concerned about overcrowding on trains. Brainstorm ways to manage these risks.

Scenario 2
Brainstorm a possible change to the way classes are organised at your institution (e.g. the timetable, length of lessons, number of students in each group).

B Prepare your ideas using the stages in Exercise 1 and the phrases in Exercise 3. Decide who will lead the session. Then begin.

C When you have finished:
- reflect on what went well, what didn't go well, and how you can improve next time.
- discuss how easy/useful the techniques were.

Self-assessment
- How successfully have you achieved the lesson outcome? Give yourself a score from 0 (I need more practice) to 5 (I know this well).
- Go to My Self-assessment in MyEnglishLab to reflect on what you have learnt.

Lesson outcome	Learners can organise information and use appropriate structures to write a press release.

Lead-in

1 Read the press release. Proofread it and find nine more mistakes. Think about spelling, grammar, wrong words and extra words. Then compare in pairs.

Beeza Airlines fully independent investigation

Beeza Airlines have made major changes to their baggage handling system but it does not seem to be working as planned. The company has just announced an ~~independently~~ *independent* review into the customer service issues which occured last week when thousands of passenger bags were transported to the wrong destinations.

Senior staff were informed that thousands of customers were complaining that, when they tried to contact customer services, they were meeting immediately with automated email replies about a system error and that the company was doing everything he could to help them. The situation quickly went viral as customers expressed there anger on social media.

Beeza is dedicated to discovering who went so badly wrong so it can avoid a repetition in the future. Dag Haugen, the CEO, said he was very sorry about and deeply regretted the situation, which may have been partly caused by the new baggage handling system. He promised he would do everything possible to ensure that all affected customers were compensated. He also reminded everyone that happy customers were the key to a company's successful.

It has expected that the review will be completed in two weeks. Mr Haugen also assured the public that Beeza would providing regular announcements on the progress of the investigation.

For further information contact: BenErikson@BeezaPR.com

Functional language

2 Complete the table using the correct form of the words in the box.

> announce   announcement   assure   be
> complain   everything   key   regret   reply
> sorry   transport   viral

News and key facts (Para 1)
Beeza has [1]_____ an independent review ... Thousands of bags were [2]_____ to the wrong destinations.

Further details (Para 2)
Customers were [3]_____ that they couldn't contact customer services. Customers were met with automated email [4]_____ ... The situation quickly went [5]_____ .

Quotation (and apology if required) (Para 3)
The CEO said he was very [6]_____ and deeply [7]_____ the situation ... The CEO promised he would do [8]_____ he could to ensure that customers were compensated. He also reminded everyone that customers were the [9]_____ to success.

Future promises (Para 4)
It is expected that the review [10]_____ completed ... Beeza [11]_____ the public that regular [12]_____ on the progress of the investigation would be made ...

➜ **page 125** See Grammar reference: Passive voice with reporting verbs

T Teacher's resources: extra activities

L The press release contains examples of the passive voice with reporting verbs. Go to MyEnglishLab for optional grammar work.

›TASK

3A Work in pairs. Read the press release on page 133. Discuss how it could be improved. Think about the title, the details and the formality of language.

B Look at the notes on page 130 about Hasfell Supplies and use them to write a press release in around 200 words.

C Exchange press releases with your partner. Did your partner organise the press release clearly? Did your partner use an appropriate level of formality?

Self-assessment

- How successfully have you achieved the lesson outcome? Give yourself a score from 0 (I need more practice) to 5 (I know this well).
- Go to My Self-assessment in MyEnglishLab to reflect on what you have learnt.

Business Workshops

1 **Keeping the workforce happy** p.88

Lesson outcome: Learners can understand details in conversations about employee retention issues and can participate in a brainstorming meeting to find solutions to the problems.

Listening: Employee suggestions for improvements
Reading: Analysing a survey
Task: Brainstorm ways to improve staff retention
Writing: A proposal confirming your ideas

2 **Quality service for all** p.90

Lesson outcome: Learners can exchange information about reports they have read, interpret a skills map and help to devise a training programme.

Listening: Regional HR Directors discussing training issues
Reading: Analysis of Regional Directors' reports
Task: Create and present an online course

3 **Investment opportunities** p.92

Lesson outcome: Learners can understand details of a meeting about venture capital and can make choices about the pros and cons of different investment opportunities.

Listening: Managers' meeting and a guide to VC investment
Speaking: Describing and analysing graphs
Task: Presenting a company that is worth investing in
Writing: A report explaining your investment decision

4 **Rise of the robots** p.94

Lesson outcome: Learners can evaluate advantages and disadvantages of different technologies, interpret feedback statistics and write a short report with recommendations.

Reading: Robots in the workplace
Listening: Incidents with robots at an exhibition
Task: Analyse feedback statistics and discuss future improvements
Writing: A report analysing feedback and giving recommendations

5 **Changing expectations** p.96

Lesson outcome: Learners can understand different opinions about how performance should be rewarded and can negotiate rewards and benefits at work.

Listening: A meeting to find new ways of rewarding performance
Task: Negotiating for change in rewards/benefits
Speaking: How the negotiations went

6 **AFhomes, Tanzania** p.98

Lesson outcome: Learners can exchange information from texts about a company's ethical issues and prepare an action plan to address the problems.

Reading: Articles on the ethics of AFhomes
Listening: A radio investigative programme
Task: An action plan to maintain ethical reputation

7 **Planning for a trade fair** p.100

Lesson outcome: Learners can understand detailed arrangements in a conference call and can plan and prioritise tasks for a trade fair.

Listening: Details of an upcoming trade fair
Task: Create a plan to exhibit at a trade fair
Writing: A summary of successful participation in a trade fair

8 **Chillhot Sauces, Malaysia** p.102

Lesson outcome: Learners can discuss the effect of change on a company based on a text and take part in a meeting about takeover rumours and staff concerns.

Reading: A change at Michelin
Reading and listening: Rumours about a company
Task: Putting a stop to rumours

1 ▷ Keeping the workforce happy

| Lesson outcome | Learners can understand details in conversations about employee retention issues and can participate in a brainstorming meeting to find solutions to the problems. |

Background

1 Read the background and answer the questions with a partner.

1 What kind of company is Schokoschatz?
2 What problems did they have when they started out?
3 What makes them different from other companies in the field?
4 Why are some Schokoschatz employees unhappy?

BACKGROUND

In 1995 a trained chocolate-maker decided to found a business in Stuttgart, Germany to produce quality chocolates. At first, Shokoschatz had problems competing with the large companies producing similar products. However, they came up with a new concept and began to produce organic and fair-trade chocolate using beans from farmers in Peru. They started creating more innovative ideas for products and began to hire specialised staff around the world, which helped them to expand into foreign markets. However, Shokoschatz remains a family-owned business with many family members in senior positions. This has caused some communication problems and led to difficulties with recruitment and retention of international staff. Several employees have recently left as they felt they had little chance of making a career and Shokoschatz are also having problems attracting the talented young graduates they need.

Discussing the problem

2 You are going to hear two managers from Shokoschatz talking about problems they are having. Based on the background, what difficulties might they have with finding new staff and keeping the staff they have?

3 ◀》BW 1.01 Listen to the conversation and answer the questions.

1 Which specific problems does Johannes have regarding staff?
2 What does Martina say about candidates she interviews?
3 What suggestions does Martina have?
4 What suggestions does Johannes have?
5 What do they decide to do next?

4 Work in pairs and brainstorm reasons staff might give for being unhappy at Shokoschatz. Think about hours, pay, benefits, training and team spirit.

5 ◀》BW 1.02 Listen to two conversations. First, Johannes talks to Tomasz, a sales representative, and Carolina, an assistant sales manager. Then Martina talks to Sirina, a finance assistant, and Andy, an accountant. Do they mention any of the problems you predicted in Exercise 4?

6 Listen again and match the speakers (Tomasz, Carolina, Sirina and Andy) to the problems they identify.

1 No discounts for free-time activities: _____
2 No flexible working hours for some workers: _____
3 Little chance for a career: _____
4 Low salary: _____
5 Insufficient or no performance-based pay: _____
6 Problems with training programme: _____
7 Strict dress code: _____
8 Not enough positive cooperation between departments: _____
9 Lack of teamwork in departments: _____
10 Quality of meals at the company: _____
11 Lack of autonomy in the job: _____
12 Not enough financial help for travel: _____

 T ▷ Teacher's resources: extra activities

The survey **7A** After talking with staff and presenting their ideas to the Board, Johannes and Martina were asked to create a staff survey. Look at the first statement from the survey. Based on the recordings, what else do you think Schokoschatz asked staff about?

Employee satisfaction survey
Please circle your responses.

1 I get a fair salary.

B Compare your ideas from Exercise 7A with the original survey on page 134.

8 Work in pairs. The table shows the results of the survey. What do the majority of staff at Schokoschatz like or dislike about what they currently get from the company?

	Strongly Agree	Agree	Disagree	Strongly Disagree
Q 1	14%	18%	42%	26%
Q 2	9%	19%	40%	32%
Q 3	28%	37%	20%	15%
Q 4	14%	9%	48%	29%
Q 5	42%	36%	13%	9%
Q 6	18%	23%	34%	25%
Q 7	41%	35%	16%	8%
Q 8	21%	18%	39%	22%
Q 9	15%	31%	28%	26%
Q 10	42%	31%	16%	11%

T Teacher's resources: extra activities

9 Work in small groups. Brainstorm five ideas which you feel the management of Shokoschatz should implement to help with employee retention and/or recruitment of new staff. You can use your own ideas or the ideas mentioned in the lesson. Discuss these points.
- why this idea would appeal to millennials
- exactly how the idea could be implemented
- specific examples of how it will help staff

10 Work with another group and compare your ideas. Agree on one set of ideas based on what will be practical and appeal to the largest number of people.

11 Write a proposal of 120–140 words for Shokoschatz management using the ideas you agreed in Exercise 10. Use these headings: *Title, Introduction, Findings, Conclusion, Proposal.*

› TASK
Improve employee retention

Self-assessment
- How successfully have you achieved the lesson outcome? Give yourself a score from 0 (I need more practice) to 5 (I know this well).
- Go to My Self-assessment in MyEnglishLab to reflect on what you have learnt.

Lesson outcome	Learners can exchange information about reports they have read, interpret a skills map and help to devise a training programme.

Background

1 Read the background and answer the questions with a partner.

1 What type of company is Consulto and who do you think their clients might be?

2 What problems are they having at the moment? How does globablisation make these problems more difficult?

3 What role do you think training and development of employees plays in this?

4 What do you think their next step might be?

BACKGROUND

Consulto is an international financial services consulting firm with over 150,000 employees in more than 100 countries around the globe. They have recently had some problems with their client base because the standard of the service offered by various offices is not consistent. Customers in one location often feel that they do not get the same quality of advice as customers in another location. In today's globalised world, it is increasingly easy for customers to find out what is going on elsewhere. This is causing problems for the worldwide reputation of the company. The Human Resources departments within the organisation are well aware that there is a problem with the type of training and development offered to employees and realise that something has to be done to address the problem.

Training and development issues

2 ◀) BW 2.01 Listen to part of a conference call between Karen, the Global Training Manager at Consulto, and some of the Regional HR Directors about the problems they are having and their ideas for the future. Match each HR Director to the problem he/she mentions. What future steps does Karen propose?

1 attendance at courses   **a** Akito

2 use of the courses to employees   **b** Frederik

3 price of courses   **c** Victoria

3A Work in groups of three. Each of you read <u>one</u> of the reports by the Regional HR Directors on pages 131, 133 and 134. Answer the questions for your region.

1 What type of training do the consultants need and why?

2 What skills do the consultants have?

3 What is special to this market?

4 How can you best summarise the report?

B Tell your group <u>in your own words</u> about the report you read. Discuss which region you think is the most problematic and why.

Teacher's resources: extra activities

A skills map

4 After the call, Karen created a skills map to send to the HR Directors. Look at the skills map on page 91 and discuss these questions with a partner.

1 How would you explain 'internal' and 'external'? How is this different from 'client-centred' and 'business-centred'?

2 Which skills are used in more than one area? Are there other skills you would add?

3 How specifically can this help HR to design a training and development programme?

4 What other jobs do you think this skills map would work for?

Teacher's resources: extra activities

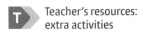

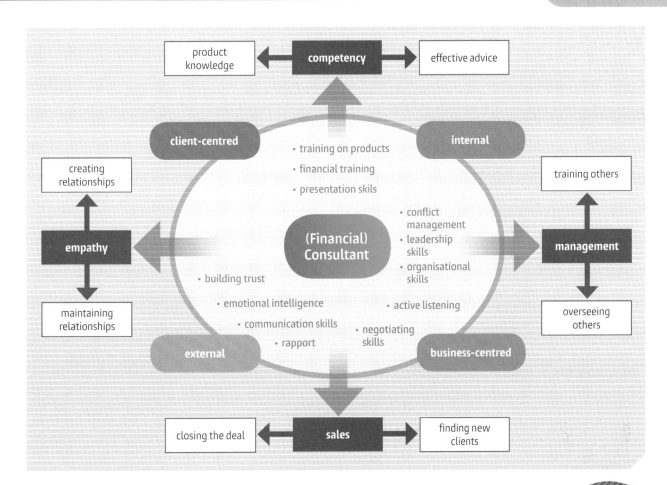

5 Work in your groups from Exercise 3 and look at these elements of a blended-learning course. Which elements do you think would work best for the training needs in the skills map? Why?

- 60-minute webinars by experts focused on particular skills
- question and answer (Q&A) periods following the webinars
- forums on the intranet platform focusing on a particular area
- questions set by presenters for participants to answer in written form on a wiki
- individual feedback from the presenters to the participants on their written homework through the wiki or email
- assessment on each of the areas presented
- face-to-face workshops on particular areas

6 Create a blended-learning course for Consulto employees around the world, to meet the needs identified in the reports in Exercise 3A. Decide:

- what skill / competency each section of the course will cover.
- which format / delivery method from Exercise 5 will be used for each section of the course.
- how participants should get feedback and be assessed.
- what the timeframe for the course will be.

7 Present your course to the class, explaining your decisions in Exercise 6. Ask each other questions and give reasons for your choices.

>TASK

Create a blended-learning course

Self-assessment

- How successfully have you achieved the lesson outcome? Give yourself a score from 0 (I need more practice) to 5 (I know this well).
- Go to My Self-assessment in MyEnglishLab to reflect on what you have learnt.

»91«

Lesson outcome	Learners can understand details of a meeting about venture capital and can make choices about the pros and cons of different investment opportunities.

Background

1 Read the background and answer the questions with a partner.

1 What kind of company is Augoose Investments?
2 Whose money do Alex, Hannah and Jo invest?
3 What kind of companies do they invest in?
4 How much do they expect to make from their investments?

"We're buying the company, the brand, the building ... but mostly we're buying the golden eggs."

BACKGROUND

After working on the stock market in Australia for several years, three colleagues, Alex, Hannah and Jo, set up a venture capital (VC) company, Augoose Investments, three years ago to help start-ups and high-growth companies in exchange for equity or a share in those companies. As the general managers, they are responsible for making decisions to invest the money of the limited partners, who are wealthy people looking to grow their wealth more quickly than in traditional stocks and shares. Their company invests the money in businesses which are considered to be quite risky but which could yield excellent returns – on average they expect to triple their investments over time. In order to spread the risk they invest in a variety of companies in the hope of finding a goose or two to lay some golden eggs.

Morning meeting

2 ◀) BW 3.01 Listen to the first part of a meeting between the three general managers and answer the questions.

1 What do Alex, Hannah and Jo need to produce for the university?
2 What are they offering the university next year?
3 What don't they want the students to believe?
4 What can a VC company provide apart from money?
5 Which famous company do they mention?
6 What don't they know?

3 ◀) BW 3.02 Listen to the second part of the meeting and complete the notes.

Guide to VC INVESTMENT

What you need to check before investing

1 Management
- can it execute a(n) ¹_____ ?
- is it experienced with a good ²_____ ?
- is it willing to ³_____ outside expertise (if not, business could fail)?

2 Product or service
- has it got a(n) ⁴_____ ?
- is it a(n) ⁵_____ solution to real-life problems?
- will it generate sales quickly?

3 Market
- is the target market right?
- is it ⁶_____ to create large revenues?
- a(n) ⁷_____ market analysis must be included in business plan

4 Risk assessment
- do a thorough risk assessment (e.g. check for possible ⁸_____ problems)
- make sure ⁹_____ can be foreseen
- is the ¹⁰_____ sufficient to take business forward?

 **T** Teacher's resources: extra activities

External factors to consider

4A There are many external events which can affect a company's performance. In small groups discuss the following factors. Think of examples of each and how they might affect business.

economic   social   legal   political   technological   environmental

economic – changes in global economy, rise and fall of living standards, ...

B Work in new groups and share your ideas from Exercise 4A. How similar were your ideas?

Gathering information from graphs

5A Work in groups of three. Each of you look at <u>one</u> of the graphs on pages 131, 132 and 134. Describe your graph to the other students so that they can complete the graphs on this page.

Company 1

Company 2

Company 3

Teacher's resources: extra activities

B Discuss what you can learn from the graphs about the three companies. Then make a list of the other financial information you would need to consider before investing in the companies.

balance sheet, expenses, ...

Investment opportunities

6A Work in three groups. Read the information about a company and decide which graph from Exercise 5A it matches. Then discuss whether you would consider investing in that company and why.

Group A: Read the company information on page 131.

Group B: Read the company information on page 132.

Group C: Read the company information on page 135.

B Make a list of the positive and negative elements of your company.

C Prepare a plan for presenting this company to your colleagues at the investment meeting.

7A Work in different groups with at least one person from each of the groups in Exercise 6. Hold a meeting to present the company you read about to your colleagues at Augoose. Follow these steps.

- Take it in turns to present the company you researched.
- Listen carefully to your colleagues' presentations.
- Answer any questions from the other group members.

B When each company has been presented:

- discuss the pros and cons of each one.
- choose the company you think Augoose should invest in (it does not have to be the one you presented).
- discuss the reasons for your choice.
- make a note of your choice and list your reasons.

C Discuss your decision with the whole class. Did you all come to the same decision? If not, try to reach an agreement together.

D Write a report of about 200 words summarising your discussions from Exercises 7A and 7B. Explain the decision made and the reasons why the company was chosen.

> TASK
Investment meeting

Self-assessment

- How successfully have you achieved the lesson outcome? Give yourself a score from 0 (I need more practice) to 5 (I know this well).
- Go to My Self-assessment in MyEnglishLab to reflect on what you have learnt.

> 93 <

Lesson outcome	Learners can evaluate advantages and disadvantages of different technologies, interpret feedback statistics and write a short report with recommendations.

Background

1 **Read the background and answer the questions with a partner.**

1 What kind of company is Stak Tek?

2 What sort of companies is the event aimed at?

3 What will visitors at the event be able to share?

4 What kind of advice will experts be giving?

5 Why is it important for companies to make the digital transformation?

BACKGROUND

Stak Tek, a technology management specialist which helps companies deal with digital change in the workplace, is organising 'Brave New World', an international event that focuses on how Artificial Intelligence (AI) is changing business today. The event will provide help in one central place for companies struggling to adapt to digital transformation and disruption. It will also allow business managers and owners access to the latest innovations and an opportunity to exchange ideas with companies that have successfully made the transformation. Top experts will be on hand to offer advice on how the latest digital technologies can work to improve a company's efficiency and effectiveness. Current evidence suggests that businesses that are brave enough to embrace digital advancements and the resulting changes to their organisations are the ones that will survive and race ahead of the competition.

Working with robots

2A **Read the article about robots in the workplace. Do you think there are disadvantages for companies using robots? What might they be?**

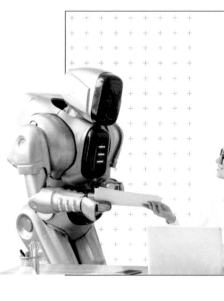

RISE ⁺ OF ⁺ THE ⁺ ROBOTS

Digital disruption is taking place all around us as more and more sophisticated apps direct consumers' lives and robots are taking over jobs in every industry from financial investments to making coffee. The manufacturing industry has successfully been using robots for many years to improve the efficiency of production processes – cars are painted by robotic arms using paint sprays, products are packaged while self-drive vehicles speed around factories with supplies. Company owners believe that using robots is the only way to bring down operating costs and to survive in a competitive market. However, many CEOs are worried that it causes distrust among employees, investors and consumers while others are convinced that today's global economy demands extreme competitiveness and, without technological transformation, companies will close and jobs will be lost anyway. Believers in this brave new world say that it is not a question of robots or people, but rather robots with people and that it is just a matter of retraining staff.

B **Look at the photos in this lesson. How would you feel about meeting or working with one of these robots at the 'Brave New World' event? What problems do you think people might have working with robots like these?**

C **Work in groups. Make a list of some of the jobs at the event which could be done by robots.**

3 **You have decided that you want to have humanoid robots at your event to demonstrate how good they can be and try to overcome people's concerns. In small groups, read the descriptions of six robots on page 95 and discuss:**

- the advantages of using each one.
- potential problems with using these specific robots.
- how you could use them at the event.

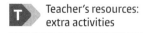

Teacher's resources: extra activities

Bob the barista
End long queues at the drinks bar while Bob prepares your favourite coffee or drink. Bob is our friendly humanoid robot barista and barman rolled into one. He has the capability of doing both the jobs for you much more quickly and cheaply than either a fully trained barista or bartender. He can be programmed to produce all types of coffee and speciality drinks and he'll even exchange small talk with you while he's working in six different languages: English, Mandarin, Spanish, Japanese, Russian and German. He'll save you time and money and is a great attraction for your guests.

Mayumi the receptionist
Our humanoid robot, Mayumi, greets your visitors with a gracious smile, and answers both the phone and their questions in various languages, including Mandarin, Russian, Spanish, Japanese, Arabic and English to name but a few. Mayumi responds to the language she hears or she can be programmed in advance for one particular language. After checking guests into your company or event, she prints the name badges required for visitors and can direct them around the building. What is more, she can also answer the phone in a human-like way so that callers do not feel they have been put through to just another robotic message.

Oskar the driver
Oskar is a humanoid robot who drives a vehicle that can transport your visitors or customers around your facilities. All they have to do is tell him where they want to go and he will get them there by the most efficient route. Although self-drive vehicles are common these days, research has shown that many people prefer to have someone at the controls, even if it is a robot. And Oskar is that robot! Not only that, he can pick up and carry luggage for his passengers and engage in some small talk, too.

Agnes the caterer*
Take the worry out of catering for any event with our team of humanoid robot caterers led by Agnes, the head chef. Each team can be programmed to produce the food you want to serve at your facility. Agnes' team will wait on the tables and take the orders, which Agnes and the sous chef then prepare. The waiting team then serves the meals to the customers with pleasant, speedy service. And after the meal the robots produce the bill, take payment and clear the tables.

Arturo the presenter
Who better to present the latest news about robotics, but Arturo, our life-like humanoid robot presenter programmed with the most up-to-date information about AI and robotics. He is constantly processing the latest data, which he includes in his presentations when relevant. He sounds human, he looks human and his facial expressions are incredibly human so that when he engages in Q&A sessions, his reactions and responses are so life-like that audiences listen to his every word and react to him as if he were a person. Give your audience the very best that robots have to offer.

Brutus the security guard
This humanoid robot is fitted with laser sensors, cameras and navigation equipment to avoid people and other obstacles as he patrols your venue. In addition, he can scan bags and people for unwelcome items hidden in their bags and on their person, so is very useful at the entrance to your event. He constantly monitors his surroundings for any unexpected or suspicious activity, such as breaking glass or shouting. If he notices anything out of the ordinary, he sets off an alarm which will sound in the control room where a real human is monitoring the cameras. Make your event safe with Brutus.

*caterer: a person or company that provides and serves food and drinks at parties, meetings, etc.

Day 1
Incident report

4A ◀ BW 4.01 **Listen to six voicemail complaints from participants about the robots at the exhibition. Note down the details of each incident.**

Matteo – pushed over, grabbed and shouted at by Brutus.

| Matteo   Hideaki   Mark   Wei Ling   Sarah   Aleksander |

B **Compare your notes with a partner. What immediate action can you take to solve these problems?**

>TASK
Final reporting

5A **Work in groups. Analyse the feedback statistics on page 133 and discuss how you could improve similar future events. Look at:**
- the visitor response to each robot.
- if it was a good decision to use the robots overall.

B **In your group, plan and write a short report for senior management analysing the feedback and giving recommendations for future events.**

Self-assessment
- How successfully have you achieved the lesson outcome? Give yourself a score from 0 (I need more practice) to 5 (I know this well).
- Go to My Self-assessment in MyEnglishLab to reflect on what you have learnt.

| Lesson outcome | Learners can understand different opinions about how performance should be rewarded and can negotiate rewards and benefits at work. |

Background

1 Read the background and answer the questions with a partner.

1 What business is Energia Renovável involved in and what do they do?
2 Which type of employees do they need in the company?
3 What areas of the job do younger workers seem to have specific expectations about?
4 What differences are mentioned between millennials and older employees?

BACKGROUND

Energia Renovável is a successful energy company in Brazil and uses renewable energy sources such as wind, solar power and bio fuels. Since the oil crisis of the 1970s the company has been expanding and today is a leader in the field. However, they rely more and more on highly qualified university graduates in a variety of fields who speak English and at least one other foreign language in order to help them expand overseas. Recently they have noticed that millennials have different expectations regarding appraisals, promotions and pay rises. While older employees expected to stay at one company for many years, millennials often leave if they don't feel that their work is valued. This is beginning to become a problem and the company needs to find a way to solve it.

Meetings

2 You are going to listen to a meeting at Energia Renovável. The participants below want to find new ways to reward performance and meet expectations but are concerned about the reputation of the company if they make major changes to the current system. Who do you think will/won't be in favour of changing the way they do things? Why?

- Clara, HR representative from North American office
- Felipe and Juliana, regional managers
- Diego, union representative

3 ◀» BW 5.01 Listen to the meeting and match the speakers with their points of view.

1	Clara	a	discuss new ideas carefully before making major changes
2	Felipe	b	not fair to older employees to make changes in measuring performance
3	Juliana	c	some ideas might be possible but some would not work in practice
4	Diego	d	feels it is necessary to work together on this problem

4 Listen again and answer the questions.

1 What does Clara say about university graduates?
2 Which two problems does the high turnover of graduates cause?
3 What reasons does Diego give for young people expecting different treatment today than in the past?
4 What does Felipe say about people's priorities years ago?
5 What does Clara feel could affect the reputation of the company?
6 What does Clara suggest they do?

5 Work in pairs and briefly brainstorm the following points.

- reward systems that might appeal to younger people
- how performance at work should be measured

6 ◀» BW 5.02 Listen to the next meeting. Were any of the ideas the same or similar to those you mentioned in Exercise 5?

7A Work in pairs. Look at the sentences. Can you remember who said them? Was it Clara, Felipe, Juliana or Diego?

1 I was thinking of something like 360° feedback so that they get feedback from different people …

2 … it is important for employees to see a connection between their personal work goals and the overall goals of the company.

3 We need to see if the projects meet the goals that were set …

4 … they could talk about any problems they might have and any suggestions they have to improve the process.

5 … we need people who work well with others.

6 … if the project teams are submitting follow-up reports that are clear and well written.

7 … make sure that all staff meet regularly with their line managers to discuss what they are working on.

8 … find ways to show staff how their jobs and tasks support our overall strategies.

B Listen again and check your answers.

8 Match the sentences in Exercise 7A with these topics.

a quality of work (two sentences)

b transparency and needs of employees (four sentences)

c interpersonal skills (two sentences)

T Teacher's resources: extra activities

Expectations

9A Work in pairs. Are the expectations in the box financial benefits, non-financial benefits or benefits to save employees money?

> flexible hours   bonus system for ideas
> free fitness facility on site
> increase in overtime pay
> seminars on career skills
> subsidised public transport

B ◀)) BW 5.03 Listen to the conversation between Clara and Diego. Note down two more financial benefits, five more non-financial benefits and two more benefits to save employees money.

T Teacher's resources: extra activities

Pair A Young staff member

Essential:

Desirable:

Willing to not have (concede):

Pair B HR staff member

Cannot offer:

Might be able to offer:

No problem to offer:

10 Work in a group of four which has two sub pairs: A and B. Complete each category of your role card with two rewards/benefits from Exercise 9.
Pair A: you are a young employee who wants to negotiate extra benefits.
Pair B: you are an HR representative for the company.

11 Work in the same groups of four but in two separate A/B pairs. Roleplay the negotiation using the role cards you have prepared.

A I feel that … is essential in order for me to …

B If I give you … , will you give up … ?

A I would really like to have …

B I am afraid that … isn't possible at the moment.

12 Work again in your group of four and compare how the two negotiations went. Find out what happened and discuss the results. Give specific examples of what you were able to achieve and how well you feel that you did.

> **TASK**
> A negotiation over rewards and benefits

Self-assessment
- How successfully have you achieved the lesson outcome? Give yourself a score from 0 (I need more practice) to 5 (I know this well).
- Go to My Self-assessment in MyEnglishLab to reflect on what you have learnt.
> 97 ‹

Lesson outcome	Learners can exchange information from texts about a company's ethical issues and prepare an action plan to address the problems.

Background

1 Read the background and answer the questions with a partner.

1 What is the nature of AFhomes' business and who are its main customers?
2 What was Mr Ndege's aim when he started the business?
3 Which elements of his business indicate that it is an ethical business?
4 What problem is the company facing now?

BACKGROUND

AFhomes is a successful construction company in Tanzania. It provides low-cost homes for people living both in cities and in more rural areas. Josef Ndege started the company 15 years ago with a vision to provide fellow citizens with modern, well-built homes with cheap electricity from solar panels on the roof. He was also determined to create an ethical business for both buyers and investors having seen how most people had been pushed out of the housing market by greedy business people. He pays his employees above minimum wage and provides them and their families with free health care and education. Recently he partnered up with a conservation agency to build offices and homes in Dodoma, the capital of Tanzania. This unusual partnership – an environmental agency going into the construction business – has called his ethical judgement into question.

Trouble ahead

2A Work in two groups. Find out more about the problems that AFhomes is having.

Student As: Read the article on this page and discuss the questions.
Student Bs: Read the article on page 136 and discuss the questions.

Student As

1 What ethical issues are mentioned in the article?
2 Why do you think these are a problem for Mr Ndege?
3 What is the aim of the joint partnership?

B Work with a partner from the other group. Tell your partner <u>in your own words</u> about the article you read. Does anything surprise you about your partner's article? If so, what?

Teacher's resources: extra activities

C In small groups discuss the current situation for AFhomes and how you think Mr Ndege should deal with the current situation.

AFhomes questionable move into Dodoma

Mr Ndege, the high profile builder who prides himself on his ethical business practices, has just found himself in very deep water indeed. His announcement that he has teamed up with the Land Conservation Agency to build offices and homes in Dodoma looks like it might be about to backfire on the entrepreneur. Ever since his first venture, Mgunga Park – named for the number of acacia trees (mgunga in Kiswahili) planted around the site – he has been hailed as the leader of ethical business in the country. But now wildlife agencies and local people are protesting against the site chosen for the new homes as it crosses the route which elephants have taken for thousands of

years when moving across the country. In addition, it will destroy the only waterhole for livestock belonging to local people and all the wildlife in the area. Local and public criticism of the Land Conservation Agency grows daily as people try to understand the fact that an organisation which should protect the environment is involved.

When Mr Ndege tendered for the work, he promised a new water supply infrastructure because Dodoma is located in the centre of the country and suffers from a lack of rain. Mr Ndege negotiated with government agencies and big water companies to develop and improve the currently very poor and irregular water

supply to homes in the city. Many people still have to buy water by the bucket from neighbours who have water piped to their homes. Mr Ndege truly knows the importance of being able to turn a tap on and get running water and the benefits it brings to health. He grew up in a rural village where he had to walk five miles every day to fetch water for his mother.

In a joint partnership with a Norwegian company, and the government, AFhomes aim to build the water and waste removal infrastructure at a cost of several millions of dollars. Unfortunately, the project seems to be coming to a halt before even getting off the ground. We wonder if this is the beginning of the end for the ethical star?

Where has AFhomes gone wrong?

3 ◄)) BW 6.01 **Listen to part of a radio investigative programme about AFhomes and complete the notes below.**

Money destined for [1]_____ has gone to local business people instead.

Mr Ndege always criticised [2]_____ of this type.

Eunice Mazula says [3]_____ from Mr Ndege has allowed schools to be built and children to be educated.

Julius hasn't been paid since he was [4]_____ to Dodoma.

Nkomo is employed as a [5]_____ on the Dodoma project and is worried about safety due to a number of [6]_____ . He says company failed to give staff what was [7]_____ .

The Land Conservation Agency insists their [8]_____ will ensure the environment and wildlife will be protected for [9]_____ .

Breaking news! Dodoma project closed for investigation into unethical business [10]_____ .

4 **Work in small groups. Read the company code of ethics and discuss:**
- where AFhomes has failed.
- if the code needs to be revised.

> ### AFhomes Code of Ethics and Company Mission
>
> *To improve the lives of Tanzanian citizens by:*
> - providing low-cost comfortable homes.
> - ensuring employees are treated and paid fairly.
> - providing health and education for employees and their families.
> - contributing to educational charities.
>
> *To protect the environment by:*
> - working with local communities to reach mutually satisfactory outcomes.
> - using sustainable energy for buildings.
>
> *To achieve the above, we expect all employees to:*
> - have integrity in everything they do.
> - communicate openly and honestly.
> - follow all health and safety rules.
> - refuse to accept or offer gifts from or to clients.

T Teacher's resources: extra activities

5A **Hold a meeting to decide what AFhomes should do now in order to maintain its ethical reputation. Discuss these possible options and suggest ideas of your own.**
- pull out of the Dodoma project completely
- have Mr Ndege give a press interview denying all the allegations and stressing his innocence
- prepare a press release denying all the allegations
- make sure that all staff have been paid properly and pay them if not
- investigate the allegations about charity funds going missing
- work with the Land Conservation Agency to plan a press campaign

B **Share your ideas as a class and decide on an action plan for AFhomes.**

> TASK
> Agree an action plan

Self-assessment

- How successfully have you achieved the lesson outcome? Give yourself a score from 0 (I need more practice) to 5 (I know this well).
- Go to My Self-assessment in MyEnglishLab to reflect on what you have learnt.

› 99 ‹

Lesson outcome	Learners can understand detailed arrangements in a conference call and can plan and prioritise tasks for a trade fair.

Background

1 Read the background and answer the questions with a partner.

1 What type of company is Khilauna, Inc. and what exactly does it produce?
2 What is the company planning for at the moment and why?
3 What things do you think the company may need to plan in order to take part in the trade fair?

BACKGROUND

Khilauna, Inc. is a toy manufacturer in India located in an industrial area near New Delhi. It manufactures fun and innovative toys for children. Its product range includes educational and musical toys as well as toys to use outdoors. As the toy market is very competitive and Khilauna, Inc. wants to guarantee its place with retail shops and chains, it has decided to take part in one of the most important toy trade fairs in Asia, which is going to be held in Hong Kong. While Khilauna, Inc. is very keen to expand into other markets in the region, it is also extremely aware that it will need to become more efficient in the future if it is to be successful and to make the most of its participation in the fair.

Conference calls

2 ◀) BW 7.01 Listen to a conference call at Khilauna, Inc., in which Rahul, the General Manager, Divya, the Sales Manager, Varinder, the Marketing Manager and Aarav, the Head of Product Development, talk about the upcoming trade fair. Complete the notes.

Notes

- Name of trade fair: [1]_____
- From: [2]_____ to [3]_____
- Number of staff going from:
  - marketing: _3_ people
  - product development: [4]____ people
  - sales: [5]____ people

- Day to set up stand: [6]_____
- Day to take down stand: [7]_____
- Number of hotel rooms:
  - from Sunday to Saturday: [8]____ rooms
  - from Monday to Saturday: [9]____ rooms
- Next conference call: [10]_____

Varinder
Marketing Manager

Aarav
Head of Product Development

Divya
Sales Manager

3A Divya, Varinder and Aarav all work at Khilauna, Inc. but come from different departments. Look at their job titles again and decide which person is likely to have each goal (1–6) while at the trade fair.

1 setting up a network _____
2 finding out what customers want _____
3 getting customers to sign sales contracts _____
4 not making products which won't sell _____
5 not having to contact retailers in future _____
6 being able to tell a large number of people about the company at one time _____

B ◀) BW 7.02 Listen to the follow-up conference call the next morning and check your answers.

C Listen again. Which specific preparation tasks do Divya and Varinda mention?

Divya: _____

Varinda: _____

T Teacher's resources: extra activities

Prioritising tasks

4 ◉ BW 7.03 Rahul checks his phone and finds seven answerphone messages with problems. Listen and note down who is speaking, the problem they are having and any action/help they need.

5 Look at the steps below which can help you prioritise tasks. Work with a partner and prioritise the tasks from Exercise 4 using this system.

- Use a matrix and decide which box to use for each of the tasks.

	Urgent	Not urgent
Important	1	2
Not important	3	4

- Look at the tasks in box 1 and categorise them.
  - prioritise them according to how urgent they are.
  - estimate which will take the longest to complete or is the most complicated.
  - decide which to do first – the long, complicated task or one of the shorter ones.
  - decide if any of the tasks can be done by someone else or cut completely.
  - set realistic deadlines for the remaining tasks.
- Repeat the process for the tasks in box 2.

T ▶ Teacher's resources:
extra activities

> **TASK**
> Create a plan to exhibit at a trade fair

6A Work in small groups. Read the advert for a trade fair which is taking place two months from now and answer the questions.

1 Why is there no cost to exhibit?
2 How many stands will there be?
3 What do you have to do to take part?
4 When will you find out if you have a place?

Trade fair on Innovation and New Ideas

Where: The new conference centre
When: Monday, 7 April – Wednesday, 9 April
Who: First-time exhibitors
What: Innovative products in the development stage
Cost: Free
How: Send in your application by 10 January

This trade fair is sponsored by the Alliance of Industrial Partners to encourage new ideas and innovation. A total of 150 places will be given to those with the most innovative ideas. Read the guidelines carefully and describe your product or idea as clearly as you can. Get your application to us on time for a place. All notifications will be sent by 8 February.

B Your group has won a place at the trade fair and will be presenting an app you are developing to help people manage their time. You have put together a list of tasks. Work together to prioritise them and come up with a realistic timetable for the next two months.

- Goals: target audience – customers, investors?
- Message: how to get your idea across quickly?
- Location: get plan of fair and available stands – choose location
- Design of stand: how to attract people?
- Staffing: 4–6 people for stand – who?
- PR: bloggers, posters, social media
- Supplies: pens, paper, bottled water, cups, laptops, adapters, etc.
- Business cards: design and print

Writing

7 Imagine you've been to the trade fair and that it was a great success. Colleagues would like to take part in the future and have asked for your help. Write a summary of your experience in 120–160 words.

Self-assessment

- How successfully have you achieved the lesson outcome? Give yourself a score from 0 (I need more practice) to 5 (I know this well).
- Go to My Self-assessment in MyEnglishLab to reflect on what you have learnt.

Lesson outcome	Learners can discuss the effect of change on a company based on a text and take part in a meeting about takeover rumours and staff concerns.

Background

1 Read the background and answer the questions with a partner.

1 What kind of company is Chillhot Sauces?
2 What was the founders' vision for the company?
3 How big is Chillhot Sauces?
4 What kind of culture does the company have?
5 Why may the company need to find an investment partner?
6 What things might employees worry about if they think the company they work for is going to be bought by or merged with another company?

BACKGROUND

Chillhot Sauces is based in Malaysia and produces a wide range of tasty spicy organic, gluten-free and halal sauces. The company was established twenty years ago by Anis Khan (CEO) and Dewi Shahar (Finance Director): food technology and business graduates, who wanted to develop a range of their favourite home-style sauces, like the ones their mothers made. Chillhot currently employs 50 staff and produces over thirty sauces in a medium-sized factory. The company owners and their staff have mutual respect and most of the employees have worked there for over 15 years. It exports to North America and the rest of South East Asia and has recently received a very large order from Europe. However, in order to fulfil this order, it needs to expand its manufacturing capability and it does not have the funds for the expansion.

How a large manufacturing company changed

2A Read the newspaper article about another well-known company that made changes. How would you feel if changes like this were made in an organisation you worked for? Discuss your answers with a partner.

FT

Power to the workers: Michelin's great experiment

Managers at Michelin's plant in Le Puy-en-Velay noticed a particularly French change in behaviour three years ago. Workers at the tyre factory exchanged the formal 'vous' form of address for the friendlier 'tu', a symptom
5 of more profound change. Michelin, the paternalistic* company that's been strong in France for more than a century, was handing more responsibility to workers at the 600-person plant and urging managers to step back into a less formal coaching role.
10 In the past, says a manager at Le Puy, 'you couldn't be a good boss if you hadn't passed through all the stages of [tyre] preparation. Now the team's attitude is "Don't worry – we'll organise production and you can check it". The manager just has to respond: "No problem, I trust
15 you".'
Michelin's experiment at Le Puy and five other plants around the world is part of a plan to reorganise the whole group – more than 105,000 employees, at plants in 17 countries – along the same lines to become more agile
20 and more responsive to customers.
Changing the way Michelin is run will require sacrifices from management and unions, and an upgrade in the skills and self-confidence of the workers themselves.
25 In 2012, Jean-Dominique Senard became the first CEO not directly tied to the family and he set up more than 70 working groups to refine the plan.
'The real risk is that management doesn't communicate with sufficient force – through explanation and training –
30 that the group should move forward as fast as possible,' he says.
Olivier Duplain, leading a working group in Le Puy trying out new ways of encouraging co-operation, left his team to prepare a presentation to senior executives in
35 early 2014. He was uneasy when they ditched PowerPoint and drew a picture of an old-fashioned driver-controlled train that transformed into a team-controlled high-speed train on a sheet of paper covered with Post-it notes. At the top the legend read: 'Before: a chore; apathy; everyone
40 for himself, lack of accountability; disorganisation; selfishness.' And at the bottom: 'After: team agreement; shared knowledge; improving results; pride; team leader's trust'. The team still shows the drawing to visitors, to help explain what changed.

paternalistic: making decisions for others and telling them what to do

B Read the article again and answer the questions.

1 What is the traditional French management style?

2 What is Michelin encouraging its managers to do?

3 Why is the company making these changes?

4 What does the CEO believe could hinder these changes?

5 How did Olivier Duplain feel about letting his team make the presentation? Why do you think he felt this way?

6 Which Michelin staff do you think might have had the most difficulty with the changes? Why?

3 **Work in pairs. Look at the comments from various Michelin employees on page 136. What do they say about the past? What do they say about the present? And what do they say about how things have changed?**

The CEO says that now he feels he is more of a mentor than before.

Unexpected news and rumours

4A Read the text below. Using the information you learnt from Michelin's experience, work in small groups and discuss why you think the staff at Chillhot Sauces are unhappy about this news.

Chillhot Sauces staff are generally very happy and management and workers have mutual respect. However, the traditional business culture in Malaysia means that the workers expect the managers to tell them what to do. Employee respect for their managers means that they expect their bosses to know more than they do. Until now, everyone has been happy with the system but the following news extract changes everything.

Chillhot Sauces hot for takeover?

It seems that Chillhot Sauces, the local success story, has become the latest takeover target of Osbruk-Basri Industries, the large food and beverage multinational. Sources inform us that Chillhot's CEO has been in talks with the company. Osbruk-Basri is well-known for its focus on profit and its asset-stripping activities.

B 🔊 BW 8.01 Rumours are spreading around the company fast. Listen to a conversation around the drinks machine and note down the things which are worrying staff. How many of these things do you think are true?

5A Work in groups of three. Decide which of you is going to be the CEO. The CEO reads role card A on page 133. The rest of the group chooses from roles B and C on pages 130 and 135. Hold a meeting with the CEO to clarify the situation and to find out which rumours are true. Take notes of what the other people say.

AGENDA	
1	Reason for meeting
2	Company plans
3	Employee concerns
4	Future possibilities

B Work in pairs with someone from another group. Tell each other what was said at your meeting.

C Work with another pair and decide what Chillhot Sauces should do to improve the situation with their staff.

〉 TASK

How to stop the rumours

"The announcement of the changes really went well."

1.1 Elements of corporate culture

1 Complete the missing words. The first letters are given.

When applying for a job with a new company, it can be very difficult to know what kind of culture exists within it, especially with regard to organisational [1]b_____ . Before you start, you might be aware of the company [2]s_____ and [3]h_____ , knowing who reports to whom, but not how people act and react towards each other. Some companies have a dress [4]c_____ , while other companies allow staff some [5]f_____ in what they wear. However, always remember that employees reflect the [6]i_____ of a company, especially to the outside world. For most people, having a good [7]a_____ in the work space is vital, especially if you are working in an [8]o_____-plan office. Employees need to work together to follow the company's [9]s_____ for the future and achieve goals. Furthermore, understanding a company's [10]v_____ is also key to a successful company.

1.2 Future Continuous and Future Perfect Simple

2 Complete the sentences with the Future Continuous or Future Perfect Simple form of the verb in brackets.

1 We _____ (work) on this for ten years by the end of November. I can hardly believe it.

2 I wonder if I _____ (still / work) here in ten year's time.

3 It looks like the company _____ (make) its biggest profit ever by the time the year ends.

4 _____ we _____ (open) the new factory before the end of the year?

5 We _____ (implement) a new policy regarding the salary structure next month.

6 By the middle of next month we _____ (install) all the new equipment in the factory.

7 _____ they _____ (train) all employees to use the new machines over the next few weeks?

8 What do you think we _____ (achieve) by the end of the course?

Functional language
1.3 Building trust

3 Complete the dialogue using the phrases in the box.

> based on your experience   can I suggest
> to be honest   we both want to
> what you're saying about   would it be useful

A: [1]_____ , the staff feel worried about the new system the company's introduced.

B: Look, [2]_____ sort this out. You know we had no choice but to implement the new system.

A: I understand [3]_____ the need for change, but staff weren't told about the changes or given training.

B: So, [4]_____ , how do you think we can solve this?

A: [5]_____ that you have a meeting with everyone to listen to their concerns?

B: [6]_____ for me to ask the training company to be there, too?

A: Yes, I think it would.

1.4 Self-presentation

4 Match the sentence halves.

1	My current job	a	you said about our strategy.
2	If you need my help	b	in Cincinnati.
3	I used to	c	to be part of such a great team.
4	I'm now responsible	d	involved with this new project.
5	I'm really delighted	e	for finding new locations.
6	I'm proud to be	f	work on product design.
7	I really liked what	g	is head of U.S. operations.
8	I'm based	h	in any way, just let me know.

1.5 A company news blog

5 Put the sentences in the correct order.

a If you are interested in taking part in this scheme, please contact the HR manager as soon as possible.

b You are sure to be delighted to learn that we are offering all staff the chance to work with our colleagues in another country for three months.

c For example, a factory supervisor in the UK could change places with a factory supervisor in Australia.

d Click on the link to find out more about the scheme and how it could work for you.

e This is part of an employee exchange scheme which gives employees in all our companies the opportunity to swap jobs with a colleague in another country.

f Great news! The company has come up with an exciting new initiative.

g The HR manager will then find out which colleagues abroad you could change places with.

2.1 Training and development

1 Complete the sentences using the words in the box. Some are not used.

> analyse analysis benchmarking
> competency development emotional
> job-related mentee online rapport

1 I want to make sure I join a company where there are lots of opportunities for career _____ .

2 A mentor can help when someone needs more specific _____ training.

3 When you are working in a team, it is important that there is _____ between team members.

4 Before offering training to employees, a needs _____ is done to ensure that the best programme is chosen for them.

5 We use _____ to ensure our performance is always of the highest standard.

6 A new manager needs to develop _____ at the job as soon as possible.

7 Managers also need to have _____ intelligence to ensure that they can empathise with others.

8 Remember you can request two _____ courses a year as part of your training.

2.2 Modals in the passive voice

2 Complete the email using modals in the passive.

From: Training director
To: Training manager
Subject: New training scheme

....

It is clear that in today's competitive climate, up-to-date training courses ¹_____ (must / provide) in order to retain staff. I've realised our training programme ²_____ (could / improve) and feel that a meeting ³_____ (must / hold) so we can discuss our specific requirements. I also think that staff ideas ⁴_____ (ought / take) into account before making a final decision. Therefore employees ⁵_____ (should / invite) to complete a questionnaire about the kind of training they would like to receive. I'd be grateful if this ⁶_____ (could / arrange) as soon as possible.

I'm aware that not everything ⁷_____ (can / do) immediately, but I think there are areas where significant changes ⁸_____ (could / make). The new training policy ⁹_____ (not need / finalise) until the end of next month and head office ¹⁰_____ (not have to / inform) about the new policy until then.

I look forward to discussing these ideas with you.

Functional language
2.3 Exchanging ideas

3 Complete the dialogue. Use one word in each gap.

A: What's the best ¹_____ to handle this situation?

B: ²_____ don't we ask a consultant to help us?

A: I don't think it ³_____ sense to do that and it'll be far too expensive.

B: Another option could be to ask for employee suggestions.

A: There are pros and ⁴_____ to that. Sometimes employees have great ideas but they can also become too involved and waste a lot of time.

B: But isn't it good to involve staff?

A: If we start from a positive viewpoint, yes.

B: Just ⁵_____ up on what you said before about how expensive consultants are. It could save the company, so isn't it worth a try?

A: Perhaps you're right. So ⁶_____ we try that?

2.4 Facilitating a discussion

4 Choose the correct option in italics.

1 What we're *looking / seeing* to do today is to finalise plans for the launch party.

2 To *make / ensure* everyone can say something, can we go *over / around* the table first?

3 Gupta, can you kick us *off / on*?

4 Patsy, you have some *experience / information* of organising events, would you mind helping me?

5 It seems that there's a *contribution / consensus* about keeping costs as low as possible.

6 I agree the budget is really important, but I want to *come / discuss* to that a little later.

7 I'm afraid we're running out of time. So just to *recap / repeat* everything …

2.5 A training request

5 Complete the text using the phrases in the box. Some are not used.

> as I am because registration could you reply
> do not have enough it be possible promoted to
> so I can would therefore like writing to request

I am ¹_____ some professional training. I have just been ²_____ manager so I am now in charge of a team but I feel that I ³_____ experience in this area. I ⁴_____ to attend the Managing Teams course next month.

Please ⁵_____ quickly ⁶_____ closes on Wednesday next week?

3.1 Finance and economic crises

1 Choose the correct option in italics.

The company has suffered severe financial [1]*crunch / losses / recovery* recently and, as a result, we have had to let a lot of staff go. There is a danger of the company [2]*going / making / dropping* bankrupt, which is very worrying. Although we used all of our [3]*debts / mortgages / savings* and took out a(n) [4]*mortgage / investment / credit* against the office premises, this wasn't enough to [5]*recover / bail / lend* us out of the serious situation we find ourselves in. We realise now that it was a bad move to invest in the new factory even though sales were [6]*dropping / bailing / booming* and everything was going well. Unfortunately, now we are in an economic [7]*depression / bankruptcy / insolvency* and the [8]*stock / rate / loan* market does not show any sign of [9]*booming / dropping / recovering* in the near future. Furthermore, the [10]*credit / debt / loan* crunch has affected us very badly. Unfortunately, the bank will not [11]*borrow / lend / bail* us any more money because we are unable to repay our current [12]*credit / investments / loans* with them.

3.2 Expressing certainty and probability

2 Look at the first sentence in each pair. Complete the second sentence with the correct form of the word in capitals so that the meaning does not change.

1 There is a possibility that the company will soon be taken over.

The company _____ over soon.   LIKELY

2 The new store is going to open next month.

The new store _____ next month.   DUE

3 I think we will to have to cut some jobs.

It _____ to cut some jobs.   LIKELY

4 You will definitely be promoted this time.

You _____ this time.   CERTAIN

5 I don't think we will be able to go.

It _____ able to go.   UNLIKELY

3.2 Position of adverbs and adverbial phrases

3 Put the word in bold in the correct position in the sentence.

1 We hope to move our offices to India next year. **also**

2 We will recruit 100 new staff next year. **probably**

3 They are likely to expand into Australia in the future. **also**

4 Costs won't rise over the next few months. **probably**

5 Prices are going to rise further in the near future. **probably**

Functional language
3.3 Responding to bad news

4 Choose the correct option in italics to complete the dialogue.

A: I'm very disappointed [1]*for / with / of* last month's results. The market response was not [2]*that / such / what* we were hoping [3]*for / in / to*.

B: To be [4]*true / fair / correct*, the results are only a little less than we expected. I'm sure that we can [5]*push / make / turn* this around next month.

A: [6]*Just / Overall, / Simply* I don't think things have gone well since we launched the new product range.

B: Yes, but I think we simply need to keep doing what we're doing.

A: I don't agree. I think we have to find a new [7]*method / approach / way* to marketing. I really think it's [8]*time / confident / progress* to look at alternative solutions.

3.4 Asking for clarification and paraphrasing

5 Match the sentence halves.

1 There are a couple of things	a here refer to?
2 OK, so that means	b mind repeating that?
3 Can I talk you	c you said about the product line?
4 Tell me, what exactly does the figure	d through the points I'm unsure of?
5 Could you remind me what	e it will be ready by the end of the month.
6 The sound went for a moment. Would you	f I'd like to clarify.

3.5 Annual report summary

6 Complete the summary using the words in the box. Some words are not used.

> caused   due   forecast   gives   increased
> mixed   of   on   optimistic   posted
> promising   recovery   result   tough

The past year has been very challenging and a year of [1]_____ results, mainly [2]_____ by poor sales in some markets. These poor sales were largely as a(n) [3]_____ of a downturn in the Asian markets, although this was offset by a steady [4]_____ and impressive growth in our South American markets.

We [5]_____ overall sales of $32 million dollars, up 1% [6]_____ last year's figures. This [7]_____ us cause to be cautiously [8]_____ and, with the growth in our South American markets, the [9]_____ for the coming year looks [10]_____ .

4.1 Digital business and technology

1 Complete the missing words. The first letters are given.

1 You can save space by storing files in the c_____ instead of on your computer.

2 Digital technologies used to market products are known as Digital Marketing P_____ .

3 Copying information from one computer to another is known as a data d_____ .

4 In digital marketing, the number of sales you get in relation to the number of visits to your website is referred to as c_____ .

5 Using computers to analyse large amounts of information is known as data m_____ .

4.1 Word building – verbs, nouns and adjectives

2 Complete the sentences with the correct form of the words in brackets.

1 Digital tools can be used to help businesses be more _____ (analyse) and also to make _____ (personalise) products for individual customers.

2 Technology gives everyone the chance to become an _____ (innovate) as well as allowing people to _____ (visual) what their product will be like.

3 _____ (disrupt) technologies help companies reach target customers more accurately, but some consumers find this intensely _____ (irritate).

4.2 Zero, first and second conditionals; Linkers

3 Look at the first sentence in each pair. Complete the second sentence using the linker in brackets.

1 If the product is user-friendly, people will buy it. (as long as)

_____ user-friendly, people _____ it.

2 There must be an internet connection for the phone to work. (if)

The phone _____ no internet connection.

3 The situation isn't improving and we're losing customers. (unless)

_____ all our customers.

4 We don't sell many products because the technology isn't reliable. (provided)

We _____ more products _____ more reliable.

5 We must get a 12% discount or we won't place an order. (on condition)

We _____ an order _____ a 12% discount.

6 My advice to you is to design a new product. (if)

_____ you, I _____ a new product.

Functional language
4.3 Keeping a meeting on track

4 Choose the correct option in italics.

1 We can *stick / come / go* back to the launch date later.

2 I'm afraid that's really outside the *plan / space / scope* of the meeting.

3 Jack, *give / allow / let* Sylvia finish the point she's making.

4 Can we *slow / go / reduce* down a little?

5 Can I *finish / slow / stop* you for a second?

6 But what do you actually *suggest / say / think* we do?

4.4 Reaching agreement in a negotiation

5 Complete the dialogue using the phrases in the box. Some phrases are not used.

accept the fact that   agree to that   sounds reasonable
from another perspective   suggestion might work
how this situation affects you   imagine this working
the best thing would be   way to approach

A: Firstly, tell me about [1]_____ .

B: Well, staff are working longer hours with no overtime.

A: Look, we need to [2]_____ this is only short-term until the company is out of trouble.

B: I'm sorry, we're not prepared to work longer hours unless we get paid more.

A: Well … how could you [3]_____ then? Is there another [4]_____ this situation?

B: I think [5]_____ to organise the system better so that we can be more productive.

A: We could have a meeting with all the staff involved and ask them for ideas. I'm sure we can find a better way.

B: Yes, I can [6]_____ . That [7]_____ .

4.5 Short business proposal

6 Match the sentences with the categories (a–e).

a Introduction or purpose   d Plan, costs and schedule

b Summary of problem   e Conclusion

c Solution to problem

1 To sum up, we recommend a further study. ____

2 This proposal evaluates the possible use of robots. ____

3 Recently, we have seen a dramatic fall in profits. ____

4 I therefore recommend that we accept the offer. ____

5 In order to solve this problem, we need more staff. ____

6 I propose that we move production to Korea. ____

7 The new equipment could be installed next month. ____

8 The most efficient option would be to send someone to negotiate with them. ____

5.1 Rewarding performance

1 Choose the correct option.

1 Companies cannot offer a _____ of lifelong employment these days.

   a guarantee   **b** recognition   **c** reward

2 The CEO _____ through the ranks having started as a supervisor many years ago.

   a achieved   **b** promoted   **c** rose

3 Young people sometimes find it difficult to _____ in the company.

   a reward   **b** advance   **c** promote

4 The company's _____ to adapt to new technology lost them market share.

   a success   **b** achievement   **c** failure

5 I had my staff _____ this morning. I think it went well.

   a appraisal   **b** advancement   **c** recognition

6 Did you get a pay _____ last month?

   a reward   **b** guarantee   **c** rise

5.2 Linking words and concessive clauses

2 Complete the sentences using the words in the box.

> although despite though in spite nevertheless
> one hand   other hand

1 We decided to sell the company, _____ we were very reluctant to do so.

2 We knew the product would be popular. _____, it took a while before sales increased.

3 _____ the fact that there is a recession, the new company made a good profit in its first year.

4 On the _____, we lost staff, but on the _____, productivity increased, so it did not affect efficiency.

5 Even _____ sales were up, profits were down.

6 _____ of being given almost impossible targets, I managed to achieve them.

Functional language

5.3 Responding to challenging feedback

3 Complete the dialogue with the phrases in the box.

> and why   not seeing the big picture
> predicted this might happen   room for improvement
> take on board   've talked about this before

A: Oscar, I'm worried that you didn't meet all your targets.

B: OK … but I'm afraid you're [1]_____ here. I exceeded my targets for the new lines.

A: That's true but we expected improvement across all sales.

B: I [2]_____ what you're saying and I agree there's [3]_____ .

A: Don't forget that we [4]_____ .

B: OK, but I really think that I can do better next quarter.

A: Yes, but you have to remember that we [5]_____ as you often fail to meet your targets.

B: I understand what you're saying, [6]_____ , but I think many of the problems have been beyond my control.

5.4 Leading and participating in review meetings

4 Complete the dialogue. Use one word in each gap.

A: As you can see from the [1]_____ , what I want to do today is reflect on how we are doing things. So, what do you think about where things have gone well and where the [2]_____ were?

B: Well … overall, it's great that we have [3]_____ all of our most important targets.

A: And what hasn't gone so well?

B: Some deadlines were missed. That mistake was [4]_____ to an oversight on my [5]_____ .

A: So what was the main [6]_____ of that mistake?

B: I misread the schedule. If I'd planned more carefully at the [7]_____ , I could have avoided this problem.

A: Yes, it's important never to underestimate the [8]_____ for good planning.

5.5 Performance review summary

5 Match the sentence halves.

1 You display great aptitude
2 You demonstrate the
3 You consistently
4 Although you have done a very good job,
5 I am impressed with what you have done so far,
6 Unfortunately, I feel that more training

   a meet deadlines.
   b for negotiating.
   c you have had some problems.
   d despite your having missed the deadline.
   e ability to use your initiative.
   f is required to help you meet your future targets.

6.1 Business ethics

1 Choose a word from each box to complete the sentences.

> clothing ethically fair-trade fashion low tough

> brands cotton conditions industry pay sourced

The [1]_____ is one where companies often have an ethical label to help sales. However, many of the workers who produce the clothes work in very [2]_____ and are often getting very [3]_____ . Well-known [4]_____ need to make sure that their clothes are being made in an ethical way. If they claim that a product is made from [5]_____ then they must ensure that they have the evidence to prove that the materials are [6]_____ .

2 Complete the sentences with suitable prepositions.

1 The company has been accused _____ not being ethical.

2 A company needs to take responsibility _____ its staff.

3 People have been campaigning _____ sweatshops for years.

4 Consumers should be aware _____ how their products are produced.

5 The bad publicity about the company has had a big impact _____ sales.

6.2 Third conditional

3 Complete the dialogue with third conditional forms using the verbs in the box. Some are used more than once.

> be find have try use

A: The problem is we didn't use ethical natural materials and as a result sales were poor.

B: If we [1]_____ natural materials, sales [2]_____ better, for sure.

A: It's a pity we had these problems. It's been bad for our brand image.

B: We [3]_____ these problems if we [4]_____ to cut costs, but we'll never know now.

A: Really? So you think that if we [5]_____ in such a hurry, we [6]_____ an ethical supplier?

B: Yes. And that might have been the difference between success and failure.

Functional language

6.3 Voicing and responding to concerns

4 Choose the correct option in italics.

A: When do we implement the changes?

B: I can't say [1]*for / with / by* certain because not all the information has been [2]*decided / concerned / confirmed* yet.

A: I see. And what do you think about the new ideas?

B: I'm [3]*honest / certain / concerned* that the customers might not be happy about them. It's just a [4]*light / thought / difficulty*. I could be wrong.

A: Well, to be [5]*important / honest / certain*, I agree with you. I don't think they'll like the changes.

6.4 Selling a product or service

5 Complete the sentences with words from the box.

> answer come enable major specialise useful

1 We _____ in digital advertising for small and medium-sized companies.

2 Could this service be _____ for you?

3 Our solutions _____ our clients to benefit from contact with a global audience.

4 Is budget a(n) _____ consideration for you?

5 So how about if I _____ over and show you some ideas?

6 Are there any other questions I can _____ for you right now?

6.5 Company newsletter

6 Put the sentences in the correct order.

STAFF COMPETITION

a As a result, we have set up a competition for staff to suggest ideas.

b Every month, we are going to choose the best idea from the box and award a prize to the winner.

c When this is done, you will be able to leave your suggestions there.

d The company has recently decided to encourage all staff to be more eco-friendly.

e We are therefore currently designing a virtual suggestion box on our website.

7.1 Managing time

1 Choose the correct option in italics.

1 They didn't *allocate* / *set* enough resources to complete the job properly.

2 You need to identify key *priorities* / *resources* if you want to be good at time management.

3 Managers must be able to set realistic *jobs* / *goals*.

4 Team leaders have to *measure* / *schedule* the tasks to be done by the team.

5 It is important to *maximise* / *allocate* efficiency at all times.

6 Managers should make sure that everyone is able to take a *time* / *break* at regular intervals.

2 Complete the dialogue. Use one word in each gap.

Daniel finds it difficult to make time ¹_____ his family. Although he tries to manage his time, he never finishes a job ²_____ of time and is always running ³_____ of time to do things. When a consultant analysed his working patterns, she found that he ⁴_____ a lot of time starting several jobs at the same time without any planning. Consequently, nothing ever gets finished ⁵_____ time. He then has to ⁶_____ time solving problems which could have been avoided if only he had planned his time better. If he learned to do one job ⁷_____ a time, he'd be much more efficient.

7.2 Adverbials and time expressions

3 Complete the dialogue using the words and phrases in the box.

> a daily basis all day any day latest never
> occasionally rarely time to time usually

Felizia had been at her desk ¹_____ since early morning trying to complete the proposal for her boss, who wanted it by 8 p.m. at the ²_____ . She worked long hours on ³_____ and almost ⁴_____ had a holiday. She explained that it was because she loved her job so much. Her colleagues did not understand why she did it because they ⁵_____ stayed late and only ⁶_____ agreed to do so when Felizia could persuade them to help her. This was ⁷_____ with an offer of more money plus extra time off if they did stay. Felizia's boss knew that Felizia could be found working hard in her office any time, ⁸_____ . However, she also knew that she would have to talk to Felizia about this, as it was not healthy to work such long hours. From ⁹_____ staff were expected to work late, but not every day.

Functional language
7.3 Discussing priorities

4 Complete the words. The first and last letters are given.

Hi Jaques,

Sorry to bother you, but I need your help. I'm ¹o_____d at the moment with so much work! Could you deal with the brainstorming of new initiatives with your team? Please ²p_____e this. It's urgent. The boss wants our ideas yesterday! The report you're writing, that's a lower ³p_____y – the ⁴d_____e is not until next week so you'll still have plenty of time to do it. The boss needs a ⁵r_____e by close of business tomorrow on the new initiatives. So, once you get a chance to give me your team's ⁶f_____k, I'll send the boss an ⁷u_____e on what's happening.

Thanks,

Joshua

7.4 Dealing with difficulties in negotiations

5 Match the sentence halves.

1 So what you're saying
2 I think we can both agree
3 I understand your
4 How about if we
5 We're going to have

a to go the extra mile to meet the deadline.
b change the work schedule?
c that saving time is essential.
d position a bit better now.
e is you don't like the idea?

7.5 An email giving reasons

6 Complete the text. Use one word in each gap.

I'm really ¹_____ to tell you that, ²_____ to unforeseen circumstances, we've ³_____ a major problem. This means that, unfortunately, we will not be able to meet the original deadline. ⁴_____ our best ⁵_____ to finish the building work on time, the problem has been ⁶_____ by poor weather conditions, which have forced the whole project to come to a complete standstill. Furthermore, we have not been able to get the extra materials we needed and this ⁷_____ has not helped the situation. I ⁸_____ propose that we look for the extra materials while everything has stopped. Furthermore, we should also find some additional temporary staff to help us ⁹_____ this problem once the weather improves. However, we will still need to ¹⁰_____ the schedule and find a new deadline which will suit all parties.

8.1 Change management

1 Choose the correct option in italics.

1 Good planning led to the actual move being very *adaptable / efficient / risky*.

2 Management have to *weigh / move / keep* up the risks and benefits of every situation.

3 If staff don't know what is happening, they can be very *adaptable / measured / apprehensive* about change.

4 Management should *cope / consult / weigh* with all staff about changes which will affect them.

2 Complete the sentences with the correct form of the word in brackets.

1 We need to ensure that the _____ (implement) of the new strategy is smooth.

2 For _____ (success) change to take place, everyone needs to be aware of the reasons for it.

3 We need to react with a carefully _____ (measure) response to avoid conflict.

4 Staff need to see that this change is _____ (benefit) for them.

8.2 Reported speech and reporting verbs

3 Rewrite the direct speech as reported speech using the word in capitals. There may be more than one possible answer.

1 'I won't be late again.' PROMISE
   She _____ .

2 'If I were you, I'd look for another job.' ADVISE
   His boss _____ .

3 'I think we should sell part of the company.' SUGGEST
   John _____ .

4 'I won't leave until the job is finished.' INSIST
   She _____ .

5 'We've just signed a new contract.' INFORM
   The company _____ .

Functional language
8.3 Coaching and mentoring

4 Complete the sentences using the words in the box.

> considered feel make should support tell were

1 How would you _____ about leading the project?

2 I can't _____ you what to do, but I can advise you.

3 Have you ever _____ working overseas?

4 No, I haven't but thanks for your _____ .

5 If I _____ you, I'd take the opportunity.

6 You _____ think it over for a couple of days before you _____ a decision.

8.4 Leading a brainstorming session

5 Match the functions (1–8) with the examples (a–h).

1 Define the goal
2 Start with questions and statements about the issue
3 Collect as many ideas as possible.
4 Ask for ideas about procedure
5 Ask people to give more details
6 Build on the ideas of others
7 Discuss and evaluate
8 Make a decision

a Feel free to make suggestions.
b Can you elaborate on that?
c Adding to that idea, we could ask the consultant for input.
d Let's go with that idea then.
e We're here today to address the design issue.
f These opening questions will enable us to identify the main problems.
g Are we all agreed that this is the best way forward?
h How would you like to group them?

8.5 Press release

6 Complete the text using the words in the box. Some words are not used.

> announcements announced assured
> complained complaints do expected
> key regretted replies told went

BSQ Supplies has just [1]_____ plans to purchase its main competitor, FDG Components. Unfortunately, rumours about redundancies [2]_____ viral last week and staff have [3]_____ about not being informed of the situation.

The CEO, Walter Grum, said he [4]_____ the lack of communication, which led to staff believing they would be made redundant. He [5]_____ everyone that this was definitely not the case and added that he would [6]_____ everything he could to retain all staff from both companies as the employees were the [7]_____ to BSQ's success.

It is [8]_____ that there will be further [9]_____ over the coming weeks.

Introduction

Pronunciation is important because even if you use the right words and the right grammar, you won't be able to communicate effectively if listeners can't understand your pronunciation easily. Awareness of the key elements of pronunciation will also help you to understand spoken English better.

Syllables, stress and intonation

Different words have different numbers of syllables:

1 syllable	*grow, growth*	4 syllables	*in·ter·view·er, co·or·di·nate*
2 syllables	*prod·uct, re·port*	5 syllables	*char·ac·ter·is·tic*
3 syllables	*in·ter·view, pro·duc·tion*	6 syllables	*re·spon·si·bil·i·ty*

In words with more than one syllable, one of the syllables is stressed, i.e. clearer, louder and longer than the other syllables, and it carries the main intonation, i.e. the movement of the voice up or down:

PRODuct   INterview   INterviewer
rePORT   proDUCtion   coORdinate

In longer words and compound nouns there is often a secondary stress, i.e. a less strong stress earlier in the word:

characteRIStic   responsiBILity   mobile PHONE

Stress is important in making words recognisable, and stress and intonation are used to highlight important information:

A: Are you still using that same old comPUter?   **B:** No, I've got a NEW one.
A: Did you get it as a PREsent?   **B:** No, I BOUGHT it.

The sounds of English

These are the sounds of standard British English and American English pronunciation. See also the section 'Varieties of English' on the following page.

Consonants		Vowels		
Symbol	**Keyword**	**Symbol** BrE	**Symbol** AmE	**Keyword**
p	pen	ɪ	ɪ	kit
b	back	e	e	dress
t	tea	æ	æ	bad
t̬ (*AmE*)	city	ʌ	ʌ	but
d	day	ʊ	ʊ	foot
k	key	ɒ		odd
g	get	ə	ə	about
tʃ	church	i	i	happy
dʒ	judge	u	u	situation
f	fact	iː	i	feel
v	view	ɑː	ɑ	father
θ	thing	ɔː	ɔ	north
ð	this	uː	u	goose
s	soon	ɜː	ɚ	stir
z	zero	eɪ	eɪ	face
ʃ	ship	aɪ	aɪ	price
ʒ	pleasure	ɔɪ	ɔɪ	boy
h	hot	əʊ	oʊ	no
m	more	aʊ	aʊ	mouth
n	nice	ɪə	ɪr	near
ŋ	ring	eə	er	fair
l	light	ʊə	ʊr	jury
r	right			
j	yet			
w	wet			

/t̬/ means that many American speakers use a voiced sound like a quick /d/ for the /t/ in words like *city, party, little*.
: shows a long vowel

Sounds and spelling

In English, the relationship between spoken and written language is particularly complicated.

The same sound can be spelt in different ways, e.g.
- /əʊ/ sl**ow** g**o** l**oa**n t**oe** alth**ough** kn**ow**
- /s/ **s**ell **sc**ien**c**e **c**ent

The same letter can be pronounced in different ways, e.g.
- the letter *u* can be pronounced /ʌ/ as in c**u**t, /ʊ/ as in f**u**ll, /ɔː/ as in s**u**re in British English or /ɪ/ as in b**u**sy;
- the letter *s* can be pronounced /s/ as in **s**ell, /z/ as in ea**s**y, /ʃ/ as in ten**s**ion or /ʒ/ as in deci**s**ion.

Using a dictionary

Once you are familiar with the phonetic symbols in the table in 'The sounds of English' section, you will be able to use a dictionary to find the pronunciation of any word you are unsure about. As well as the sounds in a word, dictionaries also show word stress. Look at this dictionary entry for *controversial*:

> **con·tro·ver·sial** /ˌkɒntrəˈvɜːʃəl/ *adj* causing a lot of disagreement, because many people have strong opinions about the subject being discussed

- The ' sign shows you that the syllable immediately after it is stressed.
- The ˌ sign shows you that the syllable immediately after it has secondary stress.
- The ː sign shows you that the vowel is long.

Simplifications

In normal everyday speech, however, words often do not have the same pronunciation as shown in dictionaries. This is important for listening. Vowels in stressed syllables are usually pronounced clearly, but otherwise speakers make various simplifications:
- Some sounds are missed out, e.g. *facts* can sound like 'facs', *compete* can sound like 'cmpete', *characteristic* can sound like 'charrtristic'.
- Some sounds are merged together, e.g. *on Monday* can sound like 'om Monday', *ten groups* can sound like 'teng groups', *this show* can sound like 'thishow'.

Varieties of English

English is of course spoken by some people as a first language, but it is spoken by much larger numbers of people who learn it as an additional language and use it as a lingua franca for international communication.

There is a large amount of variation in how English is pronounced:
- Variation among traditional 'native' accents such as British, American and Australian. There are even considerable differences between the accents of different regions of the United Kingdom.
- Variation among accents of English as a lingua franca, with many of the differences caused by the influence of speakers' first languages, e.g. Japanese speakers often do not distinguish between /l/ and /r/, and Spanish speakers often add an /e/ at the front of words beginning with /sp/, /sk/ and /st/.

Consonant sounds are generally similar in different varieties, but there is much more variation in vowel sounds – both the number of vowel sounds used and the exact quality of the sounds.

In the audio and video recordings which accompany this course – and in your everyday life and work – you will hear speakers from various English-speaking and non-English-speaking backgrounds communicating successfully with each other despite such differences in pronunciation. For example, many speakers do not use the /θ/ sound of '**th**ink' and the /ð/ sound of '**th**en', but this does not generally affect their ability to make themselves understood. Particularly important things to concentrate on include:
- word stress,
- stress and intonation in phrases and sentences, for highlighting important information,
- consonant sounds,
- groups of consonants at the beginning of words – e.g. **str**ong,
- the difference between long and short vowels.

Good pronunciation does not necessarily mean speaking like a 'native' speaker; it means being understood by others when communicating in English. Awareness of pronunciation principles and regular pronunciation practice will help you improve your speaking, but also your listening comprehension.

Lesson 1.1 ❯
Stress in compound nouns

> In compound nouns, the main stress may fall on either word. For example:
> CREDIT card company STRUCTURE
>
> Some compound nouns consist of more than two words. The main stress may fall on any of the words. For example:
> CREDIT card payment   company DAY care

1 Work in pairs. Match 1–5 with a–e to make compound nouns. Then underline the word with the main stress in each compound noun.

1	role	a	transaction
2	company	b	office
3	pay	c	model
4	open-plan	d	hierarchy
5	credit card	e	rate

2 🔊 P1.01   Listen and check. Then listen again and repeat.

3 Work in pairs. Take turns to say a word from one of the compound nouns in Exercise 1. Without looking at Exercise 1, your partner says the compound noun in a sentence.

Lesson 1.2 ❯
Auxiliary verbs in the Future Continuous and Future Perfect Simple

> When we use auxiliary verbs in speech, we normally use the contracted forms /l/ (= will) (especially after pronouns) and /əv/ (= have).

1 Mark where you think the contracted forms /l/ and /əv/ are used.
1 What do you think you will be doing ten years from now?
2 Many young people will have decided what is important for them in a job by the time they go to their first interview.
3 What position will you have reached by the time you're forty?
4 This afternoon at our weekly meeting, we will be discussing how to reduce menial tasks for junior staff.

2 🔊 P1.02   Compare with a partner, then listen and check.

3 Work in pairs and practise saying the sentences in Exercise 1.

Lesson 2.1 ❯
Stressing key words in sentences

> The emphasis of a sentence can often change depending on which word you stress when speaking. For example:
> *The Paris branch has <u>doubled</u> sales in the last six months.* The emphasis is on how much sales have grown by.
> *The <u>Paris</u> branch has doubled sales in the last six months.* The emphasis is on where sales have doubled.

1 🔊 P2.01   Listen to the sentences and repeat. Copy the intonation.
1 The share prices fell <u>after</u> the takeover.
  The share prices <u>fell</u> after the takeover.
2 <u>Induction training</u> is sometimes called onboarding.
  Induction training is sometimes called <u>onboarding</u>.
3 <u>Training courses</u> can help to drive career development.
  Training courses can help to drive <u>career development</u>.

2 Work in pairs and practise saying the sentences in Exercise 1.

Lesson 2.4 ❯
Linking between words

> In spoken English, we can link words in various ways.

1 🔊 P2.02   Listen to the pairs of words. Match them to the types of linking.

1	so_everybody	a	/v/ links the words.
2	objective_of	b	/w/ links the words.
3	more_efficient	c	/r/ links the words, even though it is not pronounced when we say the word on its own.

2 Work with a partner. Mark where there will be examples of each type of linking.
1 We communicated through our lawyers.
2 Thanks to all of you.
3 Then we'll have a meeting of eight directors.
4 How do others feel about this?
5 Please give your ideas and tell us what you want.

3 🔊 P2.03   Listen and check. Then listen again and repeat.

4 Work in pairs. Take turns to say the sentences in Exercise 2.

Lesson 3.3 ❯
The letter 't'

> The letter 't' in words can be pronounced in different ways.

1 🔊 P3.01 Listen to two versions of the phrases below. In which option (a or b) do you hear a 't'?

                      a **b**

1 Gatwick airport   ☐ ☐
2 get back   ☐ ☐
3 the money was sent yesterday   ☐ ☐

2A 🔊 P3.02 Listen to the sentences and complete the missing words.

1 The new CEO has had the _____ approach so far.
2 A 0.5 percent increase is _____ than nothing.
3 We hope to _____ our targets this quarter.
4 Revenue will increase by 50 percent _____ year.
5 In the last quarter, _____ profit fell by 15 percent.
6 The project will cost _____ million euros.

B Listen again. Focus on the words you added in Exercise 2A and decide if the /t/ is pronounced in each case.

Lesson 3.4 ❯
Strong and weak forms of *that*

> When *that* is a pronoun or a determiner, we normally use the strong form /ðæt/, but when it is a conjunction or a relative pronoun we normally use the weak form /ðət/. For example:
> *Is that /ðæt/ the one that /ðət/ you wanted?*

1 Work in pairs. Do you think *that* will be strong or weak?

1 That's it.
2 There's only one version that everyone can see.
3 That way you can be sure you're looking at the more recent version.
4 We have to change that.
5 I wrote down that the figures in row 48 are averages.

2 🔊 P3.03 Listen and check.

Lesson 4.1 ❯
Stress in word building

> When we add suffixes to words, the stress sometimes stays on the same syllable and sometimes moves. We can record the stress pattern of a word by using large and small circles. For example:
> trans·port Oo
> trans·por·ta·tion ooOo

1 Work in pairs. Look at the words. In which pairs does the stress stay on the same syllable? In which does it move?

> analyse → analysis
> disrupt → disruption
> innovate → innovation
> irritate → irritating
> predict → predictable

2 🔊 P4.01 Listen and check.

3 Work in pairs. Draw large and small circles on a sheet of paper to show the stress patterns of the words in Exercise 1.

4 Work in pairs and practise saying the words.

Lesson 4.4 ❯
Stress in phrases

> Some of the phrases and sentences in this lesson often have a characteristic stress pattern. For example:
> *You WANTED to SEE me?*

1 🔊 P4.02 Listen and underline the stressed words. There are two in each item.

1 That sounds reasonable.
2 What are your priorities?
3 You have to understand …
4 I can agree to that.
5 For some of us it's necessary.
6 Let me make sure.
7 Let's look at the facts.
8 I think I can make that happen.

2 Listen again and repeat.

3 Work in pairs and practise saying the sentences in Exercise 1.

Lesson 5.2 ❯
Intonation and linking words

When linking words are used at the beginning of a sentence, they often have a fall–rise intonation. For example:

On the one hand ...

If a linking word forms the beginning of a longer phrase or clause, the fall–rise often occurs later in the phrase or clause. For example:

Despite experiencing a number of problems, ...

1 Work in pairs. Where will the fall–rise be in these sentences?

1 On the other hand, they receive overtime pay.
2 Although he has achieved a great deal in the company, there have been a number of problems to deal with.
3 Nevertheless, it was effective to simply make pilots aware of saving fuel.
4 Even though some work can be done from home, many companies prefer to have the workers in the factory.
5 In spite of his career being so successful, he decided to try a new area of business and left the company.

2 ◀) P5.01   Listen and check. Then listen again and repeat.

Lesson 5.3 ❯
Intonation when handling challenging feedback

When giving and responding to challenging feedback, sound confident and assertive without being impolite by using falling intonation.

1 ◀) P5.02   Listen to the following sentences and underline where you hear a change in intonation.

1 I agree with you 100 percent.
2 I can see your point.
3 We've talked about this before.
4 I take on board what you're saying.
5 There's room for improvement.

2 Work in pairs. Take turns to practise the sentences. Listen to your partner and draw a line in the air with your hand to show how your partner's voice goes up and down.

Lesson 6.2 ❯
Contractions and weak forms in third conditionals

In third conditional sentences, we normally use the weak form /əv/ (= *have*), and we often use the contractions 'd (= *had or would*), hadn't (= *had not*) and wouldn't (= *would not*).

1 ◀) P6.01   Listen and complete the sentences.

1 We _____ paid such a high tax bill last year if we _____ given some of our profits to a charity for the homeless.
2 If they _____ taken on employees with disabilities, they _____ had diversity in the workplace.
3 We _____ reduced both our transport costs and carbon emissions if we _____ sourced all of our raw materials locally.

2 Work in pairs and practise saying the sentences in Exercise 1.

Lesson 6.5 ❯
Chunking, pausing and stress when reading aloud

When we read a text aloud, we divide it into chunks to make it more manageable for us and our listeners.

1 Work in pairs. Discuss how you could divide this text into chunks to read it aloud. Which words would you stress for emphasis?

Salvador Fidalgo is our 'Hero of the month' for his work on our local community programme. He has formed and coached a football team of local teenagers and the youngsters have done so well that they have just won a regional football competition. Salvador says he has had such a rewarding time working with these youngsters, that he is going to start a second team.

2 ◀) P6.02   Listen to two versions. Which was closest to your ideas in Exercise 1? Which version do you prefer, and why? Discuss with your partner.

Lesson 7.2 ❯
Stress in adverbials and time expressions

Many adverbials and time expressions, even ones consisting of more than one word, have a typical stress pattern. For example:
At first (oO), they didn't like the idea.
I don't normally (Ooo) work on Fridays.

1 Work in pairs. Draw large and small circles in the brackets to show the stress patterns of the underlined words.

1 <u>Usually</u> ( ) they finish their work by Friday afternoon.
2 <u>From time to time</u> ( ) he goes to visit customers.
3 <u>Occasionally</u> ( ) we take clients out for dinner.
4 <u>In a few days</u> ( ) we should have more information.
5 <u>Recently</u> ( ) they have started to look into making meetings shorter.

2 ◀) P7.01 Listen and check.

3 Work in pairs. Practise saying the sentences with the correct stress.

Lesson 7.4 ❯
Intonation when negotiating

Using intonation with a wide voice range can help us sound cooperative and willing to negotiate. For example:

How about if we postpone your departure for a few days?

1 ◀) P7.02 Listen to two versions of sentences from a negotiation. Which version sounds cooperative and willing to negotiate, the first or the second?

1 This is a good thing that you are offering. I am very grateful.
2 In other words, you want to continue with the project.
3 So what you're saying is that you are no longer interested in the deal.

2 ◀) P7.03 Listen to the cooperative versions again and repeat.

3 Work in pairs. Write three sentences starting like sentences in Exercise 1. Practise saying the sentences to each other, sounding cooperative and willing to negotiate.

Lesson 8.2 ❯
/s/, /z/, /ʃ/, /tʃ/ and /dʒ/

The consonant sounds /s/, /z/, /ʃ/, /tʃ/ and /dʒ/ can be spelled in various ways. For example:
/s/ promised, price
/z/ advised, size

1 Work in pairs and put the words in the correct category, according to the pronunciation of the letters in bold.

ac**t**ually an**x**ious appre**c**iate bu**s**iness **ch**anges chan**ge**s de**c**ision in**s**isted lo**se** mana**ge**ment offi**ce**s pa**ss**ion pri**ce**s que**st**ions su**gg**ests

/s/	
/z/	
/ʃ/	
/tʃ/	
/dʒ/	

2 ◀) P8.01 Listen and check.

3 Work in pairs. Take turns to point to words in Exercise 1, and say sentences containing the words.

Lesson 8.4 ❯
Voice range

A falling intonation from a high level can help to give an impression of authority, completeness or finality.

1 ◀) P8.02 Listen and mark the main stress with falling intonation in each sentence.

1 There is no right or wrong.
2 How would you like to categorise them?
3 Could you expand on this point for us?
4 These statements highlight the issues we're facing.
5 What does everyone think about that as an option?

2 Listen again and repeat.

1.2 Future Continuous and Future Perfect Simple

- We use the **Future Continuous** for **events that will be taking place at a particular time in the future**.

  *The best way to get staff members to care whether their employer **will be doing** business in the future is to convince them that they **will be working** there when it happens.*

  *This time next year I think companies **will be looking for** employees who are interested in making careers with them.*

  *HR **will be analysing** the data on staff retention once all the departments and subsidiaries have sent them the information they need.*

- We form the **Future Continuous** using **will + be + present participle** of the main verb.

- We use the **Future Perfect Simple** for **events in the future which will be finished by a certain time**.

  *By the time they have been there a few months, Morgan Stanley **will have told** top first-year analysts that they have a bright future at the bank.*

  *Hopefully, within a few years these initiatives **will have made** a real difference.*

  *By the middle of the next decade, most companies **will have implemented** a policy of paid sabbaticals for employees.*

  *We are certain that we **will have solved** the problem of employee retention before the next five years are over.*

- We form the **Future Perfect Simple** using **will + have + past participle** of the main verb.

- We invert the subject and *will* when making questions with the Future Continuous and Future Perfect Simple.

  ***Will** companies **be implementing** changes more frequently in the next decade?*

  ***Will** students **have completed** more than one degree by the time they finish university and enter the workplace?*

1.5 Phrases with *be*

- **be about to** is used for something that is going to happen almost immediately.

  *The presentation **is about to** start.*

- **be due to** is used to say something is expected to happen at a particular time.

  *The meeting **is due to** finish at 1700 hrs.*

- **be supposed to** is used for something which should happen but may not.

  *Everyone **is supposed to** come back to work afterwards.*

- **be sure / certain to** is used when something is definite.

  *Everyone **is sure / certain to** benefit from a sabbatical.*

- **be (un)likely to** is used to say that something is probable or improbable.

  *You **are likely to** have concerns about time away from work.*

  *The budget **is unlikely to** be increased next year.*

- **be to** is used for giving formal instructions.

  *Full salary **is to** be paid during the sabbatical providing you do voluntary work.*

  *Employees **are not to** take time off during the summer months.*

2.2 Modals in the passive voice

We use the **passive voice** when we don't know who or what (the agent) is responsible for an action, or the agent isn't important, or when we simply want to emphasise the importance of an action rather than the person/thing responsible for doing it.

Modal verbs indicate ability, obligation, lack of obligation, necessity, permission, possibility, prohibition or recommendation.

- We use **need to / have to / must + be + past participle** to talk about passive actions that are **necessary**.

  *This expense **needs to be explained** as it wasn't approved.*

  *She **has to be helped** with the report.*

  *These bills **must be paid** as they were due last week.*

  We use **have to** more frequently for **external rules**, and **must** more frequently for **obligations we make for ourselves**.

  *According to government regulations, these policies **have to be followed** when we lend money to clients.*

  *The training needs **must be evaluated** by this afternoon as I am leaving tomorrow on holiday.*

  We can also use both **have to** and **must** for **strong recommendations**.

  *His comments on the development programme **have to be read**, they are wonderful.*

  *The course I took **must be offered** to everyone, it is incredibly useful!*

- We use **should / ought to / shouldn't + be + past participle** to make **recommendations** and to give **advice** and **opinions**.

  *The telephone **should be answered** immediately.*

  *Business clothes **ought to be worn** in the office by staff who deal with customers.*

  *Development courses **shouldn't be offered** to everyone in the company as they may not need them.*

- We use **mustn't + be + past participle** to say that something is **not allowed or permitted** or is **prohibited by law**.

  *Your clients' personal data **mustn't be shared** with any of your colleagues.*

- We use **don't have to / don't need to + be + past participle** to say that it is **not necessary or compulsory** to do something, but that it can be done if you want. This is a **lack of obligation**.

  *The reports **don't have to be finished** till next week, but you can do them earlier if you like.*

  *All working hours **don't need to be spent** in the office, employees can work at home some of the time.*

*Note: **mustn't + be** + past participle and **don't have to + be** + past participle have very different meanings.*

*Mobile telephones **mustn't be used** in this part of the plant. (This is not permitted.)*

*Business suits **don't have to be worn** in this office. (This is not necessary.)*

- We use **can / could / may / might / would + be** + past participle to say that it is **possible** to do something.

  *This research **can be finished** tomorrow.*

  *An employee **could be moved** from one department to another.*

  *This training programme **may/might be implemented** to help new employees.*

  *A more intensive development training **would be considered** if enough people needed it.*

- We use **can + be** + past participle to say that the ability exists to do something.

  *The language in this manual **can** easily **be simplified**.*

- We also use **can + be** + past participle to say that permission is given to do something.

  *This door **can be used** in the afternoon but not in the morning when the assembly line is running.*

2.5 ❯ Linking words for reason and purpose

We use the following linking words to introduce a reason or purpose.

To introduce a reason: *because, because of, as, since*

*Please could you let me know by tonight **because** registration for the course closes tomorrow.*

*The supplies were late **because of** a transport strike.*

***As/Since** I have just been made a project leader, it is important for me to attend a project leadership training course.*

To introduce a purpose: *to + infinitive, in order (not) to + infinitive, so as (not) to + infinitive, in order that, so (that)*

*Could you stay late this evening **to** help us prepare tomorrow's presentation?*

*I am interested in developing skills **in order to** deal with conflict.*

*We worked overtime **so as not to** miss the deadline.*

*It is vital to develop my skills **in order that** I can effectively motivate my team.*

*We worked overtime **so that** the project was finished on time.*

3.2 ❯ Expressing certainty and probability

(un)likely to, certain to and due to

- We use the expressions *(un)likely to, certain to* and *due to* to talk about certainty and probability.

  be + (un)likely/certain/due to + infinitive

  *The new sales strategy **is likely to increase** profitability this year. (= This is probable.)*

  *He **is unlikely to meet** his sales targets by the end of this month. (= This is improbable.)*

  *They **are certain to gain** market share. (= This is certain.)*

  *The meeting **is due to start** at three o'clock. (= This is planned for a fixed time.)*

- These structures are often used with time expressions, e.g. *at the end of the (month), by (2030), by/before the end of the (year), over/in the next (three years),* etc. We usually put the time expression at the end of the sentence.

  *The group is certain to expand faster **over the next five years**.*

  *We are due to review our market position **by the end of the second quarter**.*

It is (un)likely/certain + clause

- We can also use *(un)likely* or *certain* with a clause.

  It is + (un)likely/certain + (that) + subject + will + infinitive

  ***It is likely (that) we will have** to review our online sales.*

  ***It is certain (that) the footwear brand will sign** an NBA star.*

Position of adverbs and adverbial phrases

Position of *also*

- We put the adverb *also* <u>after</u> the verb *be* but <u>before</u> the main verb with other verbs.

  *Adidas's online sales are **also** due to rise.*

  *Adidas is **also** likely to sell off unwanted businesses.*

  *The new CEO has **also** said they are aiming to boost sales.*

Position of *probably* with *will/won't*

- We can use the future form *will* to talk about future probability. We use the adverb *probably* when we are less certain something will happen.

Be careful with the word order:

- We put *probably* after *will*, but <u>before</u> *won't* in negative sentences.

  *The group **will probably** continue to invest more. (= This is probable.)*

  *Our online sales **probably won't** rise significantly. (= This is improbable.)*

- We put *probably* after *be*, but <u>before</u> *isn't/aren't* in negative sentences.

  *The group **is probably** going to continue to invest more.*

  *Our online sales **probably aren't** going to rise significantly.*

3.5**>** Articles: *a/an, the*, no article

Talking about people or things in general

- There is **no article** with plural nouns or uncountable nouns. (Uncountable nouns don't have a plural form, e.g. *information, knowledge, money*.)

    Lower operating costs mean that we finished more strongly than expected.

    Information about the project is now available online.

- We use *a/an* with singular countable nouns. (Countable nouns have singular and plural forms, e.g. *factory - factories*).

    It was a year of mixed results.

    An assessment of the market for the coming year indicates that sales will increase.

- We use *the* when we know which thing we are talking about either because it is unique or has been referred to before.

    This was caused by a slow-down in the global economy. (= The global economy is unique.)

    Here is the information you asked for. (= This refers back to information which was requested previously.)

    Last year we decided to build a new factory. The new factory is now up and running. (= This refers back to the factory mentioned in the first sentence.)

4.2**>** Zero, first and second conditionals; Linkers

Zero conditional

We use **zero conditional** sentences to talk about **consequences of actions that are always or usually true**. The usual structure of a zero conditional sentence is:

If + Present Simple, Present Simple

If you click here, the different functions appear.

First conditional

We use **first conditional** sentences to talk about **potential consequences of actions and real possibilities**. The usual structure of a first conditional sentence is:

If + Present Simple, *will* + main verb

If you use this app, you'll be able to understand instantly.

We can sometimes use the Present Perfect instead of the Present Simple.

If you've seen the advert, you'll know what I'm talking about.

We can also use a modal verb or imperative instead of *will*.

If you click here, you can see all the language options. (modal verb instead of *will*)

Record the dialogue on your smartphone if you have one. (imperative form instead of *will*)

We can use *unless* in zero and first conditional sentences to mean *if not*.

Unless you can afford an interpreter, this is the device for you. (= *If you can't afford* …)

Second conditional

We use **second conditional** sentences when we feel **less certain of potential consequences or to talk about imaginary or 'unreal' situations**. In these situations, we consider the action more difficult to achieve and so less likely to happen. The usual structure of a second conditional sentence is:

If + Past Simple, *would/could/might* + main verb

If I had a digital personal assistant now, it could make my life much easier.

We can sometimes use the Past Continuous instead of the Past Simple.

If we weren't using voice recognition now, you might have problems understanding me.

In the second conditional we usually use either *were* which is more formal or *was* in informal speech, after *I, he, she* and *it*.

If I wasn't / weren't so busy, I'd stop to chat more often.

But we always use *were* in the phrase *If I were you*.

We can sometimes use either the first or the second conditional, depending on how likely we think the situation is.

If you buy 50 headsets, we'll offer you a discount. (I see this as a real possibility.)

If you bought 50 headsets, we'd offer you a discount. (I think it's unlikely you will buy these.)

Linkers

We can use a variety of linkers or conjunctions instead of *if* when talking about conditions.

- We can use *provided/providing (that)* to say that something will only be possible if something else happens or is done.

    We'd buy this product provided/providing (that) you gave us a two-year guarantee.

- We can use *as long as* to say that one thing can happen or be true only if another thing happens or is true.

    We could start the project next month as long as you signed the contract.

    We can also use *as long as* to say that one thing will continue to happen or be true if another thing happens or is true at the same time.

    We will become one of the world's most revolutionary companies as long as we don't stop innovating.

- We can use *on condition (that)* in formal situations to say that something will only happen if a particular point is agreed upon.

    As discussed in our meeting, we will be happy to order 50 headsets on condition (that) you offer us a 10% discount.

Note: Like *if* and *unless*, we can use *provided/providing (that)*, *as long as* and *on condition (that)* both in the middle and at the beginning of a conditional sentence as the two clauses can appear in either order.

4.5❯ Noun phrases to replace verb phrases

We often use noun phrases to replace verb phrases in formal writing.

- A **verb phrase** is more personal than a noun phrase and is about what we do.

  We measure the medication very carefully when we dispense prescriptions.

- A **noun phrase** is less personal than a verb phrase and focuses more on the topic.

  The measurement of medication is very important when dispensing prescriptions.

- We can make **nouns from verbs** by adding suffixes. For example:

  *measure → measure**ment**   produce → produc**tion***

- Some verbs have the same form as nouns. For example:

  change → change   release → release

Prepositions used with noun phrases

If there are two nouns in the phrase then we use *of* or *in*.

*The automated measurement **of** medication has improved safety.*

*There have been complaints about an increase **in** waiting times.*

5.2❯ Linking words and concessive clauses

We can use a range of linking words or adverbials to introduce contrast or concessive clauses, but the language structures following them and punctuation associated with them vary.

- ***Though*** adds a fact or opinion that makes what you have just said seem less definite or less important. It can be used to link two clauses or at the beginning of the sentence. We can also use ***though*** at the end of a second sentence which shows contrast to the sentence before. When it is used at the beginning of the first clause, there is usually a comma before the second clause but not when it appears in the middle or at the end of the sentence.

  *Employees did not expect to receive pay rises **though** a number of them hoped they would get them.*

- ***Although*** contrasts one clause with another in the same sentence. It can be used to link two clauses or come at the beginning of the first clause. The clauses are usually separated by a comma, both when it appears at the beginning and in the middle of the sentence.

  *It was found that setting targets helped improve performance, **although** some people preferred to be rewarded financially for their efforts.*

- ***Even though*** is used to introduce a statement that makes the main statement coming after it seem surprising. It is used to show a stronger contrast to the two clauses than *though/although*. It can be used to link two clauses or come at the beginning of the first clause. The clauses are usually separated by a comma, both when it appears at the beginning and in the middle of the sentence.

  *Executives often receive performance-related pay, **even though** their performance on the job is hard to evaluate.*

- ***However*** and ***nevertheless*** are often used to begin or end a sentence to provide contrast to a sentence which came before. They are also occasionally used in the middle of a sentence. They are usually followed by commas when they come at the beginning of a sentence and are usually set off by commas (have a comma before and after), when used in the middle of a sentence. There is usually no comma when they come at the end of a sentence.

  *Performance incentives are usually only given to managers. **However,** this year we all got a bonus.*

  *He earns a six-figure salary, but he feels he should be paid more **nevertheless**.*

- ***Despite*** and ***in spite of*** are used to say that something happens or is true even though something else might have prevented it. They can be used to link two clauses or come at the beginning of the first clause. They are similar to *although* but are followed by a noun, noun phrase or verb form ending in *-ing*. When they are used at the beginning of the first clause, there is usually a comma before the second clause but not when they appear in the middle of the sentence.

  *Job satisfaction is quite high **despite** the number of hours people are working at the moment.*

  ***In spite of** receiving a promotion last year, she decided to leave the company.*

- ***Despite*** and ***in spite of*** can also be followed by ***the fact that*** and a clause. They can be used to link two clauses or come at the beginning of the first clause. The two clauses are usually separated from each other by a comma, both when they appear at the beginning and in the middle of the sentence.

  *Many people at my company who didn't get raises are looking for new jobs, **in spite of the fact that** the economy is slow at the moment.*

- ***On the one hand, … on the other hand,*** are used to present a main idea which is then contrasted in a second sentence or clause. These expressions are usually followed by commas or set off by commas. *On the other hand* is often preceded by *but* when it comes in the second clause. There is no comma between *but* and *on the other hand*.

  ***On the one hand,** he is a hard worker, but **on the other hand,** his performance does not seem to improve from year to year.*

5.5❯ Phrasal verbs

Phrasal verbs are a group of words that are used like a verb and consist of a verb with an adverb (e.g. away, forward) or preposition (e.g. off, on) after it. The meaning of the verb + adverb/preposition changes the meaning of the verb.

Here is a list of some common phrasal verbs and their meaning.

The ↔ sign indicates that the adverb or preposition can go in two places in a sentence:

*He **worked out** the cost. He **worked** the cost **out**.*

carry on continue doing something

*Sorry, I interrupted you. Please **carry on**.*

catch up spend time finding out what has been happening while you have been away or during the time you have not seen someone

*Can we meet to **catch up** about the project?*

copy somebody in (on) send someone a copy of an email message you are sending to someone else

*Can you **copy me in** on the memo you're sending to Chris?*

fall behind make less progress than others in a competitive situation

*Small firms that **fall behind** technologically can be rapidly wiped out.*

keep something ↔ up continue doing something

*I don't think I can **keep this up** any longer.*

look forward to be excited and pleased about something that is going to happen

*He **looked forward to** the end of his shift.*

run something by/past somebody tell someone about an idea or plan so that they can give you their opinion

*You'd better **run it by your manager** first.*

take off if an aircraft takes off, it rises into the air from the ground

*I felt quite excited as the plane **took off** from Heathrow.*

sign something ↔ off / sign off on something show that you approve of a plan or that something is finished by signing an official document

*A qualified engineer needs to **sign off** major repainting work.*

work something ↔ out 1 think carefully about how you are going to do something and plan a good way of doing it

*UN negotiators have **worked out** a set of compromise proposals.*

2 calculate an answer, amount, price etc

*He **worked out** the cost of the new project.*

6.2 ⟩ Third conditional

Describing hypothetical past actions or situations

We use **third conditional** sentences to talk about **hypothetical past actions or situations**. In these sentences, we are **speculating about past possible actions or situations that didn't happen** for one reason or another.

*She would**n't** have **chosen** that supplier if they had**n't used** fair trade products.*

(But she **chose** them because they **used** fair trade products.)

*If I had **known** they weren't an ethical company, I would**n't** have **bought** their products.*

(But I **didn't know** and I **bought** their products.)

The usual structure of a third conditional sentence is:

If + Past Perfect, *would/could/might have* + past participle

Like zero, first and second conditional sentences, the two clauses can appear in either order.

*If they **had considered** the TBL of people, planet and profits, they **would have been** an ethical company.*

*We **would have reduced** our carbon footprint and **saved** money if we **had gone** on fewer business trips last year.*

Note: If you begin a conditional sentence with *if*, then you need to put a comma after the conditional clause. You do <u>not</u> need a comma if you start with the main clause.

Question forms

When asking questions, we invert *would* and the subject in the main clause. Remember always to use the Past Perfect tense in the *if* clause whichever position this clause appears in.

*If we **had had** more video conferences instead of international meetings, **would** we **have saved** money on travel?*

***Would** customers **have bought** their clothes **if** they **had known** they had exploited workers in sweatshops?*

would/could/might

We can substitute *would* for the modal verbs *could* or *might*. When we use *would*, we are **more certain** of our hypothesis.

*If you had recycled more responsibly, you **would have reduced** your carbon emissions. (I see this as very likely as a past possibility.)*

However, if we use *could* instead of *would*, the possible outcome of a past event or situation was **less likely** in our opinion, and **refers to a past opportunity which was not fulfilled**.

*If we had developed a sustainability statement, we **could have been** on the list of most ethical companies but we weren't. (I see this as less likely than 'would'; it was a missed opportunity.)*

If we use *might* instead of *would*, we think the outcome was **even less likely** to happen.

*Our brand **might have been** more successful if we had considered its carbon footprint and the impact on the environment. (I see this as an unlikely past possibility; the brand's success depended on different factors.)*

Passive forms

When we use the passive form in the third conditional, remember always to use the past participle of the auxiliary verb *be*, i.e. *been*, in the main clause.

*If Kao hadn't developed the Kao way, they might not **have been listed** as one of the world's most ethical companies.*

*If our annual report **hadn't been published**, we **wouldn't have been seen** as a responsible company.*

Contractions: *would've* and *wouldn't've*

Native speakers usually use contracted forms of *would have* (*would've*) and *wouldn't have* (*wouldn't've*) and of the past perfect tense (*'d*) when speaking.

*If they**'d** taken on more female managers, they **would've** (/ˈwʊdəv/) had diversity in the workplace.*

*If you**'d** listened to me, we **wouldn't've** (/ˈwʊdəntəv/) had problems with the audit!*

6.5 ⟩ Linking words for causes and results

We can use words and phrases like ***therefore**, **as a result**, **so**, **such**, **so/such ... that*** and ***so much/many ... that*** to link causes and results.

- We use ***therefore*** and ***as a result*** to introduce a sentence that describes a result.

Therefore, if you are interested, please contact the HR manager.

As a result of the community project scheme, staff are more motivated.

- We use **so** to join a cause and a result in one sentence.

  We are going to run a competition next month, **so** staff can suggest ideas.

- The word **so** can also mean *very* before an adjective or adverb.

  The cost of the new system was **so** expensive.

  The energy bills were **so** high.

  Such is similar to *so* but we use it before a noun phrase.

  It was **such** an expensive system.

  They were **such** high energy bills.

- We use **so/such … that** to introduce a clause that describes a result.

  The team has done **so** well **that** they have just won a regional football competition.

  It was **such** an expensive product **that** we couldn't afford to buy it.

  So much/many can be used in the same way.

  There were **so many** people in the room **that** we had to move to a bigger one.

  There was **so much** waste **that** we did not have enough bins.

7.2 ❯ Adverbials and time expressions

Adverbials of frequency

A range of adverbials can be used to express how often an event occurs or something is done.

- **Always**, **seldom**, **rarely**, **hardly ever**, **almost never** and **never** are used in mid-position in a sentence:

  - before the main verb in a sentence, and after the auxiliary or modal verb.

    They **always** plan the events of the month in advance.

    We have **seldom** spent the weekend in the office.

    His line manager can **rarely** keep a meeting short.

  - between two auxiliary verbs (e.g. *has* and *been*).

    She has **hardly ever** been given a sensible answer when she asked how to manage her workload.

  - after the verb *be*.

    Employees at our company are **almost never** trained in time management.

- **Normally** and **usually** come in mid-position or at the beginning of a sentence.

  Our manager **normally** plans the assignments for the month.

  Usually we look over the timetable when we get to work in the morning.

  Note: When **normally** is used at the beginning of a sentence, it is followed by a comma.

- **Frequently**, **occasionally,** **often** and **sometimes** come in mid-position or at the beginning or end of a sentence.

  They **frequently** reassign jobs.

  Occasionally upper management suggests time-management seminars to our boss.

  We don't **often** work from home.

  I see him in the breakroom **sometimes**.

  Note: When **frequently** is used at the beginning of a sentence, it is followed by a comma.

- **From time to time** and **now and then** come at the beginning or end of a sentence.

  From time to time they attend extra courses.

  I manage to leave the office early **now and then.**

Time expressions

Time expressions can be used to indicate events taking place in the past/future and to specify the timeframe.

- **At first** is used to talk about the beginning of a situation in the past, especially when the situation is different in the present. It can come at the beginning or end of a sentence or after the phrase it defines. When it comes at the beginning of a sentence, it is followed by a comma.

  I felt overwhelmed with the job **at first**. Now I really enjoy it.

- **Recently** is used to indicate events which happened in the near past or not long ago. It can be used with the Past or Present Perfect tense. It can come in mid-position or at the beginning or end of a sentence.

  Our boss **recently** gave us news about our new schedule.

- **In a few …** is used to indicate a particular period of time in the future. It can be combined with any noun in its plural form indicating time, e.g. *minutes*, *hours*, *days*, *months*, *years*, etc. It can come at the beginning or end of a sentence.

  In a few months this project will be finished.

- **At the latest** is used to indicate that something must happen or be finished not later than the time mentioned. It can come at the beginning or end of a sentence or after the phrase it defines. When it comes at the beginning of a sentence, it is followed by a comma.

  At the latest, this work needs to be completed by tomorrow.

Expressions with *day*

Various expressions with *day* are used to indicate different periods of time.

- **All day** is used for events, actions or situations which take place from the morning to the evening. It can come in mid-position or at the end of a sentence.

  It isn't good to sit **all day** at a desk.

- **Any day** is used to indicate an event or action which can take place at an unspecified day and time in the future. It can come in mid-position or at the end of a sentence.

  You can call me **any day** at my office number.

- **Every day** is used to indicate events, actions or situations which take place throughout the week. It can refer to the work week or all seven days of the week. It can come at the beginning or end of a sentence.

  Every day we start with a 'to-do' list.

- **On a daily basis** is used to indicate events, actions or situations which take place every day of the week. It can refer to the work week or all seven days of the week. It usually comes at the end of a sentence.

  *We all put in too many hours **on a daily basis**.*

  When a sentence has more than one clause, we may use more than one adverbial or time expression. In such cases, each adverbial or time expression is positioned according to the rules above in the part of the sentence it relates to.

  *Some of my colleagues work overtime **on a daily basis**[1], but I **almost never**[2] have to stay in the office after 5 p.m. ([1]refers to how often the colleagues work overtime; [2]refers to how often the person stays in the office past 5 p.m.)*

  *In **a few weeks**[3] the system will be going live, but there are **always**[4] problems for the first few days. ([3]refers to when the system goes live; [4]refers to how often there are problems)*

7.5 ❯ Prepositions of time

A range of prepositions can be used to talk about when things happen and how long they last.

- **At** is used for times and with *time*, *weekend* and *night*.

  *At breakfast **time** this morning there was a major electrical failure.*

  *He's travelling to Costa Rica **at the weekend**.*

  *Sometimes they have to work **at night**.*

- **In** is used for other parts of the day and months, seasons and years.

  *The project will finish **in December**.*

  *The factory was built **in 2017**.*

- **In** can also be used to indicate how long something took.

  *I finished the report **in two hours**.*

- **On** is used for days.

  *We're meeting **on** Monday morning to discuss the project.*

  Note: In some cases **no preposition** is used. For example, we don't use *on* with *last* or *next*.

  *The relocation took place **last** year.*

  *Work started on the project the **next** day.*

- **For** is used to answer the question *'How long …?'*

  *We were negotiating the contract **for** three days.*

- **During** is used to answer the question *'When …?'*

  *The equipment was damaged **during** the power surge.*

- **From … until** (or informally **till**) are used to mark the beginning and end of a period.

  *We worked **from** 6 in the morning **until** 10 in the evening.*

- **Within** is used to express the idea of 'less than'.

  *The task must be completed **within** two hours.*

- **By** is used to express the idea of 'some time before'.

  *I assure you that the final product will be ready **by** Friday.*

8.2 ❯ Reported speech and reporting verbs

Changes in reported speech

When we tell someone what another person said, we usually change the verb tenses from direct speech: **Present Simple** becomes **Past Simple**, **Past Simple** becomes **Past Perfect**, etc.

Modal verbs also change: **will** changes to **would**; **can** changes to **could**; **may** changes to **might**; **must** changes to **had to**, etc.

We often use the verbs *say* and *tell* when reporting what someone said. Both verbs can be followed by a clause with or without *that*.

Changes to pronouns and adverbs of time and place

We often need to change the pronoun and the adverbs of time and place when we change from direct speech to reported speech: **I** becomes **he**, **yesterday** becomes **the day before**, **tomorrow** becomes **the next day**, etc.

Adverbs of place and demonstrative pronouns also change: **here** becomes **there**, **this** becomes **that**, etc.

Note: When we report what someone said on the same day, or if a person says something which is still true, we can often retain the verb tense used in direct speech.

*'I**'m looking forward** to my retirement.'*

*She told me (that) she **is looking forward** to her retirement.*

Reporting verbs

We often use other reporting verbs, such as *advise, complain, confirm, suggest,* etc. instead of *say* or *tell*. These make reported speech shorter and less repetitive.

Note: It isn't necessary to report every word.

'I don't think changing offices has come at a good time,' my manager said.

*My manager **complained** (that) changing offices **hadn't come** at a good time.*

'We'd like to let you know that the website will be down as from 10 p.m. tomorrow,' the technician said.

*They **confirmed** (that) the website **would be down** as from 10 p.m. **the next day**.*

Common reporting verbs include:

- **advise** someone to do something

  *My parents **advised me** to follow my passion.*

- **complain** (*that*) + clause

  *The students **complained** (that) the university had given them too many exams.*

- **confirm** (*that*) + clause

  *Management **confirmed** (that) the offices were closing.*

- **inform** someone (*that*) + clause

  *Our manager **informed us** (that) she was leaving the company.*

- **insist** (*that*) + clause

  *They **insisted** (that) we planned everything in advance.*

Note: With some reporting verbs it is possible to use various structures.

- **promise** to do something

  He **promised to let** me know.

  promise someone (*that*) + clause

  They **promised us** (*that*) there wouldn't be any further changes.

  promise (*that*) + clause

  She **promised** (*that*) she would phone as soon as she got there.

- **suggest** (*that*) + clause

  My friend **suggested** (*that*) I started my own company.

  suggest (*not*) doing something

  My friend **suggested starting** my own company.

  My tutor **suggested not leaving** college until I had completed the year.

8.5 ❯ Passive voice with reporting verbs

Passive voice with reporting verbs is often used in formal communications.

- **reporting statements with the person as the subject**

  This pattern can be used with the verbs **tell** and **inform**.

  I am told that the company will change its recruitment policy.

  Staff were immediately **informed that** thousands of customers were complaining.

- **reporting statements with the topic as the subject**

  1 This pattern can be used with the verbs **say, think, know, expect, believe, understand** and **consider**. Note that the reporting verb is followed by the infinitive.

  The company is said to be experiencing difficulties with its computer systems.

  The changes are expected to take place next month.

  2 We use the **perfect infinitive** if the infinitive refers to a time before the reporting verb.

  The company **is believed to have started** negotiations for a merger with its main competitor.

- **reporting statements beginning with the word 'it'**
  We use this pattern if we do not want to use the person or topic as a subject.

  It is expected that the review will be completed in two weeks.

  It was thought that customers should be contacted immediately.

Lesson 1.3 > 9A

Student A

Your preferred candidate is Mike Preston.

About Mike: did well on 3 other similar projects, has been with company for over 10 years so knows all the processes well, is a team player, gets on well with people, works a 6-hour day and often takes days off at short notice because he is a single parent.

Lesson 2.3 > 9A

Team-building event ideas

- A social event outside office hours: bowling, karaoke or a weekend picnic for staff and their families.

- A social event within office hours: a catered lunch at the office every month or networking breakfasts.

- A one-day team-building event run by a specialist company: staff work in competing teams on a range of activities, e.g. mud runs, blindfold trust trials, circus skills, memory games and analytical puzzles.

- A charity event: small groups of staff participate in community volunteering together, e.g. at a food bank or a beach clean-up, or fundraising events such as sponsored runs or walks.

Lesson 2.4 > 4B

Student A

Internationalisation ideas

- Organise intercultural training seminars in the company so people can learn about German and French business culture.

- Send the management of the company to an international business school to learn about international strategy and leadership.

- Subsidise holidays to France and Germany for staff members to encourage them to experience and learn about the countries.

- Create intranet resources about culture and trade rules / regulations for staff to read and use on a daily basis.

- Select the best Texan staff from the U.S. to go to Germany and France to create local offices there which promote AIRCON and manage sales and marketing.

- Your own idea(s).

Lesson 1.4 > 4B

Personal profile

Name: ....

Location of office: ....

When you joined company: ....

First job(s): ....

Current role: ....

Main tasks/responsibilities: ....

Travel in the job: ....

Extra

Family: ....

Familiarity with other team members (who you know): ....

Positive thoughts towards the team members and the project: ....

Lesson 1.5 > 3A

Sabbatical news

One month to travel around the country afterwards

Next year's sabbatical schedule to be finalised by end of month

Company sponsoring overseas volunteer projects

Contact HR if interested

Please submit your project ideas!

Australia

Learn how to surf!

Project idea
Marine charity

Great Barrier Reef

Learn about marine life

Lesson 2.5 ❯ 3A

> ## Learn how to negotiate
> **more effectively**
>
> **This course is for:**
> - those negotiating already but without formal training.
> - those new to negotiating.
>
> **The course teaches you to:**
> - recognise the changing nature of negotiations.
> - read the reactions of people involved.
> - learn how to listen carefully and ask the right questions.
> - build a broader understanding of the negotiation process.
> - realise the value of careful planning and preparation.
> - develop strategies for each stage in a negotiation.

Lesson 3.5 ❯ 3B

KEY NOTES

- Group sales best ever – £48 bn (last year £40 bn)
- Economic downturn in some European markets
- Entered new, more buoyant markets (India, Japan)
- Cash flow from operations £4.5 bn (last year £4 bn)
- Annual dividend £1.34 (previous 3 years £0.99/£1.02/£1.23)
- Total number stores worldwide – 2,000
- New stores: 5 in Russia (existing market); 10 stores in India and 4 in Japan (new markets)
- Successful launch of new high-end brand in Europe
- Future plans: major restructuring to reduce operating costs. Buy back £1 billion worth of shares over next three years.

Lesson 4.5 ❯ 3A

New management system proposal

a I would therefore recommend that we contact the company to discuss suitable dates for the installation.

b The manufacturer also provides a 24/7 helpdesk.

c Although the initial costs are high, the return on investment would be very great.

d After some research we found a management system which we believe would be suitable for our organisation.

e This proposal aims to analyse and recommend a new management system for the company.

f Furthermore, the supplier can install the system within three weeks.

g As the company has grown so fast, the current system is unable to support the number of operators working in the building.

h It offers a fast and efficient integrated system, connecting every part of the organisation.

Lesson 3.4 ❯ 5A

Student A

Task 1 – Financial Forecast for Business Unit TT

Look at the information below and prepare to call your partner to ask for clarification.

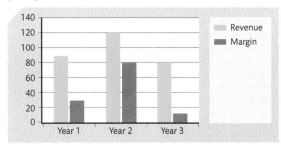

You're not sure why the margins will increase so dramatically from Year 1 to Year 2. And why is everything going to fall off in Year 3? Surely with such low margins in Year 3 it's better to simply stop sales and focus on other areas of the business. Think of one or two other points to clarify.

Task 2 – Growth Forecasts

Your partner calls you to ask for clarification on some points in a growth forecast you sent them earlier. Look at the information below and answer their questions.

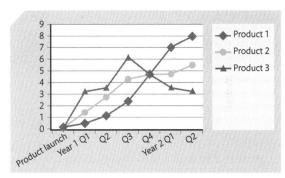

You're planning on launching three very different products which should each behave differently and bring returns at different times.

- Product 1 is one which will take time to generate sales. It is a traditional product with very good levels of quality. However, there are many similar products on the market so it will take time before customers realise that it is better and make the switch from their existing competing products.

- Product 2 is an upgrade on an existing product. It should sell well and consistently over the first year after which revenue should level off at a good level around the end of the year. It might even rise slightly in Year 2.

- Product 3 is version 1 of an innovative product with new technology. It is likely to get a lot of interest in the beginning and be our best seller. However, as with many version 1s, some problems are likely to appear after around nine months and sales will fall dramatically while we prepare a version 2 for launch the following year.

Lesson 1.3 > 9A

Student B

> Your preferred candidate is Alice Andrews.
>
> About Alice: did well on one similar project, has brought experience from another company, has a very direct style of communication, which some colleagues have found off-putting, goal oriented, sometimes works too many hours and gets over-stressed.

Lesson 3.5 > 3A

> Things were a bit up and down last year, I'm afraid, because the dollar was very strong. So we bought cheaper materials and closed some factories. We sold 7% less in the first quarter but then things got better for 6 months and we finally sold 1% more in 2018 than 2017. The market in India is getting bigger so things are looking good for next year.

Lesson 4.3 > 8C

Student B

> You have the strongest views on the logo, but are not very interested in discussing the dessert menu.
>
> You want to go through the agenda as quickly as possible because you want to discuss some other things in this meeting.
>
> Look for an opportunity to interrupt and discuss the following:
> - more staff for the kitchen
> - longer opening hours

Lesson 4.5 > 3B

Willow City Proposal

Aim: to solve traffic congestion and pollution

- long-term strategy: ban gas-powered vehicles from centre in 3 years + encourage more people to use public transport
- traffic congestion in centre bad = high levels of pollution
- solution = driverless, battery-powered people-movers instead of trains and buses in city centre
- cheaper travel for customers – more would use
- no new infrastructure needed
- much less pollution
- personal vehicles parked 95% of time – car parks use valuable land
- initial investment would be high, but running costs cheaper and less pollution
- buy a few vehicles and run trial before end of year

Lesson 5.3 > 9A

Student B – Roleplay 1

> The results are for the last six months. You are new in the department and only joined five months ago. You feel it's too early to judge your performance, so it would be reasonable for you to push back on challenging feedback, though it's also an opportunity to learn where you can improve.
>
> Decide which approach you will take: resist or accept the feedback. Whichever option you choose, aim to have a successful outcome of the discussion and keep your relationship intact.

Lesson 5.5 > 3A

Positive comments or criticism?

1 effective organisational skills
2 needs to support team more
3 meets targets
4 should try to exceed targets
5 must listen more actively
6 decisions are well thought out
7 always late for meetings
8 can handle large projects
9 staff not given enough authority
10 sometimes chooses inappropriate communication methods
11 has established new procedures

Lesson 6.3 > 10A

Student A

> **You are concerned about the following points.**
> 1 You might not receive this month's sales figures by the end of the week.
> 2 The launch of the new product could be delayed.
>
> **You know the following information.**
> 1 The customer wasn't happy with the quality, but the 'official' information is that the customer wanted product features the company doesn't and cannot provide.
> 2 There won't be enough space for everyone at the new office so some people will get a permanent desk while others will have to hot desk. You don't know who will have to use hot desks and the management has asked you not to discuss this until all the information is confirmed.

Lesson 3.4❯ 5A

Student B

Task 1 – Financial Forecast for Business Unit TT

Your partner calls you to ask for clarification on some points in a financial forecast you sent them earlier. Look at the information below and answer their questions.

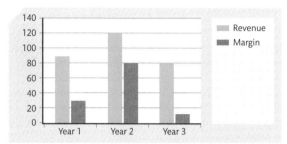

- In Year 1 the revenue is expected to be 90 with a margin of 30, which represents a 33 percent margin.
- In Year 2 there is the expectation that revenue will increase by 33 percent to 120. Margins should increase considerably to 80 as the main product investment will be made in Year 1. This means that the costs will be a lot lower in Year 2 and this should dramatically increase the margin potential to 66 percent of overall revenue.
- Finally, in Year 3 there will be a downturn as the market becomes mature. More marketing and sales costs will be needed to keep the revenue at a level of around 80. These additional costs in Year 3 will mean a sharp fall in margin to around 15. Still, it's better than nothing and worth it before this business unit becomes unprofitable in Year 4 and we stop sales.

Task 2 – Growth Forecasts

Look at the revenue information below and prepare to call your partner to ask for clarification.

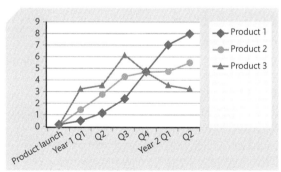

- You're not sure why there is such a difference in performance between the three products over the 1½ year period. Product 1 seems to be very slow to grow up until Q3, but then starts to outperform the other two products at Q4 of the first year. You don't understand its very fast growth in Q3.
- Product 2 seems to perform well and grow steadily throughout the period. What makes it different and more consistent than the other two products?
- Product 3 seems very erratic and unstable. It is characterised by very fast growth and an almost equally fast decline. This doesn't seem to make sense.

Lesson 2.4❯ 4B

Student B

Internationalisation ideas

- Offer in-company language courses to train staff to speak German and French.
- Invite managers from other Texan companies which work internationally to hold 'breakfast meetings' with staff to present and answer questions about working internationally.
- Pay staff to travel to Germany and France to take foreign language courses.
- Recruit a new international sales director for AIRCON with experience of France and Germany, and who can drive international sales and marketing.
- Create a French and German language version of your website and sales literature for potential customers in these new markets.
- Your own idea(s).

Lesson 7.3❯ 9A

Student A

Scenario 1 You sent your partner an email last week and still haven't heard back. Their lack of response is now putting pressure on you, though it may be because they are also very busy and under a lot of stress at their end. Maybe if you can support them with something, they will find the time to respond to your email from last week. Call them to discuss the situation, but it's not a very high priority so don't go too hard on them.

Scenario 2 You get a call from your partner following up on an email they sent this morning. You've been busy and have hardly had time to check your emails, and definitely haven't had time to do any work on the topic they emailed you about. You can understand it may be a priority for them, so do your best to help them.

Lesson 7.5 ❯ 3B

- problem with equipment for new factory – opening could be delayed
- supplier gone bankrupt – no equipment – can't afford to miss opening
- deposit paid when ordered – probably lose that money
- look for different supplier – need quick delivery at reasonable price
- will collect information by end of week

Lesson 4.3 › 8C

Student C

You have the strongest views on the the dessert menu, but are not very interested in discussing the logo.

You want to go through the agenda as quickly as possible because you want to discuss some other things in this meeting.

Look for an opportunity to interrupt and discuss the following:

- which advertising company to use
- modernising the interior design

Lesson 5.5 › 3B

SALES MANAGER – PERFORMANCE REVIEW NOTES

- good communication skills – clear and concise
- good listening skills – quick to understand
- team management – develops individuals' skills and helps them solve problems
- responsibility – takes responsibility for team actions
- relationship with team – praises individuals or gives constructive feedback
- goal achievement – all, sometimes exceeded
- good work – could be improved, more training
- leadership skills – lacks confidence, not good under pressure
- time management – can be poor

BUSINESS WORKSHOP 8 › 5A

Role card B

Production manager

Time with company: 10 years

Your objective: to tell the CEO about your worries and get assurance that it would be a good move.

You are worried that Osbruk-Basri:

- recruit staff without the correct qualifications.
- have a poor safety record.
- do not offer a good career path for staff.

Lesson 7.4 › 5B

Student A

Scenario 1   You have worked every weekend for the last five weeks so that the new website will be ready by the deadline. However, you need to visit your mother, who has not been feeling well, and would like to take a couple of days off and need to ask Student B to do overtime to cover your absence. You usually get along well with them though don't usually talk about your private lives.

Scenario 2   You think these meetings are a complete waste of time, though you need to be diplomatic not to say that openly. They're too long, not structured, never really have an outcome, and anyway, it's a Monday morning: you're tired from the weekend and feeling stressed as you always have a lot of other things to do on Mondays.

Lesson 5.3 › 9A

Student A – Roleplay 2

The results are for the last six months. You've been overloaded recently with too many projects and you also had to train a new team member. They didn't pick things up as quickly as you expected, so you had to spend more time with them than you had planned. You feel it would be reasonable to push back on challenging feedback, though it's also an opportunity to learn where you can improve.

Decide which approach you will take: resist or accept the feedback. Whichever option you choose, aim to have a successful outcome of the discussion and keep your relationship intact.

Lesson 8.5 › 3B

- Hasfell Supplies now part of multinational group
- Hasfell Supplies – moving HQ to Mumbai – media say will cause job losses
- When: December – new building ready
- Facts: all offered other jobs in company – several people happy to take redundancy
- Quotation/Apology: CEO, Raj Singh told staff before announced publicly – many new and exciting career opportunities available
- Future – next week discussions with staff re options – next month interviews in Mumbai

Lesson 7.5 › 3A

Problems	Reasons	Actions
1 payment will be late	a not enough items in stock	i ask for short extension
2 work won't be completed on time	b bad publicity / faulty product	ii source from other suppliers
3 sales figures really bad	c big customer not paid	iii product recall / new marketing campaign / repair brand image
4 can't fulfil customer order	d accident occurred	iv chase customer / promise to pay supplier within 2 weeks

BUSINESS WORKSHOP 2 > 3A

Akito's report on Asia

In speaking to our consultants in the area, one thing has come up several times and that is how diverse the market is. We have places in Asia which are highly developed economies and there our products sell well and our consultants are considered to be experts in the field. However, we also have emerging economies and we need to start looking at the technical skills and knowledge we give to our consultants for these areas. They have to be informed on micro-loans and be able to give advice to people starting small businesses, an area we have not been concentrating on. We also need to train our consultants on how to explain financing to clients who may not be familiar with the basics of how markets work. This is an area we definitely need improvement in.

An additional challenge we have in the market is the growing importance of Islamic financial products. A number of banks now have departments specialised in these but we also need to train our staff about them. They need to know which of our funds they can sell to certain customers as there are strict regulations about the types of companies which can be invested in. Our products also have to fit the 'no-interest' rule which is a basic principle of Islamic financing. With some basic training this could open many doors for us here in Asia.

My recommendation is that we set up training to improve the competency of our consultants and provide them with widespread knowledge that they can use to reach a broad base of clients. We might want to use a company-wide wiki for this which would enable staff to share their knowledge with others. There is enormous potential here and many of our consultants have excellent relationships with their customers and can close the deal. They just need more specific information about the different aspects of the products we sell in order to help them in their jobs.

Lesson 8.1 > 11A

Scores for quiz: How adaptable are you?

Mostly As

Your answers suggest that you can sometimes be too flexible, or too dependent on others. You often feel you are not in control and that whatever you do you think you probably won't be successful. Remember, whatever you want to change will remain just a daydream unless you take action. To change things in your life, start with small, achievable goals in your work or personal life and then build up your experience of planning and implementing bigger changes in your life. It might be helpful to read about how successful people changed their lives, or you could consider working with a life coach.

BUSINESS WORKSHOP 3 > 5A

Company 1

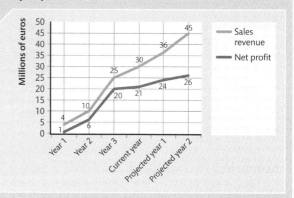

BUSINESS WORKSHOP 3 > 6A

Group A

Belezflor Cosmetic retailer

Belezflor designs and sells a range of chemical-free, organic cosmetics and runs a chain of 10 beauty salons in Brazil. Very popular with young and middle-aged professional women with a large disposable income. Plans to open 15 beauty salons in other South American countries over next three years but main objective is to break into the North American market. Although not cheap, customers are prepared to pay more for the excellent quality of the product and first class service in the salons. Looking for an investment of $20 million.

Current annual revenues: $25 million

Projected sales growth: 20% expected each year for next two years.

Market: fast-growing market but may be dependent on fashion.

Pricing: Good middle-to-high price range, but also reflects quality.

Customers: love the products. They Tweet about the salons and the new products and post features on social media. The company produces videos demonstrating how to use each product and it seems that social media has been a crucial part of the impetus for the rapid rise of this business.

Social responsibility: donates 2% of net profit to charities which protect the environment.

Lesson 7.4 > 5B
Student B

Scenario 1 You are very committed to this project and making it succeed. You don't have a very good relationship with Student A, but they do their job well and you're happy to keep your relationship functional. You have been working all the weekends since this project started and you are very tired. However, you are holding out until the project ends in a couple of weeks and hope to take a week off, if Student A can do some overtime for you.

Scenario 3 You recently got a promotion to become the team leader of a small team of four people. It's been going well, but one of your team members has become quite difficult. They're older than you and have been with the company longer, but that shouldn't matter. Talk to them and try to find a better way of working together.

Lesson 7.3 > 9A
Student B

Scenario 1 Your partner gets in touch to follow up on an email they sent a week ago about something not very important. They always put a 'High Priority' note on all of their emails though. You've been busy and have hardly had time to check your emails, and definitely haven't had time to do any work on the topic they emailed you about.

Scenario 2 You sent an urgent email this morning and haven't heard back from the other person yet. It's now the middle of the afternoon and you need their input before the end of the working day. They are often very slow to respond and you are losing patience with them now. Maybe you need to put a little pressure on them – call them to discuss the situation.

Lesson 6.3 > 10A
Student B

You are concerned about the following points.

1 Why did the customer decide to halve their order?

2 Your company is moving to a different location where there won't be enough desks for everyone so there will be a hot desking policy.

You know the following information.

1 You hope to send this month's figures by Friday this week. However, you are still waiting for data from one department, but you don't want to stress your colleague.

2 The new product hasn't passed some safety tests, but this is being fixed so the launch might not necessarily be delayed. However, only your team knows this.

BUSINESS WORKSHOP 3 > 5A
Company 2

BUSINESS WORKSHOP 3 > 6A
Group B

Seklok **Home security systems and apps**

Seklok produces, sells and installs smart home security systems and apps for controlling everything in your home. The company is based in The Netherlands and its products sell very well across Europe. Seklok has developed an app with total connectivity to every aspect of the home security system. The new app includes live streaming from house cameras to mobile devices; it controls the security panel, locks and unlocks doors, controls lights and thermostats, sends alerts when the doorbell is rung or when cameras detect movement around the house and provides flood, fire and carbon monoxide alerts. The company also offers software that detects attacks on mobile and computer systems. Looking for an investment of €35 million to compete in Asian markets.

Current annual revenues: €30 million.

Projected sales growth: 20% next year and 25% in the following two years.

Market: buoyant market of young tech-savvy professionals who love the comprehensive connectivity of the systems.

Pricing: lower than major rivals for a more digitally advanced and comprehensive system.

Customers: say the company has excellent customer service and has dealt with any initial technical faults efficiently. They feel much safer with the system and recommend it to their friends.

Social responsibility: supports homeless projects and provides technical equipment for schools.

BUSINESS WORKSHOP 2 ⟩ 3A

Frederik's report on Europe

Our consultants are very well-trained and know their products well. At least 90% of the clients say that our consultants are experts in their field and that they get the advice they need. This is a sales-oriented market and our employees have always been good at selling new products and finding new customers. There are other areas where we need to do more to help our employees, however. In speaking with our consultants I have come to the following conclusions.

We have always offered excellent training although it is quite expensive. Therefore, we are starting to offer more online training. We have developed a series of webinars – specialised seminars which employees can access over our intranet. They can then continue to work on those skills in intranet forums. We feel constant training on our products is necessary as our customers expect the best and know we offer excellent advice. What this type of training does not cover, however, are the communication skills our consultants need when something goes wrong in a sales call. Although we have been offering these courses, some of our consultants still need work in this area as customer retention is a problem. They need to learn that the job is not just about selling but about gaining trust and setting up long-term relationships. Several consultants have said that courses which address this issue would be helpful.

Our main concern at the moment is how to support new talent. Our managers are all at the top of their field, something clients are also aware of. This means that they sometimes ask to speak to a manager rather than their personal consultant but this is not the way we can move forward. We need to make sure that the training includes further development for all our consultants and not just those at the top. We need to develop our young talent, make them feel they are important to us and help them to have the careers they want through efficient and cost-effective training.

Lesson 8.5 ⟩ 3A

Working in Malawi

Big changes in the company. Dingbell Construction has won a big contract to build schools in Malawi. The contract is worth a lot of money.

The company has sent a project team to Malawi to recruit local workers.

We will provide them with accommodation and regular work for three years.

The Project manager says that if this goes well, there will be similar contracts in other African countries. This is big for the company.

Watch this space!

BUSINESS WORKSHOP 8 ⟩ 5A

Role card A

Chillhot CEO

Your objective: to keep your staff onside, give the facts and deny any silly rumours about working conditions.

The facts:
- You had an informal meeting with Osbruk-Basri to find out what they could offer.
- You don't know how the press knew about the meeting – supposed to be secret – just exploratory at this time.
- Funds are needed for expansion.
- Chillhot staff jobs and contracts are safe.

Changes needed:
- new operating systems
- more training
- relocation of staff to new premises

BUSINESS WORKSHOP 4 ⟩ 5A

Feedback statistics on use of robots

Questions	Bob	Mayumi	Oskar	Agnes	Arturo	Brutus
Did you use/interact with this robot?	95%	100%	45%	94%	88%	65%
Was it a bad experience?	8%	5%	10%	30%	3%	76%
Was it a good experience?	54%	68%	80%	54%	70%	24%
Was it an excellent experience?	38%	27%	10%	16%	27%	0%
Would you consider using this robot in your company?	8%	10%	1%	4%	17%	22%
Statements						
I think the robot enhanced the conference experience.	79%	82%	30%	54%	81%	2%
I don't think the robot enhanced the conference experience.	21%	18%	70%	46%	19%	98%

Lesson 7.4 ▶ 5B

Student C

Scenario 2 It was your idea to have the team meetings on a Monday morning as a way of updating everyone on each other's week ahead as well as identifying where anyone may need support or have capacity to support others. You think Student A is always very negative and difficult in these meetings, though you need to be diplomatic about how you communicate that. Student A looks bored and disinterested and never really gets involved other than to interrupt or disagree with others.

....

Scenario 3 You were passed over for promotion recently and the person who got the job is younger than you and joined the company more recently. You also think they're not at as committed to the company as you are and they are just using the company as a step on their career ladder.

BUSINESS WORKSHOP 1 ▶ 7B

Employee satisfaction survey

1 I get a fair salary.

2 I get a satisfactory bonus when I do a good job.

3 I find the training programme meets my needs.

4 I have the chance to make a career in the company.

5 I have flexible hours that adapt to my needs.

6 I get useful discounts for free-time activities.

7 I get meal vouchers for places I like to go to.

8 I get enough financial help with travel.

9 I have enough autonomy in my job.

10 There is positive cooperation between employees in the company.

Lesson 6.5 ▶ 3A

Notes on environmental situation in office

1 plan to put in new light systems

2 report shows energy costs too high in the past year, e.g. lights left on

3 investigating more eco friendly systems

4 intend to have paperless office by this time next year

5 plastic coffee cups and 50% of paper not recycled in last 6 months

6 developing plan to reduce waste

7 staff could suggest ideas for reducing waste – competition next month

8 failed to achieve environmental targets

BUSINESS WORKSHOP 2 ▶ 3A

Victoria's report on South America

South America is an interesting market because the growing economies mean there are many opportunities for business development. The feedback from staff and customers has been very helpful and I am certain we can find a way to improve our performance in this market.

When consultants or managers join us from other parts of the company, they need to learn that it is essential to have face-to-face meetings in order to understand clients and have rapport with them. In some markets it may be possible to speak to clients over the phone or in a conference call, but that does not work here. Consultants have to understand that they need time to set up long-term relationships with clients and work at them. Some of our consultants are very knowledgeable but they do not always have the ability to make a client feel comfortable and important. They need to learn to do this with every client, the small private ones as well as the large corporate ones. This is the area in which we can succeed and move forward in the future.

Although our consultants have always managed to sell products to existing clients, we sometimes have a problem keeping clients and in finding new ones. We work through a network of people who recommend us and these recommendations need to include the personal element.

We often have a problem with training and development as our younger employees are not always interested in taking part in development courses. Our managers are very generous with their time and have offered to work as mentors for new and less experienced staff but new employees do not seem to want to put in the time needed to begin planning for their future careers, a situation which I feel may turn into a big problem soon.

Therefore, my suggestion is to look for courses which emphasise the personal touch in consulting work, something I feel will attract our young employees.

BUSINESS WORKSHOP 3 ▶ 5A

Company 3

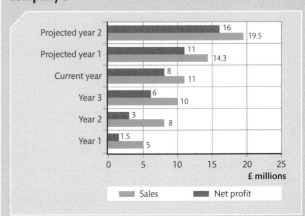

Lesson 8.1 ⟩ 10

///

Quiz: **How adaptable are you?**

1 **How do you usually adapt to change?**
   A You prefer to go along with what other people decide.
   B You persuade others that your way of doing things is best.
   C You are pretty good at adapting to different people and circumstances.

2 **Your organisation/company is moving its main office. How do you feel about it?**
   A It's inconvenient but it's a management decision.
   B It's really inconvenient and you're very worried about the move – it's unnecessary.
   C You're worried about your journey time but you help your team plan the transition.

3 **A colleague asks to change the date and time of a project meeting. What do you do?**
   A Ask him/her to propose a new date and time that suits him/her best.
   B Say you're sorry but it isn't possible; the meeting needs to go ahead as planned.
   C Suggest some new dates and send an email to all participants.

4 **Your boss has asked you to take a position in a different department. What do you do?**
   A You feel obliged to accept, although the new position is not in your field.
   B Decline politely. You enjoy doing what you know best.
   C Accept the position. You need a change and like learning new things.

5 **A new product designed by your department has been recalled. What do you do?**
   A Ask your team to brainstorm a new model.
   B Argue against the recall: the problem lies with manufacturing.
   C Work with the team to improve any faults and defects.

Lesson 5.3 ⟩ 9B/C

Student A/B

The results are for the last six months. Tell your employee that they are not meeting their targets. Remember to stay professional. You can use expressions like:

'What do you think are the causes for … '
'Can you explain why … ?'
'I'd like to hear the reasons why … '
'Can you offer me an explanation for … ?'
'I'd like some more details concerning … '
'Why do you think that is so?'
'I'm interested in hearing about … '

BUSINESS WORKSHOP 8 ⟩ 5A

Role card C

Factory worker

Time with company: 7 years

Your objective: to express your worries about the working conditions in Osbruk-Basri companies.

You have heard rumours that:
- the uniform is made of cheap material which makes you very hot.
- there is no air-conditioning in their factories.
- you cannot ask for help if you have a problem.

BUSINESS WORKSHOP 3 ⟩ 6A

Group C

EVFill **Electric Vehicle charging stations**

This young company focuses on manufacturing and selling electric vehicle charging stations. As more electric vehicles are appearing on our streets, they are going to need stations to recharge their batteries. The company has developed one of the fastest and most efficient systems and has already become the market leader in the UK with its main target customers being large workplaces and supermarket and hotel chains. The company is looking forward to rolling out the stations across Europe where some countries have been slower to invest in these charging stations. They want an investment of £12 million in order to do this.

Current annual revenues: £11 million.

Projected sales growth: 30% next year and more for the following five years.

Market: still young market and plenty of opportunities worldwide.

Pricing: very competitive for the quality provided.

Customers: say there have been a lot of teething problems with the new stations, but on the whole are generally very happy with them. However some of their bigger customers, supermarket chains for example, say that sales of electricity have not made them the huge sums of money promised, but EVFill expects this to change soon.

Social responsibility: working with local governments to improve air quality in towns and cities.

BUSINESS WORKSHOP 6 〉 2A

Student B

Ethics versus Economics – AFhomes in deep water

It seems Mr Josef Ndege's partnership with a conservation agency to build homes in Dodoma is upsetting both conservationists and local people. However, Mr Ndege has hit back by saying that that he will deliver everything he has promised and more. 'We've hit a few bumps in the road, but they're only teething problems,' he says. 'Although the land chosen for the development falls within the traditional paths of elephants and other animals, we've consulted with experts to solve the problem. Apparently elephants hate bees and are as vulnerable to bee stings as humans, avoiding them at any cost, so we will locate beehives at regular intervals along the boundary. The beehives will also provide employment for locals who will look after the bees and collect the honey, which can be sold.'

This solution may have satisfied the elephant lovers, but the waterhole used by both farmers and animals is causing an even more serious problem. Conservationists and local farmers are worried that the waterhole will be severely reduced by the new scheme. Mr Ndege responded by explaining that the water would be returned to the farmers at a small charge. However, they are very unhappy about having to pay for water which is currently free.

When Mr Ndege was asked if what he was doing was really ethical, he replied: 'It's always a balance between economics and ethics. We need to create businesses so communities can thrive and, sometimes, our plans are going to bring us into conflict with certain elements of society. I'm doing my best to ensure that we adhere to our vision as well as we can.'

Student Bs

1 How does Mr Ndege react to the accusations about his company?
2 What two benefits do the beehives have?
3 What problem does Mr Ndege face regarding the water supply?

BUSINESS WORKSHOP 8 〉 3

What the staff thought

1. Chief Executive Office, Jean-Dominique Senard
'I see myself now much more as a mentor … supporting the teams as well as guarantor of group strategy and investor relations.'

2. The site director for the last 7 years
'My role is changing, my decision-making changes: I'm not micro-managing, I'm more of a coach of people.'

3. A team member who has worked for the company for over 30 years
'Workers used to take orders from the team leader and cope day to day with absences and changes. Now the team plans production a week in advance, deciding how it should organise itself to meet targets and absorb absences. Staff can solve safety problems and cut waste more quickly.'

4. A manager
'The manager must learn to work with the team. They have to bring the challenge, but not the solution. Sometimes you have a feeling of losing power but we [managers] get 10 times as much back from the team.'

5. The team leader responsible for maintenance for the last 6 years
'Before we had a top-down system: we applied the rules and that was that. Now there's an enormous energy. It can be frightening to work in this system because sometimes you have a feeling of losing power.'

6. The technical secretary for the last 30 years
'There's a clear difference between my first years working here and now. We used to have less right to say what we thought.'

7. A worker for over 30 years
'The team leader gives us all the elements – number of tyres for a week, absences – and we can do what we want. We have everything we need to prepare production a week in advance. Before we found things out day to day. I was always sceptical about the plan to give us more autonomy. If you're taking guys away for meetings in the morning, afternoon and night, they aren't on the production line and producing tyres.'

General comments
Team members at Le Puy describe the bosses who used to issue orders as 'coaches', 'referees', even 'judges'. The manager 'gives direction', says one. He or she is there 'to take the big decisions', adds another.

Team leaders point out that workers still need someone to say 'that went well'. Fellow managers agree they are using more soft skills than hard ones.

1.1.1

**P = Presenter K = Korinne Ward D = Dan Price
A = Alyssa O'Neal M = Michael Wheeler
T = Tom Osborn**

P: Different businesses have different styles. We talk about the 'culture' of a company – and this might mean its dress code, or the way in which its staff communicate with their managers. Gravity Payments is a credit card processing company based in Seattle. It organises the authorisations of fund transfers for credit card transactions. Its clients are retailers who accept card payments for purchases, and it aims to cut the cost of processing card payments.

K: Gravity Payments, this is Korinne.

P: Gravity Payments has grown quickly from a small start-up to a profitable mid-size operation. Company culture changed for the hundred employees of Gravity Payments when their boss, Dan Price, announced the company's minimum salary would go up to 70,000 dollars a year.

D: Effective immediately, we are gonna put a scaled policy into place, and we are gonna have a minimum 70,000 dollar pay rate for everyone that works here.

P: And he cut his own salary from one million dollars a year to 70,000.

D: Curious if anyone has any questions?

K: Let me see if I can find that for you.

P: Korinne Ward, in customer support, used to have a long commute. Now she can afford to live close enough to walk to work.

K: I'm able to afford, you know, the cost of living in Seattle, which is incredible.

A: Gravity Payments, this is Alyssa.

P: Alyssa O'Neal, used to make 21,000 dollars a year before coming to Gravity Payments. Now she makes almost 60,000 a year as a customer support representative. She's paid off her car loan, credit card debt, and moved into a better home.

A: It's something I never ... never could've imagined.

P: Following the announcement, Dan Price was praised as 'America's best boss' and the company received a flood of job applications and new client enquiries.
But there were negative effects as well. Gravity lost a few of its most senior staff. They felt their skills and experience were not recognised in the new more equal pay structure.
Over time, however, Gravity reported a 75 percent increase in revenue and 67 percent increase in new clients. Harvard Business School researched the changes at Gravity Payments.

M: Some of their success might be attributed to increased productivity on the part of the workers now, who, you know, feel respected and understand that they are gonna have a hard time finding another job that pays so well, but it also has generated a lot of publicity, and that has been good in terms of pulling in business.

P: Tom Osborn is a client of Gravity Payments.

T: To me, if they're running their business in a way that their...that their staff feel better about being part of the company, work harder with their customers, to me as a vendor, that's a good thing.

P: And another good thing seems to be happening at Gravity's headquarters. The staff are up to something.

A: We had tried to think of a way that we could thank Dan for what he's done for us.

P: Customer support representative Alyssa O'Neal got the ball rolling.

A: We have one more gift for you.

D: All right ...

A: Um, it's outside, though.

P: Alyssa convinced the other employees to contribute hundreds of dollars each. They bought Dan a Tesla car worth 90,000 dollars.

D: Are you kidding me?

A: No ...

A: What happened it was ... it was like it was meant to be.

D: Oh my gosh!

A: I'm really surprised by his reaction.

D: Thank you!

P: In the short term, Dan Price's strategy seems to have been a success, particularly in creating a new culture at Gravity Payments. And only time will tell if it's going to be a long-term success or whether other companies will take the same approach.

1.3.1

K = Katie S = Sanjit

K: Careful. You're overflowing.

S: Yeah. Thanks.

K: Something on your mind?

S: Some things. Mainly about this meeting with Claudio today. It's just that I don't really know Claudio or Emma very well, or the whole Go Global set up for that matter. Things have gone so fast these last five weeks and it's such a big, big step to go in with these guys and commit to the finance. They come from a very different world. Different values. And well I'm worried they're going to take over the project completely. Their number one priority will always be maximising profits, and that isn't always the case with us.

K: So you don't trust them.

S: Is that a bad thing? I guess it is. I'm just trying to figure out how to handle things properly. I want to do things our way. EN-Tek stands for something.

K: Even if you don't trust them, pretend you do. Otherwise, they may well just walk away from the deal.

S: And if we make the wrong choice?

K: At least we tried to make the right one. That counts for something. Ah ... I gotta deal with this. Let me know how it goes. See you at five. OK?

S: OK, and thanks. Appreciate all your advice!

K: Here's a bit more advice. Have some coffee instead. Perk up!

1.3.2

C = Claudio S = Sanjit K = Katie E = Emma

C: So, there's been lots of discussion with our management here at Go Global and, I'm pleased to say, they loved the proposal. I think we both want to go forward with this project. There's just a couple of issues we need to nail down. Firstly there's the production location – China or Bangladesh? Secondly there's the feasibility of using the local distributors you've suggested.

S: Well, Claudio, firstly, let me say that I really appreciate the effort you've made to drive this forward. A great product is nothing without a great partner. I understand what you're saying about the distributors. Katie, you've been in touch with them recently, haven't you?

K: Yes. We're working hard to get the information we need. You'll appreciate, these are small companies with very few people: they will struggle to put together all that documentation you've asked for. How soon do you need the data, and how much detail do you need?

E: Well ideally, we need full annual reports for the companies – for regulatory reasons. But, maybe one way to solve this is to send our financial risk analyst.

K: OK, that sounds more realistic.

C: Great. Erm ... then there's the production location issue. What's the deal there?

S: To be honest, I feel a little worried about some aspects of your proposal to go with China. Locating things in Bangladesh would both support local jobs and keep the end price down.

E: Mm look, there are major issues here with quality and reliability. Our auditors have looked at local production as an option and they say there are numerous risks. We'll get a full report next week.

S: I respect that. But ... for me ... the issue is a wider one. It's connected to the values of EN-Tek, and who we are. Based on your experience, how do you think we can address these issues with the local producer?

C: OK. Here's my suggestion. I think we wait for the detailed quality report and then we discuss that and decide next week.

S: OK. If this makes most sense, let's wait.

K: I like your suggestion to get more data. That's fine.

1.3.3

C = Claudio S = Sanjit K = Katie E = Emma

C: So – as you can imagine, there's been lots of discussion with our management here at Go Global around the financing of the project. I'm pleased to say they loved the proposal. I think we both want to go forward with this project ...

S: That's great news Claudio. If I may? Well, to come straight to the point, well I think there are only really two key topics to focus on today – production location and the choice of distributors. Right now, we need to know if our position to go with local people is being considered.

C: Erm ... yes, well, both topics did come up in discussions ...

S: So, what's the feedback? Sorry. But you must understand, these are very important issues to us.

E: Sanjit. It seems like we have two main problems here. The product is excellent, yes – but if you produce locally we feel you risk quality issues. Producers in China can guarantee better standards. As for the distribution partners you want to work with, we just don't think they're good enough. They're small. Limited finances. Frankly, a risk to sales.

S: But have you fully analysed these risks? Where's your data? We know these markets and partners very well, and we're confident.

C: That's true, yes. We do have less experience in this market – which is precisely why we're being so cautious. We're happy to take a look at any numbers you might have.

K: I can't give you any financial information from the partners at the moment. The data you need is very difficult for them to put together. They're not used to these kinds of management processes. They need more time.

E: And in the meantime? What do we do? We need the data to make decisions.

C: OK, look, these are not easy discussions, but they are useful. EN-Tek clearly has a focus on local partners ... and we're open to that, in principle.

S: Good.

C: But we do need that data. What shall we do? I actually emailed a couple of times last week. No response.

K: OK, could we help you with that? Let me call them. I'll see what we can realistically get for next week.

C: OK, that would be useful. By next week we'll also have the auditors' report on quality at the local production site. Then we'll be better placed to discuss this again. Right, moving on ... I had some questions about sales forecasts ...

1.3.4

In Option A, Sanjit has more of a 'trust first' approach and he decides to be very collaborative and respectful and he openly shows his appreciation. This helps to create a good atmosphere and to establish a positive working relationship quickly. The disadvantage, however, is that the important topics are not really dealt with and the decisions regarding the distributors and production location get postponed.
In Option B, Sanjit is less focused on developing trust with his partners and is more interested in pushing forward his own objectives. And we see the risks of this approach; the conversation gets a little heated, there's an uncomfortable atmosphere and the relationship is put at risk. However, this tension allows people to be honest, to talk about real concerns openly with each other and then to cooperate on finding solutions, which is another way to develop trust.

2.1.1

**P = Presenter LG = Laura Guttfield L = Lucrece
D = Dale Thoroughgood K = Kina A = Ashley**

P: In the world of work, training is important for companies and for employees. For companies, good training ensures that their staff have up-to-date skills and knowledge. For employees, training can drive career development and open up new opportunities. Let's have a look at the most common types of training and development.

This international company has recently hired five new team members. They will be working in a variety of roles across the organisation. Before they start in their individual jobs, they are undertaking induction training together.

Induction training, which is sometimes called onboarding, helps new staff members get to know the company and its systems as well as their new colleagues.

LG: A key part of our induction programme, and the importance of it, is to help new members of the team understand and feel a part of our company's culture. We structure the programme in a way to give them the skills and the knowledge to do this. And our aim is that they can become effective team members as quickly as possible.

P: Induction training usually includes learning about company policies and procedures. It may also provide information about how the business operates and its key markets.

L: The induction was just amazing. We were able to meet all the key people in the company. And able to ask them questions and for them to ask us about ourselves. So there was a real sense of belonging.

P: Mentoring can be a very successful way of helping individuals develop their careers. A mentor is an experienced professional, either from inside or outside the company, who develops a relationship with a more junior member of staff.

The mentor is there to act as a guide and offer support, usually on a one-to-one basis.

D: We think mentoring is really valuable. With so much great experience in the company, it is important we find ways to pass that on. It is a very personal and focused form of staff development and it is great at building confidence. It shows them that we are willing to invest time and expertise in them and their career.

P: Mentoring can be used for specific, job-related training or more general career development.

K: What's great about a mentor is that they were once in my position and so they can advise me as to what the best skills would be to learn and the best departments would be to work in, in order for me to progress in my career.

L: The biggest benefit of mentoring for me is being able to measure your progress and to come up with solutions for your problems.

K: One of the really useful things about being a mentee is that my mentor introduces me to very important people within the British broadcast industry, and as I am just starting out in my career, that's really important for my personal network and to sort of keep my eyes open for further opportunities.

P: More and more training is being conducted online using e-learning technology. It allows people to learn at their own pace and in a more flexible timetable.

D: Online training has become popular because it is so flexible - staff members can access it anytime anywhere. They can access it from home or whilst travelling and use the time that otherwise would have been wasted. It is also very cost-efficient.

A: I had to do an online course which covered health and safety. Um … it mainly covered the health and safety regulations that the company had, as well as … um … telling you about what different health and safety signs in the building actually meant … um … so that way, in the example of a fire, we'd know exactly where we needed to go. For me, the best thing about online training is that it's completely flexible. You can do it on any device – on a computer at home, on a mobile phone maybe when you're on the bus or the train, um … and it means that you can really approach your training when it's suitable for you.

P: Many companies offer programmes that mix online with face-to-face sessions. This is known as 'blended learning'. Whatever the type or delivery method, training and development is a critical function in a modern business. As the world changes, we all need to adapt and learn to stay effective and efficient.

2.3.1
E = Emma C = Claudio

E: So the auditor's quality report has come in and the message is very clear. Local production is not an option; their facilities are too poor. We need to go with production in China for this. We can't put product quality at risk like that.

C: Sanjit won't be happy.

E: Well … well, he should be happy – happy I've indulged him this far. We have to take the lead here. It's our money behind the project, and we know the production chain like the back of our hands.

C: Yes, we are the experts … but Sanjit looks at this very much as a kind of partnership. He likes to be involved, to pitch ideas around, to collaborate. It's the EN-Tek team culture. We've seen this from day one so I think the best approach here is to be consultative and include Sanjit in the decision-making.

E: Yes. But we can't get production location wrong, Claudio. We just can't. It's been a major project risk from day one. A wrong decision will kill this whole thing.

C: OK, gotta go. But think, Emma. And think carefully. It's your call on how to handle this in the meeting tomorrow.

2.3.2
E = Emma C = Claudio S = Sanjit P = Paweł

E: You might not like what I'm about to say, but there are major concerns here. You asked me to analyse the two production site options. I did that and came to a very simple conclusion; we have to go with China as a production location. Sanjit, I agree that the local company is very capable … but not capable enough for this project. My role in the project is to give the best advice on finance and quality, and as such, I am saying this loud and clear; China is the only option.

C: OK, thanks, Emma, for your openness. Sanjit, any thoughts on the matter?

S: Emma. Erm, I'm sure you've guessed that I'm disappointed by your recommendations. Er but … I understand. Really, er … Paweł and I have gone through the report – and your conclusions are sound. I was wondering, however – is there some way of coaching the people working locally? You know er training them, developing their skills …?

P: If I can add to that, it will ensure that quality is implemented. We've done this in other projects.

E: I don't think that makes sense. It adds time and money that we just don't have. Also, who knows what the end result will be? It just creates more risk.

S: OK … I understand. It's just that it was part of the vision to have the local community involved as much as possible.

C: Emma, can you walk us through the report step-by-step? Just to take a look at the numbers and make sure everything's clear?

E: Sure. Let's start on page three.

C: Happy overall?

E: They agreed to go with China, so … yes. I'm happy.

C: It's strange. They weren't exactly thrilled but they did warm to the idea, more so than I expected.

E: Great. They saw sense … finally.

C: Just remember – it's their product and concept and we need to respect that. Sanjit in particular is very sensitive about the idea of losing control. I'll probably call him later just to check in. Good job today by the way.

E: Thanks.

2.3.3
E = Emma S = Sanjit C = Claudio P = Paweł

E: You might not like what I'm about to say, but there are major concerns here. You asked me to analyse the two production site options. I did that and came to a very simple conclusion; we have to go with China as a production location. Sanjit, I agree that the local company is very …

S: Sorry to interrupt, Emma, but I'm not happy with it. I don't know what data the auditor's working from but to date we've had very good experiences with the local producers in Bangladesh. I have a lot of trust in their abilities.

E: Sanjit. We all want the same thing here: efficient production, good product quality, a successful project. Now – there are pros and cons of both production locations: China and Bangladesh. I'm sure you'll agree. All of which makes this decision a complex one for everyone here.

S: Absolutely.

C: So, Sanjit, what do you think we should do?

S: Well er Paweł had a great idea earlier. Paweł?

P: Yes er, one option could be to create a clearer and more detailed set of requirements for production.

S: If we do that, then it will lead to higher standards of production.

P: I think it makes sense to have a look at the requirements again.

E: Do we really want endless paperwork holding things up?

C: No one wants that, I agree. Sanjit, what's the best way to handle this? I am always willing to listen to new ideas. Try me.

S: OK, well, just picking up on what Paweł said, why don't we let my local guys try using the more detailed requirements? Give them an opportunity to prove themselves. Let them do a small production run. At the same time, do the same with the guys in China, as is recommended in this report. Then we check the results and we decide.

E: Sounds fair. So shall we try that? Do we all agree with the idea to run two pilots in parallel?

C: Yep.

E: Fine. Let's flesh this out …

C: Happy overall?

E: Seriously? No. Anything but. Now we have another delay. So much for effective teamwork, Claudio. I mean, I did the whole 'listening' thing. I tried not to be pushy. And now what? Now we're stuck with this double production pilot idea. And we all know what the result will be, don't we? China will come out on top. A total waste of time.

C: We don't know that. Look, it was a good meeting. People listened. The team is together. You handled it well.

E: We can't do everything by committee, no matter how much those guys wish we could. *We* have to lead this project.

C: Let's pick this up tomorrow. You … *we* did well.

2.3.4

In Option A, Emma is very direct, and pushes her ideas very strongly. She reminds Sanjit and Paweł that her role is to give the best advice on finance and quality, and basically says that China is the only option. Sanjit, surprisingly, agrees – the data is clear – but it goes against his core values and the vision he had to help the local community in Bangladesh. So, while Emma is very happy at the end, Sanjit isn't fully convinced and the team is a little divided.

In Option B, Emma is more collaborative; she stresses a common interest and is more open to ideas from Sanjit and Paweł. It's this openness that gets the team to a creative place as they agree to set up two pilots to see if production could run in Bangladesh. Emma is not happy with the outcome and with the delay it will cause. But Claudio points out that the result is good from a team point of view, the approach was collaborative, and new ideas were produced.

3.1.1
P = Presenter D = Des Dearlove
H = Howard Stringer

P: Stock markets can go down as well as up, and that's something every investor should know. There will always be movement in a market, but what are the effects on business and the real economy when the stock market suffers a devastating drop in value? And for that, we need to look at the past.

The Wall Street crash of 1929 led to at least ten years of worldwide economic depression. It was the most severe financial crisis of modern times. It came after a period when markets had been booming and shares had been steadily increasing in value.

: So on Black Tuesday, the 29th of October 1929, the 'good times' came to an end. As more and more people sold their shares, the New York stock market went into freefall. By the end of the day, it had lost 12 percent of its value. By the time it stopped falling the Dow Jones had lost 90 percent of its value. It meant that banks failed across America, companies went bankrupt, and individuals lost their investments and sometimes their life savings.

P: The effects were not only felt in America. Stock markets in Europe and around the world also fell. What followed became known as the Great Depression. Production slowed, factories were closed and staff laid off. Construction and manufacturing went into decline.

D: No part of the western world was left unaffected by the depression. It lasted all the way through to the Second World War. Luckily, there's never been a global depression as severe as that since then.

P: However, stock market crashes don't always lead to economic depression. On Black Monday, October 19th 1987, a rapid fall in the Hong Kong stock market spread to Europe and then the United States, where five hundred billion dollars were lost in a day.

D: In 1987, the market losses were the biggest in history, by percentage, but the markets recovered quite quickly. So there was no economic depression.

P: In contrast, in 2008 a different type of economic crisis occurred – a banking crisis that went on to affect financial markets and the global economy. For a number of years, banks in the United States and elsewhere had been giving loans to buy houses to people with poor credit ratings.

When high numbers of people were unable to pay their mortgages, banks and their investors suffered losses, and ordinary people lost their homes. This meant banks stopped lending more money. It became known as the 'credit crunch' and its effect was global.

D: A lack of credit – to banks, companies and individuals – has the effect of freezing the economy. Investment and growth slow or stop, which means recession, job losses and bankruptcies. Many economies around the world were badly hit. Portugal, Italy, Ireland, and Greece were very badly affected.

P: Governments around the world were forced to bail out their financial institutions. But it wasn't enough to prevent a global economic downturn. Business leaders were concerned.

H: We are in the worst economic depression in my lifetime; *economic recession*, we're not supposed to call it a *depression* yes, but it feels pretty depressing.

P: Movements in financial markets are part of the normal operation of the economy. When falls are severe, they can have a lasting effect on people's lives. But share prices and effects across the whole economy are not always directly linked.

D: If you look at the history, you see that there've been more crashes than there have economic depressions. The reality is that the financial markets don't always predict how the real economy behaves. By 'real economy', we mean the parts of it concerned with the production of goods and services, rather than the buying and selling on financial markets. One thing you can be sure of, in your working lifetime, is that you will experience a crash of one kind or another.

3.3.1

P = Paweł K = Katie

P: Did you get a text from Barsha? Not good. Not good at all. Go Global won't be happy.

K: Relax. It sounds worse than it is. We've dealt with worse.

P: 20 percent over budget? I think Claudio will see that as a major problem. He's a cautious guy, especially when the numbers don't work in his favour.

K: I'm meeting him in half an hour. I'll talk him round. The numbers aren't that bad.

P: To you they're not. To Claudio it will be the end of the world. We're the ones who insisted on doing the production pilot in Bangladesh. Any more figures like this and there are going to be

problems – like Go Global stepping in, stopping local production and going straight to the China option.

K: OK …

P: Just try to tone down the 'glass half full' approach a little.

K: What do you mean?

P: You can't just focus on the positives. I'm just saying – I know none of us here are ready to give up on Bangladesh, but convincing Claudio won't be easy. Try to see it from his point of view – and maybe reign in some of your optimism. Think about the issues he's likely to bring up – you're going to need a good alternative plan to keep him on board. I need to take this. Think about it. OK?

K: OK. Will do.

3.3.2

C = Claudio K = Katie

C: So. How do we move forward? I am very disappointed with the first quarter numbers. I think we need to bring them up at the next full project meeting – as well as a recommendation to confirm that we will work with the producers in China. I'm afraid trying local production has turned out as Emma and I expected it might. Now it's time to get things back on track.

K: Erm, to be fair, we're only a little over budget. It's not a bad result. And I'm happy to say we are on schedule, at least. Give these guys a chance. I'm sure we can turn this around and get local production up to standard. These figures are just due to project start-up problems which we've now overcome.

C: Katie, we can't run projects like this. This budget is simply too high. I can't justify these costs to my management. We can salvage this – but only if we act now. That means acknowledging the truth. Clearly, mistakes were made with the budgeting and planning. I don't think you can say it's just because of start-up problems. We have to change our strategy on this.

K: Alright. It's true, we didn't manage to reach all our targets. But the earthquake led to a lot of problems last month. I think we should continue to help the guys locally and give them a chance. The culture there is different and the project just needed more time to get going.

C: Going where, Katie? Bankruptcy? We have to find a new approach to this.

K: Claudio, please. I'm going out there in a week or so. I can help turn things around, I know it.

C: OK. Say that's true. When will we see improvements exactly? End of this month?

K: Yes. Yes.

C: OK. Here's the deal. If we have things back on track inside four weeks, I can sell that internally. If not … I honestly don't know. I'll be very open, I'm not sure that we'll be able to continue with the local production idea.

K: OK Claudio, that's fair enough.

C: OK, see you at this week's project meeting.

K: Yes, see you then.

C: Bye. End of the month, Katie. I'm counting on you.

K: End of the month. No problem.

3.3.3

C = Claudio K = Katie

C: So. How do we move forward? I am very disappointed with the first quarter numbers.

K: I understand. It isn't good enough. We won't reach our targets unless we change something.

C: I'm not sure that we'll be able to continue with the local production idea. I think we're going to have to go with China.

K: I see where you're coming from. 20 percent over budget is too high, but, I'm really happy with the progress we've made in a number of areas. I mean, we are on schedule and the quality report is very positive. I just feel that if we give up now, we may miss an opportunity to set up a new production centre not only for Bangladesh but also for the wider region.

C: Perhaps – but this is costing us a lot of money.

K: Maybe we should offer them more support? That would be more cost-effective than shutting down production.

C: Maybe. What support did you have in mind?

K: Send a couple of technical people down there, just for a week or so, just to see what's going on. Let them help. I think it would bring about the turnaround we're looking for …

C: Interesting. That would help us keep an eye on people …

K: Well … yes and hopefully motivate people to perform better. This would be about *support* …

C: Of course … OK, leave it with me. I'll talk to Emma and give you a call later.

K: Fine. Bye.

C: Bye.

3.3.4

In Option A, Katie is herself – optimistic, kind and maybe a little naive – she wants to give the guys in Bangladesh a second chance. This approach of focusing on the positives can be very motivational in projects but it can seem to others, in this case Claudio, that the real issues aren't being acknowledged. But, ultimately, when Katie guarantees to deliver in four weeks, Claudio becomes calmer. It's the results that matter to him. However, Katie now has to deliver on her promise. In Option B, Katie is more careful. By acknowledging the fact that costs are 20 percent too high, she gives Claudio the impression that she's practical and this makes him more open to her suggestions. The result of this approach is that they find a way to agree on managing the risks effectively, and together decide to send experts to the local area to monitor the situation.

4.1.1

T = Toon Vamparys F = Frank Verbist
I = Ian Maude E = Eileen Burbidge

T: Today everybody is almost carrying a smartphone. Smartphone has a lot of nice tools in it, a lot of sensors. We try to make those smartphones more intelligent by mining the data, meaning getting all the data in one platform, looking for patterns and so we can find out if you are moving on a bike or on a – walking or on a tram or on a train or in a car and you can see where you are, you can see how fast you move, and those patterns give a good visualisation of what you are as a person and our clients can use that to offer you a better mobile experience.

F: So let's say we have a client that has a coffee shop and wants to sell more coffee. And as a promotion he offers a brownie with every coffee, so he wants to target people commuting to work. He would isolate in our audience all people that work in the city close to the shop that come by public transportation and walk the last mile to their work, that is not enough. Now you need to find the right time to target these people and the right time is just before they will arrive at work, getting out of their commute. The early people that I identified will now get a trigger right at this moment, which is the promotion from the coffee shop. What's important here is that a morning routine is different for everybody, at different times, we call that semantic time.

T: Semantic time is important; mobile interactions need to be spot on, if you want to have a positive reaction. If you do that at the wrong moment, then you irritate; irritation is not good for customer engagement. In semantic time, the right moment is gonna become crucial. Customers should not be afraid of the data that is being gathered around them and from them, they should be afraid of who's using them and for what are they used. I'm in start-ups already for more than 30 years – 20 years ago we were talking bits and bytes, ah, on a … on a tape or so, today we are talking about terabytes or, in the cloud.

I: It's essentially a really new thing because it's only made possible by the fact that we now have smartphones in our pockets all the time and we carry them around with us. So it's a, it's a whole new field, but it is, it's very competitive. Sentiance are one of a number of companies in this space and, um, they have an interesting take on it but then, you know, they're not the only game in town.

E: The challenge for Sentiance is to deliver actionable insights, um and not just more data for marketers. Marketers want to have really useful data if it's going to help them with conversion and with transactions, and frankly in making more money and getting more commerce out of users. But if what Sentiance does is just deliver more data, more data dumps, oh now we're able to break down your customer segment by this time, by this journey and by this location, that may in and of itself not be of value to marketers. If it can actually say this offer's gonna be more interesting and there's more take-up as a result, that's hugely interesting.

T: It's all about personalisation, anticipation and prediction, and the use of that will increase immensely in, in the next coming years. Disruptive means that you approach a problem in an industry or a sector completely from a different angle: you have an idea, you have a dream about approaching that, and then you go for it and you dream big.

4.3.1
S = Sanjit C = Claire P = Paweł

S: I'd better take this. Claire, how are you doing?
C: Good, you?
S: Good, good. I'm just here with Paweł, putting our heads together.
C: Well, I won't keep you long. Just to let you know, Claudio asked me to arrange a conference call with Gary Roach, an independent marketing expert we sometimes work with, to discuss the recent marketing campaigns.
S: OK.
C: Gary's been brought in as an expert and he's got some new thoughts on how to improve branding and where we advertise. Just a word of warning – Gary is always full of ideas but ... how can I put this? He can be very direct and not always easy to handle.
S: I'll manage.
C: OK well I'll be on the call as well so, see you later.
S: OK.
P: All good?
S: Yes, I have a meeting with Gary Roach later.
P: Gary? Good luck with that. He's a nightmare.
S: So I've been told.
P: I can't work with him. He thinks he always knows best.
S: I've worked with people like that before. I might take control of the conversation or let him speak freely; I'll see how it goes. I'll also have Katie on the call with me.
P: Trust me, though ... it still won't be easy.

4.3.2
G = Gary C = Claire S = Sanjit K = Katie

G: Hi.
C: Hi? Gary?
G: Yeah, hi, hi.
C: I'm here with Sanjit and Katie.
S: Hi.
K: Hi.
G: OK, Sanjeet, Claire has filled me in, so no need for hello-how-are-yous. Let's go through the branding document I sent you. It's really important you rethink the branding.
S: I actually had an agenda I thought we could stick to ...
G: Can I go on?
S: Yes. Your document. OK Gary, carry on.
G: As you'll see, I've proposed some changes. There's a load of ideas you should look at – really good stuff, even if I say so myself. One key thing. I've done some detailed analysis of your potential customers. Interesting results, very interesting. And so I've put together a few marketing ideas on page ... 23. Got that?
G: Anyway, and I know you're not gonna like this but, you know, the little product logo, the one with the sun you've gone for – awful. Customers hate it. It simply has to be changed. Pronto.
S: Can you elaborate on that?
G: Yeah, yeah, I will come to that. I'm also worried about the marketing budget. It's totally unrealistic, so I've created a new budget which when you take a look at the ...

S: OK, OK, but if we could focus back on the logo ...
G: Just let me finish.
S: Alright. Brand and marketing spend. Go on then.

4.3.3
G = Gary C = Claire S = Sanjit K = Katie

G: Hi.
C: Hi? Gary?
G: Yeah, hi, hi.
C: I'm here with Sanjit and Katie.
S: Hi.
K: Hi.
G: OK, Sanjeet, I've been briefed by Claire, so no need for hello-how-are-yous. Let's go through the branding document I sent you.
S: Er, Gary, it's Sanjit actually. Er, can I stop you for a second? I'd like to stick to the agenda and discuss the advertising concept first. I think it's very interesting and we can come back to the brand topic later.
G: Erm, OK. I mean, I don't have much time – and I really want to talk about changing the marketing budget. It's a disaster.
S: Can we slow down a little? Gary, I think that's really outside the scope of the meeting today. As I said, I want to stick to the agenda. So, coming back to the advertising concept ...
K: Yes, we have some ideas we want to run past you.
C: Gary, I think Sanjit has some ...
G: Fine, fine, whatever, but ...
S: Gary, let her finish what she's saying, please. Her views are important.
C: Gary, I think Sanjit has some good points which you'll be very happy with so I agree: it's probably best to start there.
G: OK. Shoot away.
S: I actually had a look through your branding document before the call. Some great ideas, thanks Gary. It really matches with some of my own ideas for promotion using local sporting events as a media platform.
G: OK. Great. This is all budgeted?
S: Yes, I'll come to that in a second. Let's first talk about ...

4.3.4
In Option A, Sanjit adopts an 'accept and adapt' approach which gives Gary the opportunity to express his concerns, to challenge the team and offer creative solutions. However, by being allowed to speak so freely, Gary ends up dominating the others and makes them frustrated. The advantage is that his ideas, which could help to innovate, are heard by everyone straight away.
In Option B, Sanjit is more assertive. He decides to intervene and insists on a more structured approach. He stops Gary interrupting and controls the meeting. This approach is collaborative; he acknowledges Gary's ideas; the discussion is more focused and the meeting isn't so one-sided, and everyone is allowed to contribute more freely. However, Gary's ideas do not get heard.

5.1.1
P = Presenter TO = Takato Oku
TS = Tetsuhito Soyama E = Expert

P: Out on the street, 29 year old, Takato Oku has got his groove on, but in the corporate world he had a frustrating start. He knew that his turn for promotion and pay rise was decades away. There was a long line of older workers the company needed to reward first.
For Japan Inc., that's been the tradition for over half a century, so he quit his first job and joined an online media and advertising firm in 2013. Within two years, he rose through the ranks to become a manager.
TO: Initially, I was surprised to have staff who were older than me, or to have a boss who was younger than me, but I like the fact that CyberAgent rewards its workers based on our performance, not our age.
P: Tetsuhito Soyama is in charge of human resources at CyberAgent.

TS: Many of our executives worked at companies where the oldest got the biggest salary, and we all felt that was unfair; our model means more competition, it's natural for older staff to feel awkward to see their younger colleagues being promoted first, but because it's been our policy from the start, I think it was easier for us, compared with older companies.
P: During Japan's economic boom of the 80s and 90s, companies could afford to keep raising salaries for all the workers as a reward for their loyalty. But since the economic bubble burst, even household names, such as Sony and Panasonic had to reconsider their policies. Jobs were cut, which came as a shock to Japanese workers who were expecting the guarantee of lifelong employment.
E: It's like a couple who just found out that your partner was cheating on you. They are feeling betrayed but companies which revise their policies have not all been successful, because unless you can turn your business around, you are just creating unhealthy competition among your employees.
P: For young companies like CyberAgent, the new salary model has, so far, paid off, and its success is what the rest of Japan Inc. is also hoping to achieve. But it's much trickier for bigger and older companies to adjust to the new economic reality.

5.3.1
Cr = Claire Cd = Claudio S = Sanjit K = Katie

Cr: Claudio.
Cd: Hey.
Cr: Have you see the latest sales figures from Sanjit?
Cd: Yeah. Not what we expected, right? What happened?
Cr: Their marketing campaigns. They happened. We shouldn't have trusted them to handle the campaigns themselves. I mean, did you see them? Really badly designed. And now sales haven't taken off.
Cd: Well ... are we sure that's the reason for the poor sales?
Cr: I'm sure it is. I think we should pull the plug and do a full re-design from this end. Top to bottom.
Cd: I'll need to think about that ... I know we're concerned but we have to stand by the decision we made to let them do it.
Cr: I still disagree, but keep me posted. Whatever you decide.
Cd: Sure
S: Hey Katie.
K: So ... I just had an 'interesting' chat with Claire. She thinks I owe you an apology.
S: What?
K: She told me my marketing campaigns shared a lot of the blame for low sales figures and that I'm not doing my job properly.
S: Oh.
K: Which isn't fair. I mean we knew there was a risk of lower numbers from Bangladesh this quarter. And analytics say they'll pick up in the next few months anyway.
S: Claire may be stressed about the sales figures, but that doesn't mean she can talk to you like that. Well, I'm having a meeting with Claudio later today. Things should be clearer after that, but I'm sure he won't be in a good mood either.
K: I know. Sorry.
S: Not as sorry as I'll be feeling later.

5.3.2
C = Claudio S = Sanjit

C: I've pretty much got two reactions to these sales figures. First: surprise. Second: disappointment.
S: I understand. Er, there's often a mismatch between forecasts and actual results –
C: That may be, but if there's a difference in figures it should be with *higher* sales, not *lower*. We can't go on like this.
S: I'm afraid you're not seeing the big picture here, Claudio. The market has been slow to respond to new environmental initiatives by the government. We thought more people would be buying our product by now.

: And we're only hearing about this *now*? You told me that Katie had this under control; that she made realistic estimates.

: She does. I assure you.

: Sanjit, if this is 'under control', I'd hate to see what 'out of control' looks like.

: Well, you have to remember that we predicted this might happen. This should not come as a surprise. We expected lower figures this quarter and warned you about them. Katie is very good at what she does and she is very close to the market in Bangladesh. She's very confident that Bangladesh will be a huge success. We just need to give it a little more time to pick up.

C: Really?

S: Come on Claudio. We've talked about this before. We just need a little patience … and maybe a little more respect, too.

C: Excuse me? 'Respect'?

S: We're all professionals here. We all care about the quality of our work. We're very passionate about it – sometimes it even causes arguments. You know, Claire confronted Katie earlier today and suggested that her marketing campaigns are to blame for the poor sales.

C: Claire may have a point, if you ask me.

S: Well I'm not sure what you're saying is necessarily accurate. You know we implemented your expert Gary's new ideas on those campaigns. That still didn't help. Nothing changes the fact that Bangladesh takes a little more time to react to marketing. We shouldn't change the campaign now.

C: So you're telling me that sales will increase … just very slowly.

S: That's right. Everything will be OK.

C: If you say so. We'll hold off on any changes to the campaign for now.

5.3.3

C = Claudio S = Sanjit

C: I've pretty much got two reactions to these sales figures. First: surprise. Second: disappointment.

S: Er, why so?

C: Why do you think? They're way too low. I think we should consider redesigning the marketing campaign … the whole thing.

S: OK. I understand what you're saying, and why, but you also have to acknowledge there's often a mismatch between forecasts and actual results.

C: Yet the situation stays the same. If there's a difference in figures, it should be with *higher* sales, not *lower*. This can't continue.

S: I can see your point. I'll be honest. We'd really hoped sales would pick up faster following the new government environmental initiatives.

C: Hope all you like, Sanjit – they haven't. You told me that Katie had this under control. You told me that she made realistic estimates. Are you sure she's the right person for the job?

S: I'm happy to accept *what* you're saying; I appreciate the point you're making, but not necessarily *how* you're making it.

C: What do you mean?

S: There's room for improvement. I agree. But I can assure you, Katie is very good at her job. She wouldn't work for us otherwise. And she's also very close to the market in Bangladesh. She's very confident that Bangladesh will be a huge success. It'll pick up. We just underestimated how long it would take to see the benefits from the marketing campaign.

C: Sanjit. I'm worried that your team is seeing this too much from a local perspective. Maybe there are opportunities for you and your team to learn from the experience we have in other countries and markets.

S: That's useful to think about. Look, we can always learn more. Nobody is perfect. Katie is great – but, thinking about it, maybe we can all benefit from what you've done in other countries in the region. How about this? Before proceeding any further, we set up another meeting between Katie and Claire. We can bring all the information and our perspectives together.

C: OK. Fine. But we need to do it quickly. We can't afford to waste any more time.

S: I take on board what you're saying. We'll hurry this along, I promise. I just wanted to get some feedback from you first.

C: I appreciate that.

S: Perhaps we also need to communicate better in this team, especially when the pressure's on.

C: Agreed. Stress never brings out the best in anyone, does it? Look, I'll get in touch with Claire now to see what time she can make tomorrow. Can you do the same for Katie?

S: Yep, sure. I'll do that now.

5.3.4

In Option A, Sanjit politely but firmly pushes back against Claudio's critical feedback, and stands up for Katie when suggesting that Claire may need to be more respectful, especially in her own feedback delivery style. It's a little tense, which could negatively affect their relationship, though Sanjit has stood his ground and protected his team member Katie, both of which are positive things. In Option B, Sanjit also stands up for Katie and her experience, but this time is more accepting of the overall feedback, and shows openness to learn more, though could he be perceived as being a bit too quick to accept criticism?

In both options the marketing campaign will remain unchanged for now, and the team will work on their communication and collaboration, so the outcomes are the same. But the team relationships are impacted differently in each option.

6.1.1

P = Presenter I = Interviewer M = Maxine Bédat
D = Domenica Delfini Arroyo MB = Mike Barry
A = Alienor Taylor PI = Peter Ingwersen

P: Many companies like to claim they are ethical businesses. This can be because they believe in a moral approach to commerce. It might also be because ethical is a label that helps them increase sales.

How can we discover if a business is ethical? We've been looking into the fashion industry – and why your clothing has become an ethical matter. In the fast fashion industry, clothing brands compete to offer new trends as quickly and cheaply as possible. Pressure on time and cost is intense: it means tough working conditions and low pay rates for factory workers.

I: Let's start off by talking about, what is 'Fashion Revolution Day'?

M: Fashion Revolution Day is a global movement; over 70 countries are participating; it's citizens around the world asking what should be a very basic question: who made my clothes – using the hashtag 'who made my clothes'.

P: Protest movements like Fashion Revolution Day start because of scenes like this. In 2013 a factory building, the Rana Plaza, collapsed and killed over a thousand workers. This tragedy made the public aware of the dangerous conditions the victims had been facing at work.

D: The Rana Plaza case made consumers really want to know where their clothes were coming from and how they were made. Um, critics accused fashion brands and consumers of being responsible for the deaths. Many brands felt they had to guarantee their products were not coming from Rana Plaza style sweatshops.

P: British fashion designer Katherine Hamnett was one of many who campaigned against the clothing industry for its unethical conduct.

D: The campaigns against unethical fashion started a movement where some labels and designers began to try to brand themselves as ethical. Um it's been popular to focus on the environmental side of ethics – 'green' and 'natural' is a nice message for consumers.

P: Fashion retailer Marks & Spencer would like to sell its customers more ethical clothing but sourcing enough fair-trade cotton to produce the garments is a problem.

MB: The amount of fair-trade cotton in the world is … available … it's tiny. There's probably less than a thousand tonnes actually available at the moment. M&S's total use of cotton at the moment is fifty thousand tonnes, so even if we took every piece of fair-trade cotton in the world, it wouldn't even touch the amount we actually need as a business.

P: At the London College of Fashion, the students who'll be the next generation's designers are reacting to the problem. They are trying to use only ethically sourced materials.

A: The more I found out about the fashion industry, the more I kind of, I thought it was really horrible, the environmental and ethical impacts that has on the world, I just … I just don't think are acceptable. You know I wanted the products to be beautiful in every aspect of them, so not only do they look good, but … the … when you look behind the scenes they're good as well.

D: The ethical debate in the fashion business has created a tension between the top priced labels and the mainstream brands. So the top designer labels can usually pay good wages, so they will sell you an item and might also try to convince you that no one got harmed for you to get that shirt. But high volume brands need the garments to be inexpensive and some of them prefer you close your eyes to whatever harm might have been done. So looking across the whole of the industry, we don't have an ethical solution yet.

P: But fashion now has strongly ethical players. After his range of ethical clothing was shown at a fashion show, Danish designer Peter Ingwersen told news cameras that fashion will become an ethical business.

PI: In the future I actually believe that we won't see any separations between ethical fashion and more mainstream fashion, I think it's all gonna be one. Anything that you wear will actually come under the same umbrella with very high standards, I think that's the way it's gonna go.

P: Ethics in fashion might be a genuine moral effort to abolish bad practices and make more ethical products. Or it could be just a kind of marketing. But if consumers become more responsible, the ethical dimension of fashion looks set to grow.

6.3.1

E = Emma C = Claudio

E: Just in time! Got a minute?

C: Sure.

E: I've heard some news that might not be good.

C: Go on.

E: Well, I have this friend in finance in the South East Asian region who told me SendAll are in trouble.

C: SendAll? The distributor we recommended to EN-Tek?

E: Apparently they're struggling with cash flow and debt and are quietly looking for a business partner.

C: Right. Right. I suppose I should warn Sanjit next time I see him.

E: No, no, no – I'm not convinced that's a good move. *We* recommended SendAll as the distributor … so that might not reflect very well on us and we don't want to unnecessarily concern him at this stage. It's just a rumour, after all.

C: You may have a point but, frankly, I'm not entirely sure I'd feel right keeping this from him. It feels dishonest.

E: Your call. But if I were you, I'd keep this quiet.

6.3.2

S = Sanjit C = Claudio

S: Hi there, Claudio, it's good to see you again.

C: Good to see you, too. How are things?

S: Great. Yeah – thanks again for suggesting SendAll. Those guys are the best! We couldn't have asked for a better distributor.

C: That's … great. Really.

S: Just thinking out loud here … but maybe we can benefit a lot from having them as more of a strategic partner and not simply our distributor. What do you think?

C: I'm not entirely sure at this stage, Sanjit.

S: Er, but …

C: I don't think we should do that at the moment. We're still in the early stages of working together.

They're good, yes, but it could be good to wait for a while

S: But everything's going so well! Why shouldn't we give them a little more incentive? You know, a good sign? I'm absolutely certain that this will be a long and successful relationship. Aren't you?

C: Just hear me out. Yes, maybe I'm playing devil's advocate here, but I'm not sure that would be a good idea. There might be new issues that come to light. It's just a thought. I could be wrong.

S: Hold on. Back up. What sort of new issues?

C: Sorry, I have to take this.

S: Yeah, sure …

6.3.3

S = Sanjit C = Claudio

S: Hi there, Claudio, it's good to see you again.

C: Good to see you, too. How are things?

S: Great. Hey – thanks again for suggesting SendAll. Those guys are the best. Things are running really smoothly. In fact, you know what? I strongly believe we can benefit a lot from having them as more of a strategic partner and not simply our distributor. What do you think?

C: Well, I don't want to worry you, but I feel I have to tell you this.

S: What's up?

C: Well, I'm sorry to say that I've heard SendAll might be having some financial difficulties.

S: Really?

C: I know, I'm still processing the information myself, but it's important to be open, so I want to let you know what I've heard.

S: I appreciate that. So what do you know?

C: Well, apparently they're now having cash flow problems. They're quietly looking for a business partner. I'm not saying I agree, but some people think this is a sign that the company is in trouble. I'm sorry about this. I know it was us who suggested them and I'm aware this may cast us in a bad light. This information isn't confirmed, but I think you should know.

S: That's OK, Claudio. I appreciate the honesty. Now, correct me if I'm wrong, but … shouldn't we be pre-emptively looking for another distributor?

C: To be honest, I don't think it'll be a problem either way. I'd say hold off on that for the moment, until we know more.

C: Sorry, I have to take this.

S: Yeah, sure …

6.3.4

By now Claudio has built a good working relationship with Sanjit. It's understandable that he doesn't feel good about keeping the information from him.

In Option A, Claudio decides not to tell Sanjit in an attempt to avoid any concerns that Sanjit may develop. He's vague and he talks around the topic, which in itself arouses Sanjit's suspicions. He senses that Claudio isn't being fully open with him, and may develop some trust issues.

Option B is almost the opposite. Claudio's openness and transparency strengthens their relationship, and Claudio emphasises that he isn't currently worried about the situation with their distributor. However, we can clearly see that Sanjit has interpreted this news with more concern than Claudio, and has called an emergency meeting for the next day.

7.1.1

P = Presenter A = Agata Wisniewska
E = Eleonora Pessina M = Matthew Dickin
EM = Eben Maasdorp

P: Time is money goes the saying and this is especially true in the business world. With production targets and project deadlines to meet, effective time management is a top concern for business leaders.

Over a hundred years ago, when carmaker Henry Ford pioneered the industrial assembly line, he realised the connection between the time taken to make each car and company profits. Measuring and managing the time spent on tasks became part of a management approach known as Fordism.

Today the Fordist concept of time management still operates in some places. At many distribution warehouses, for example, workers are required to pick and pack orders at lightning speed. Elsewhere in the workplace time management, in the sense of setting goals, prioritising and scheduling in order to maximise efficiency, is an important feature. At this publishing company there's a weekly team meeting to discuss and schedule all the jobs that have to be done. Agata Wisniewska is the Content Development Manager.

A: This week we'll probably need to deal with er second proofs first. … My main role in the team is to organise a schedule, to allocate resources and set the goals for the team members. Time management is very important for our business because, if the team takes longer than expected, it has an impact on the budget, and therefore the company loses money. When it comes to managing the time of each of the members of my team, I do not get involved too much. I prefer them to decide how they prioritise their time and also to communicate to the rest of the team on their progress and any issues they may have.

P: One member of the team, Eleonora Pessina, is an Instructional Designer. How does she manage her time?

E: I work across many different projects. So, what really helps me is … um … making a to-do list at the beginning of the week … um …where I really jot down everything that I need to do for that week. But then I also identify key priorities, key tasks that I want to get done. I use a digital calendar and I use different colours to identify what is meeting time and what is … uh … desk time. Another thing I use to manage my time is post-it notes … um … and I use them just to remind myself of things that I wouldn't normally do, so that they're there on my desktop looking at me.

P: Time management for employees of global companies brings new challenges. Matthew Dickin is the Director of Design and Production.

M: I work with teams and stakeholders spread all around the globe. So the first thing to say is I have to be very aware of where everybody is and that I have to be very aware of what that means in terms of time zone. So, for calls with Australia, Asia, India, I aim for very early in my morning, which is afternoon or early evening for them. And then calls to America … um … tend to happen at the end of my day which is very early in the morning for them. Certainly there are times, particularly during busy periods, where it feels like there aren't enough hours in the day. Um … so I have to be very careful to try and manage that within my own diary to make sure that that's not too often.

P: There's a growing demand from employees for more flexibility in their work schedules, and some people like Eben Maasdorp, a translator, are choosing to work on a freelance basis.

EM: As a freelance you actually have more time to work because you don't have to commute to work, for example. You also have more time to spend with your family because you can work in the evenings or early mornings depending on what suits you best. I do have to stay focused, so my strategy tends to be to commit myself to one hour, to see how much I can do in one hour – so, don't take any breaks before the 60 minutes are up. And then sit down the next 60 minutes and see if I can hit the same target.

P: Organising one's own time as a freelance is worlds away from the experience of workers on Henry Ford's assembly lines. But whatever the role and whatever the industry, good time management will continue to be essential to business profitability and an individual's career success.

7.3.1

K = Katie S = Sanjit

K: You look worried, Sanjit. What's the matter?

S: Well, you know how we heard that SendAll, our regional distributor, may be having financial problems … I've been looking into it. It's worse than we thought. They've expanded too quickly and are in trouble now.

So I collected the financial details and any other information I could find and sent them over to Emma Berg, the Financial Analyst at Go Global. I did that yesterday and even though this is obviously urgent, I still haven't heard back from her yet.

K: OK. The way I see it, I'd say you have three options here. First up, you could trust that she's seen the mail, understands the urgency and will get back to you as soon as she can.

S: Or?

K: Push her for a response, like with a call or an email, and be clear about your expectations for a timely response.

S: Right. I like that better. I don't want to just sit and wait. Wait – that's only two. What's the third option? Did you leave the best until last?

K: You tell me. The third option is you could escalate it and go over her head.

S: You mean go straight to Claudio?

K: Yes – to get clarification on what's going on with SendAll, and to raise the issue of responsiveness, but it would need to be handled sensitively though.

S: Sounds risky. I'll think I'll get in touch with her. Thanks.

7.3.2

S = Sanjit K = Katie

S: What should I say?

K: A friendly email ought to do it. Something like, 'Let me know when you'll get a chance to send me the information.' Email's definitely the best option. A phone call with no warning can be a bit of an imposition – she'll see the email as less pushy.

S: Sounds good. Erm, 'Hi Emma, I'm just resending my mail from yesterday. I'm worried that if SendAll goes bankrupt we'll have a big problem. When do you think you'll be able to get back to me? Thanks, Sanjit.'

K: OK, good. Now let's see what happens. I mean, we're their business partners. They really should be getting back to us, especially with something important like this. I'd be surprised if there was a further delay.

S: Me too.

K: Then again, they're very busy, so they may have a different perspective than we do. Maybe they have different or more information and don't think that this is urgent.

S: Oh, she's just replied.

K: And?

S: Hi, I saw your original email, but I'm overloaded at the moment. Nothing to worry about. All is OK. Can I get back to you by tomorrow morning?

K: Great.

S: Absolutely. Just the reply I needed. Thanks for your help.

K: It's no worries.

7.3.3

S = Sanjit E = Emma

S: I'll call her now. No point waiting any longer.

E: Hi, Sanjit.

S: Emma. Hi. I'm just calling about my mail from yesterday. Did you get it?

E: Your mail? Erm, yes, I got it.

S: Well I'm just wondering why I haven't heard back from you yet. I was expecting to hear from you within a few hours of my mail. It's really urgent.

E: Huh? You only sent it yesterday afternoon. Well, I didn't get back to you because I haven't had time to go through it in detail. Sorry. No offence, Sanjit, but I'm juggling a lot of work right now.

S: So is there any more news on SendAll? Should we be looking for another distributor?

E: Sanjit. Slow down. Take a breath. I've been travelling since Monday, I'm running on zero sleep right now, and I have another meeting in about two minutes. I'm not ignoring you, I'm just busy. OK? I've seen your email and I will respond by tomorrow morning. I assure you.

S: OK, sorry. Please prioritise this. It's urgent. And yes, I need a response ASAP.

E: I didn't mean to react like that. Sorry. And I'm sorry for not getting back to you earlier Sanjit, but everything is fine. No need to worry. You have my word.

: OK, thanks.
: Bye!
: Bye!

7.3.4

In this scene, Sanjit and Emma clearly have different opinions of how quick a response to an urgent issue should be and of what 'urgent' actually means.
To help improve clarity and understanding, here are three tips for dealing with urgency. One: write the word 'urgent' in the subject line and mark the mail with high priority as a sending option. Also indicate by when you need or expect a response. Two: when receiving such emails, quickly acknowledge that you have received the mail, even if you're busy, and indicate when the sender can expect a response. And three: follow up quickly, from either side, if the response date is missed. Focus on the information needed and not specifically on the delay or reasons for it.

8.1.1

P = Presenter G = Greg Smith T = Tommy Bryant
P: Change is a fact of life for everyone, whether it's starting school or college, moving house or beginning a new job. Companies also constantly face the need to change. It may be to improve efficiency, increase profits or to adapt to new regulations. Whatever the reason, change can bring uncertainty and risk, so it needs very careful management. Brompton Bicycle is the UK's largest bicycle manufacturer. The company designs and makes a rather special kind of bike – one that can be quickly folded up, which makes it ideal for commuters. Eighty percent of the bikes are exported, mainly to Japan and East Asia, and to Europe. A few years ago, it became clear that in order to keep growing, the company would have to move to a much larger site. Greg Smith is the head of Health, Safety and Facilities and was one of the team managing the change.
G: Brompton Bicycles has been growing ever since I joined in 1998. There were 24 people in the company at that point, we're now nearly 230, so as we expanded we needed more and more space.
P: The company formed a team of six people, to plan and manage the change. One of the main tasks was to weigh up the risks and benefits of different locations.
G: We considered that the biggest risk to the business, was losing the staff that we'd spent many years training, so we concentrated our efforts in looking for sites in West London, rather than elsewhere in the country. We've ended up six miles or approximately 10 kilometres away from where we were.
P: It's important for any company introducing change to make sure all the staff are onboard. Tommy Bryant is the Trade Marketing Executive.
T: I was quite apprehensive at first, when the company first informed us about the move. One of the main issues was the journey time; um … it was already an hour and a half by tube … um or a 45-minute cycle, which was quite long. And moving to the new site um, caused me some concern 'cause I didn't want to extend that journey time.
G: We made sure we er consulted with all our staff and told them about the potential location, before we actually signed the lease. So we brought all our employees to the new site in buses, so they could see the local area and see the new factory and the much better facilities that this site has. The moves themselves were actually quite quick. Er we split it up over a period of months. We moved some departments before Christmas 2015 and others during January 2016.
T: When the company actually moved it was a very quick and efficient process, and we were very excited about the new site as well. A big change to what we were used to.

P: The company measured the success of the move in two main ways.
G: We only lost two days production for each of the departments as we moved them. And in personnel terms, we lost approximately six people out of the total 230.
T: I'm coping well now with the … the journey time. Initially when I was living um in my house share, er the commute to our new site was er very difficult. So I had to move back home with my parents, which reduced the journey time by quite a bit, so now it takes me um around er 40 minutes to cycle, or even 40 minutes part by bicycle part by bus.
G: So we've been at the new site for 18 months and people really have adapted well to this new location.
T: The working conditions on the new site are much better. It's much more open, er there's a lot more windows, which actually makes it a much nicer view altogether. We have a canteen where everyone can sit together and have lunch. And as a whole, there's just a lot more space.
G: One of the major benefits of moving to the new factory site, is that we've now got all our employees working on one site and the morale of the staff has improved enormously as a result.

8.3.1

P = Paweł S = Sanjit K = Katie
P: You're looking happier than the last time I saw you!
S: I'm feeling great. We've had a successful launch, the product is selling well in Bangladesh now. Everything's going brilliantly, both in the market and our cooperation with Go Global.
P: It's great, isn't it? So what now?
S: Well a partnership opportunity has arisen in Vietnam with a key distributor. I'd like Katie to lead on this and work with them.
P: Sounds like a good opportunity, both for EN-Tek and Katie.
S: Exactly. I'm a little concerned though, as she was really looking forward to expanding the Bangladeshi market as it's her specialist area, but we can't miss this opportunity in Vietnam. She's a good fit and certainly capable – she just needs to be convinced to step out of her comfort zone.
P: Agreed. How are you going to tell her?
S: Well … I'd better do it sensitively. I'm just trying to decide here: should I take a direct approach and tell her it's a good career move? Or should I gently try to coax her towards the idea …
P: … and see how keen she is?
S: Mm … I'll figure it out.
K: I'm just about to head into a meeting with Sanjit. Bangladesh was a success … so I have a feeling he's gonna ask me to grow the Bangladeshi market further. I'd be quite comfortable doing that and it's definitely something I know how to do. In fact … I think I'd be really good at it!

8.3.2

S = Sanjit K = Katie
S: Thanks again for all your support on the launch in Bangladesh. Your hard work really paid off.
K: No problem … really enjoyed it.
S: Well, that's good to hear – 'cause I've got a new opportunity you might also enjoy.
K: Great. What is it?
S: We've got a great opportunity to partner with a leading distributor in Vietnam to launch our products there and I'd like you to lead the initiative.
K: Vietnam?
S: That's right. It'll be great.
K: Oh. Right. I just … I mean … I'm really familiar with the Bangladeshi market, but Vietnam is … It's really not a market I know anything about.
S: Well, you would need the relevant market intelligence and maybe you should get some further training as well. You'll be fine.
K: I'm not sure. It's all very sudden …

S: If I were you, I'd take this opportunity. Just think of what this will do for your career. The only way is up.
K: I guess, but … there's a lot to think about, Sanjit. It'll mean more travel, won't it? Maybe even moving there for a while?
S: Yes, it will – and I understand. It's a big choice to make. But I'm sure you'll be great at the job. Tell you what – I think it would be best for you to sleep on it, mull it over, and get back to me later in the week. I don't want to pile on too much pressure, but you need to make a decision about this soon.
K: OK. Will do.
Wow. *That* was unexpected. I'm really not sure about this. I think I might be in over my head. And I'm a bit disappointed that Sanjit didn't really hear my concerns.

8.3.3

S = Sanjit K = Katie
S: Thanks again for all your support on the launch in Bangladesh. Your hard work really paid off.
K: No problem … really enjoyed it.
S: Well, that's good to hear – 'cause I've got a new opportunity you might also enjoy.
K: Great. What is it?
S: Well, we've got a great opportunity to partner with a leading distributor in Vietnam to launch our products there and I'd like you to lead the initiative.
K: Me? In … Vietnam?
S: Yes. How would you feel about the idea of going abroad for a while or, if not, going on lots of business trips there?
K: Er … I'll be honest, Sanjit, this is a lot to take in. I mean, what do I know about the Vietnamese market?
S: Let's see that as a challenge to overcome, rather than a barrier stopping you. How do you think you could best approach this? Do you think you should look at what made Bangladesh a success?
K: Well … I could see which of the strategies I used in Bangladesh would also work in Vietnam and then decide what further training I might need.
S: Perfect.
K: What do you think I should do then?
S: Well I can't tell you what to do, but I can help you decide. Bear in mind this would mean a pay rise and a massive boost to your career.
K: I like the sound of that. I could start by doing some research and learning about the market as I did for Bangladesh.
S: Absolutely, and what kind of support would you need?
K: Well … a local expert would be ideal. But we would also be in touch regularly, wouldn't we?
S: Of course. I'll always be on call. And we can look into trying to find a local expert.
K: OK. I really need to think about this, Sanjit. It doesn't seem as daunting now, I suppose … but it's still something of a leap into the unknown.
S: It's a great opportunity.
K: I know!

8.3.4

The concepts of coaching and mentoring have become increasingly important at all levels in organisations. It can be tricky to decide which approach to take.
In Option A, Sanjit is direct and encouraging. As a mentor, he tells Katie what he thinks she should do and what he thinks is good for her. Katie, however, feels that he hadn't really heard, or listened to, her concerns. As a result, she doesn't seem too positive at the end.
In Option B, Sanjit takes a coaching approach and asks Katie a number of questions to help her think about how she would like to approach the new role and what she feels she needs in order to succeed. She is apprehensive at the end of this version also, but is more positive overall about the challenge.

1.01 S = Sue M = Martin A = Angela

S: Is that coffee?

M: Yes, it is. You want some?

S: Yes, thanks.

M: Here you go.

S: Thank you. Let me introduce myself. I'm Sue, from the London office.

M: Martin Kabatnik, from Germany. This is Angela.

A: Hello.

S: And where are you from, Angela?

A: Portugal.

S: Are you based in the Lisbon office?

A: No, Porto.

S: So do you both work in local finance teams?

A: Yes. Er, for one year.

M: Yes, finance. One year.

S: Oh really? Me, too – I joined the company last year. So how have you found it so far?

M: Hah – well it's certainly been a learning curve. In such a big company there are so many different systems and every team seems to have its own way of doing things, you know?

S: Yeah, I know what you mean! But I have to say in general people have been pretty supportive and patient while I've been getting up to speed.

M: Yes, same for me, actually.

S: So I guess we'll all be together in the finance part of the meeting this afternoon. Should be interesting, I think.

M: Yes, I think so.

S: OK, I think we're going to start soon. I'll talk to you later. I just want to meet a few of the others quickly. It's important to say hello. See you later.

1.02 T = Team lead S = Sue A = Angela M = Martin

T: So, er to start … could you all say a few words about yourself as a short personal presentation to the team? Er, who wants to begin?

S: Sure, I'm happy to start. I'm Sue Jacobs, and based in the London office. I've worked in this industry for ten years now. I was with a competitor for many years and then I joined Hansens at the beginning of last year. My background is in finance. My current job is Head of Financial Controlling in the UK and I report to Mike Keats, who's the Head of Group Finance. I've worked a lot on international projects which is why I am here – full time on the project. I'm really delighted to be part of this team and think we can achieve a lot in this project. It's important to create a common platform for finance across Europe. Happy to be here.

T: Thanks, Sue. Er, Angela.

A: OK. Angela from Porto. Er, been in the company a short time. I am only 50 percent on the project with my colleague who is not here. And also finance, yes.

T: OK. Er, Martin?

M: Er, Kabatnik. Martin Kabatnik. I'm Head of Finance in Germany, and will work on the project 20 percent. I studied finance in Berlin so worked in finance all my life. I agree. I think this is an important project for the company.

T: OK, so can we now hear a little from …

1.03 S = Sue A = Angela M = Martin

S: OK, Angela, lovely to meet you today. Really looking forward to working with you.

A: The same for me. It was a pleasure to meet you.

S: Yes, and I really liked what you said about your approach to projects in Portugal. Can you send me the slides you used in the afternoon?

A: Sure. I have your card.

S: Great. And Martin, also very nice to meet you.

M: Nice to meet you.

S: If you need any help with tickets for the theatre in London, just let me know. I can help.

M: I will be in touch. I promise.

S: OK, bye. See you next month. And I'll bring some tea for you from London. Only the best.

M: Ah, don't forget!

2.01 T = Teresa M = Mike

T: Welcome to Brazil, Mike. I hope you are settling in comfortably.

M: Thanks. It's great being here. I'm still waking up very early but I guess that's just the time difference.

T: Yes, I have the same problem when I travel. Has everyone been helpful so far?

M: Yes, they have and I appreciate it. This is my first trip here so everything is new.

T: I know the feeling! So, tell me what I can do to help you.

M: OK. Well, as I think you know, I've been asked to start work on a global strategy for training and development across the whole company. It's a big initiative and I want it to be based on best practices that are already in place. Every country has a different approach at the moment so I'm visiting our biggest sites to find out more about the different approaches and if there's anything that ought to be done that we are not doing at the moment. I'm starting here in Brazil and then I'll be heading to Asia on Wednesday.

T: OK, well the way we do things here works well for us – I'm very happy to talk about it.

M: Great. So um, let me check, are you the HR Director for all of Brazil or just for this plant?

T: Um, I'm actually in charge of all the HR Departments throughout the country. We feel it's important to have one strategy for both long-term and short-term goals regarding training and development.

M: Thanks. That clarifies that for me. I'm really interested in your input on both training and development and what you consider to be the main differences between them.

T: Um well, training for us means looking at areas specific to a job. It's a functional approach, meaning it's used in one job or department. These training sessions are used to make sure that employees have the skills they need to do their job. These types of courses are job- or task-oriented with short-term goals.

M: Can you give me an example?

T: Um sure. If we hire a newly-graduated engineer to work with suppliers, we may have to give him or her some specialised training on autoCAD drawing programs. The supplier might ask how a part could be improved, so the engineer has to be taught how to use these 3D computer programs or be brought up-to-date on the latest version.

M: Of course, that makes sense. But what about deciding whether a large group should be trained or just a few people? How is that done?

T: Training a small group versus a larger group is a strategic decision every company has to make. This would be considered carefully as it depends on the available budget. We might want to train a large group, but the budget doesn't provide for this, so smaller groups may be less costly. We, of course, look carefully at who exactly needs the skill in question for their role.

M: Mm that's clear. And what other factors have to be taken into account?

T: Well, there are often materials that need to be handed out so they have to be prepared in advance. It also has to be decided where the training should be held and who the trainer should be. We have to consider if it's better to do this in-house with one of our own employees or rent a space outside and bring in an expert from the field. It may also be possible to do a form of blended learning, some of it online and some of it with a trainer, or a mentor. There are lots of possibilities now.

M: So, in general, you're in favour of this type of job-oriented training on skills?

T: Absolutely. I would say that specific skill training is always seen as worthwhile. Whether it's skill training for a new program or new equipment I believe it's valuable. It's also important for the organisation that the training be successful. I guess I would say that skill training is pretty cost effective.

M: And general development of staff?

T: OK, now that's another story. When we look at development in business theory and skills that can be used across departments, it may only be beneficial if the trainee has the proper mindset for growth. It mustn't be decided without thinking carefully about a number of aspects first. Development is an important part of company strategy and long-term goals.

M: I'm not sure I follow you.

T: Um, let me give you an example. If we take an experienced manager and give them training on how to provide motivation for their staff, that may not be worthwhile because this person almost certainly has the skills to do their job already. Training for a young and inexperienced manager, however, might be very helpful as development deals with preparing employees for future challenges and fits well into our long-term goals of developing talent. It's also a cross-functional approach meaning that we might develop someone who is currently in one department with the idea that the person might be moved to another department if we needed to replace a manager for any reason.

M: So, what you're saying is that development is really helping employees gain general business skills or concepts they can use elsewhere in the company and for their future careers. Did I understand that correctly?

T: Exactly right. And we still have the option of using the same methods of delivery as we have for training, namely in-house courses and blended learning, mentoring or finding an external trainer. The difference would only be in content.

M: And how do you decide then who gets training and who gets developed?

T: Um, that depends on who needs to be developed and how this will help the company. In the end, we need to make sure that the subject matter is relevant to their level of experience and knowledge.

M: OK…Thanks so much, Teresa. That's clarified quite a few things for me and I've made a note of everything you said. If I have any follow-up questions after I get back, I'll get in touch.

2.03

I've worked a lot with teams in my professional life, and, you know, there are a lot of problems caused by different approaches to teamwork. In the end, I think there are two very different team cultures; one is more focused on the individual, each person having a clear and specific role and place in the team – this is team culture A. People like this because it's, well, clear roles – people know what they have to do and what the other does, and then they communicate like this – they have clear personal objectives, they make clear recommendations to the team based on their expertise – simple. And, there's a leader role, who can confirm any final decision. For Team culture B, this isn't actually a team. What this culture values is interaction and collaboration – working together to offer and share ideas, to have a lot of discussions and take creative decisions. In these teams, roles overlap with each other; there are no clear borders for roles; lots of discussion. And you see no separate leader role. Yes, of course, there is a leader, but shared leadership is more important to have a culture where everyone is responsible for the final decision. Which is better? Well, that is a whole other question. All I will say is that people often have very strong beliefs about this, which can make it difficult for people from these different cultures to work together.

2.04 T = Takeshi S = Sam St = Steve

T: OK, let's get started. So, just to confirm, we have Sam and Paula here in the room, and Steve joining from the USA. As you know, what we are looking to do here today is to decide how to digitalise the training and learning we do in the company, moving away from traditional classroom training, which still dominates the way we do learning here. This means finding ways to bring in new technologies, to become more flexible, and more efficient and effective in the way we do learning. Now, you all had the task of preparing a few ideas based on your country needs. Just to ensure everyone can say something, can we quickly

o around the table, and hear everyone one by
ne, and then discuss?

All: Fine.

: Takeshi, can we talk about budget as I really
think this has a massive impact on what we can
and can't do?

: Sam, er I agree budget is really important, but
want to come to that a little later. I really want to
focus on hearing the country presentations and
getting a clear picture of the needs we have in the
countries first; then we can think about the budget
constraints.

S: OK.

T: Great. And just to say, we have Steve dialling
in today but as we discuss things, it's important
for everyone to speak up, give your ideas and get
involved. I really want us to share the facilitation
so everybody – step in, clarify, summarise – this is a
team meeting.

St: OK, no problem.

T: Great, well, let's begin with you then, Steve.
Can you kick us off with …

2.05 T = Takeshi S = Sam St = Steve P = Paula

T: Thanks for that, Paula. So, er we've now heard
from everyone on their country needs. Where does
that leave us in terms of next steps? Anyone got
any thoughts on this?

S: Listening to what people have been saying, it
seems that there's a consensus to reduce spending
on soft skills training. That technical training is the
main demand from the company.

T: What do you mean by that? Which soft skills?

S: I guess it's the usual things like presentation
skills, negotiation skills, time management, and all
that. Probably some of the leadership training, too,
we could push to e-learning and save money.

St: Steve here. If I can just come in on that. I
actually really disagree, particularly on the
leadership side of things and e-learning. Of
course, people always look at technical training
as the priority, but I think it's our job to defend
soft skills and leadership. And I really don't think
it's the training to digitalise. It needs a classroom
situation so people can reflect and experience
things together. If we do change, we need to be
very careful. Sorry, I don't want to be negative, but I
really feel strongly about that.

T: No, thanks, Steve. Um, feel free to say what
you really think because it'll help us to be creative.
Um, how do others feel about this? Paula, you
have some experience of developing e-learning
leadership training from your last company. What
do you think?

P: Actually, we had an effective blended solution
with a mix of e-learning and classroom training.
But in that case we were able to implement it
carefully over several years, to create a learning
culture where that worked. We don't have that
here. People expect classroom training, and don't
want e-learning.

T: OK, so that's important. So, just to recap
everything. Sam, you feel we have an opportunity
to move to more e-learning. Steve, you are
sceptical. Paula, you have seen this work in
your previous company, but it needs to be done
carefully. So, listening to you all, I think we actually
agree that there are good options for change here,
but there are still a lot of details to work out and
we need to be careful how we do things. Perhaps
the next step would be to look carefully at some of
the risks of using e-learning in soft skills and …

2.06 S = Sam T = Takeshi St = Steve

S: So, what we're doing in my area is to hold in-
depth discussions with heads of all departments to
gauge their response to e-learning. As I said, this is
really important because it helps us to …

T: Sam, can I stop you there? Buy-in from
department heads is definitely important, but I'm
afraid time is pressing and we need to come to a
decision on next steps so we can move forward. I
realise that we still have different views on some
points. So, Sam and Steve, my proposal would be

that you two work together on this for the next few
weeks and come up with a plan on how we move
forward. I think with more thinking, we can take a
final decision. Sam? How does that sound to you?

S: I agree.

St: Fine with me.

T: Great. Sorry, but I need to rush to my next call.
Thanks very much for this. I think we have made
really good progress. I'll email round some possible
timings for the next meeting very soon. And also,
thanks to all of you for being so proactive and
sharing the facilitation. As I said at the beginning,
it makes a big difference if everyone steps in and
clarifies, summarises and so on. And it really helped
me and the discussion a lot this time. Good stuff.

All: Great. / Fine. / Thanks. Speak to you soon.

3.01 P = Pat S = Sam

P: Hello, Pat speaking.

S: Hi Pat, it's Sam calling. I'm just looking at what
I need to prepare for the test next week and I was
wondering if you could help me with a couple of
things because you know more about this area.

P: Sure, no problem.

S: I'm having a little difficulty understanding
the concept of overall strategy and would like to
understand it better. This is all new to me.

P: Oh, OK. How can I help?

S: Well, there are a couple of things I'd like to
clarify regarding specific figures in a financial
forecast. When I better understand them, I'm
sure I'll be able to get the bigger picture too. I've
emailed you the file that I'm trying to make sense
of.

P: OK, well I'm happy to help. And perhaps I can
send you a couple of printouts that I have with a
list of words and expressions used in finance.

S: OK. Great. Thanks. Can I talk you through the
points I'm unsure of?

P: Sure. I've just downloaded the attachment you
sent me.

3.02 P = Pat S = Sam

P: Right, I've got it open. Where should we start?

S: Well, can you look at the section on the top
right? Specifically the total projected sales figures
for each product line and each quarter.

P: Right.

S: I'm looking at column J. Are those figures gross
or net?

P: They're gross. They're the total revenue you
expect to get from each product.

S: OK, thanks. And tell me, what exactly do the
figures in column L refer to? What's EBIT?

P: They're the margins on each product line.

S: Sorry, I don't follow. What are margins?

P: Margins show us how profitable the various
product lines are. We calculate that by subtracting
the operating costs from the revenue to get the
operating profit. The operating profit is our margin.

S: I see.

P: We often use the term EBIT when thinking
about the operating profit. It stands for earnings
before interest and taxes.

S: Thanks, I've heard that before when people are
talking about finance, sales and profits. Also, I don't
know if my notes from the lecture are right. I wrote
down that the figures in row 48 are averages. Is
that correct?

P: Yes, you're right. They're averages of all of the
products in each category, A, B and C.

S: Hmm. Can you go over that again for me?

P: Sure. So, for example, we add up the projected
revenue from the six products in category A and
then divide that number by six. That gives us the
average revenue for each product in that category.

S: So you mean that you get the averages to see
how profitable, on average, that overall category
is?

P: Yes, that's it.

S: And if I remember correctly, I think we use the
combined totals in each category to see where we
should concentrate our sales effort? Is that right?

P: Exactly.

3.03 S = Sam P = Pat

S: Thanks for your help, Pat. It's been really useful
to speak to you. I often find it difficult to keep up
with all the terminology, there's so much of it.

P: Would you like me to share with you a glossary
of standard terms for you to use as a reference? I'll
send you the link.

S: Yes, that would be great, but can I not find it in
one of the books I am reading?

P: No, this is my own live glossary that I have been
developing since I was in your year.

S: Really? What do you mean by live?

P: Oh, when I say live, I mean that it's cloud based.
I share it with my study group so that they can
update it too. Of course, we now know what words
like margins mean but we haven't deleted them
from the glossary. Everything you are learning
about now is still in there.

S: Oh, thank you Pat. That's really kind of you.

4.01 L = Lina J = Jimena MB = Multi-Babel

L: The Multi-Babel app translates your
conversations in real-time. The Multi-Babel app is
great if you want to network at conferences with
people who don't speak your language, if you need
to have business conversations, or if you want to
socialise with people of different nationalities.
Forget about spending hours on learning grammar.
If you wear these wireless earphones, which are
connected to the app, you'll be able to understand
instantly with simultaneous translation using voice
recognition.

If you click here, you'll see all the language
options. At the moment we have English, Spanish,
Portuguese, Italian, French, and Cantonese Chinese
but later this year we'll also be offering Arabic,
Hindi, Japanese, Korean, German, Polish and
Russian.

Unless you use it through the earphones,
everyone else will be able to hear your
conversation! But, if you use the mute function, you
can hear the translation through your earphones
not the speaker.

There is also another neat feature if you make
a mistake – here, you can pause it and it won't
translate the words that you said in the last three
seconds. It's extremely useful if you accidently say
the wrong figure, or when you get a new client's
name wrong. Cool, isn't it?

You're probably wondering, 'All this is great,
but how much will it cost me?' The Multi-Babel
app with earphones retails at only 250 euros. But
we're offering a special promotion this week for all
participants at the trade show: you can purchase
three apps with headsets for the price of two.
Earphones are available in a range of colours:
black, white, blue, purple and red.

This app is really best used for one-to-one
conversations. It isn't suitable for meetings with
lots of people. However, I would recommend it
for networking, daily conversations and smaller
meetings. When you've tried it, you won't be able
to live without it! And you'll want to get one for
all your family and friends. I'm sure they won't be
disappointed. The technology is changing so fast,
we'll be able to offer you more languages and
faster translations next year with the help of more
advanced voice recognition, sensor technology
and improved artificial intelligence. Let me just
add that the whole process is done remotely in the
cloud so it doesn't slow down your device, but you
do need to be online.

Who would like to try it? Any volunteers? Yes,
you, madam. Can you um put on these earphones?
That's right. What's your name?

J: Jimena.

L: What nationality are you, Jimena?

J: Mmm, española.

L: Right, let's choose Spanish–English then. I'll
turn the mute function off so that everyone can
hear. I promise you, you'll be amazed! Start talking
when you hear the beep, OK?

J: Qué tengo que hacer?

MB: What do I have to do?

J: Qúe maravilloso!
MB: How marvellous!
J: Quiero tres!
MB: I want three of them!

4.02 E = Eamon C = Chris

E: So, what's new with our smartphones? At Dawnbreakers, we've developed a phone that's way smarter than any phone anywhere, combining the latest artificial intelligence, voice recognition technology and the ultimate digital personal assistant. But more of that later.

Since our last smartphone model, I'm pleased to tell you that we've upgraded pretty much everything: we've improved connectivity, we've upgraded the camera, and increased the pixel count. If you've seen the new screen, you'll notice it goes to the very edge of the phone. And of course if it didn't have high definition screen resolution, we wouldn't see video images so clearly. What else? We're currently developing the remote control function for interconnected home devices. This means you'll be able to operate all your home devices from your lights to the air conditioning, using your phone. And next year we'll be supporting more virtual reality content with 'wearables'. So, if I were wearing goggles now, I could see the images in virtual reality. We're also going to be adding an improved 'priority' function. At the moment, unless I prioritise events carefully, the assistant over-rides my work schedule with my social engagements! My boss might not be very pleased if he found out about that!

We're already making smartphones more like robots. Let me show you a demonstration of how. My new personal assistant can help me with booking appointments and managing my schedule. Some of you will remember our demonstration last year with a prototype of the digital personal assistant. Since then, I'm very pleased to announce, we've improved battery life for voice recognition to work more effectively. ... Ladies and gentlemen, I'd like to present my assistant, ... Chris! Say hello to everyone.
C: Hi everyone, I'm Chris, Eamon's digital personal assistant.
E: Chris, you can help me with a number of tasks, can't you?
C: That's correct, Eamon.
E: Just give us three examples please.
C: I can search for stuff on the internet. If you like, I can control your home devices remotely, and I can remind you of important meetings or birthdays.
E: So, when's the next birthday I need to remember Chris?
C: Oh, that's easy, it's yours! Next week, on the 8th of March.
E: Mmm, I'd like to celebrate that. What about an Italian restaurant in Dublin? For Wednesday the 8th of March at 7p.m.
C: OK, that's the 8th of March at 7p.m. For how many people, Eamon?
E: A table for six.
C: Searching ... for ... you ... now... I've just found ... five options within 30 minutes from you. Let me know which one you prefer and I'll book a table.
E: Great thanks. I'll let you know when I've finished the presentation.
C: Sure. At 12...15.
E: You can take a break now, thanks.
C: Thanks. I will!

Ext4.01

1 You'll be able to understand instantly with simultaneous translation using voice recognition.
2 You can pause it and it won't translate the words that you said in the last three seconds.
3 You can purchase three apps with headsets for the price of two.
4 Earphones are available in a range of colours.
5 The whole process is done remotely in the cloud.
6 We've developed a phone that's way smarter than any phone anywhere.

7 You'll be able to operate all your home devices from your lights to the air conditioning, using your phone.
8 Next year we'll be supporting more virtual reality content with 'wearables'.
9 If you like I can control your home devices remotely.
10 Let me know which one you prefer and I'll book a table.

4.04 M = Mandy I = Isabella

M: Hi Isabella. You wanted to see me? What's up?
I: Hi, Mandy. Well, I'm not happy about this new policy of not being able to access our work emails after 8 p.m.
M: Uh huh.
I: We're a digital agency with clients all over the world. It's simply not reasonable to expect me to do my job and then limit me like this. I have to be able to access my emails in the evenings.
M: OK, hold on a moment, Isabella. You have to understand that the company policy is for everyone. This new system has been put in place for the benefit of the employees. There's an unhealthy culture of people still working electronically long after they have left the office and sometimes into the night.
I: Yes, but for some of us it's necessary, especially when our customers are on different continents. The servers are now holding incoming and outgoing emails after 8 p.m. until the following morning. You need to unlock my emails in the evenings.
M: Yes, but can't you just send your outgoing mails before you leave the office around 6 p.m., and then reply the next morning to any that come in during the night?
I: I can, but I need to leave earlier than 6 p.m. every day, and it also means I lose a day when communicating with some of our clients.
M: OK.
I: And it also means my inbox is already filling up by 8 a.m. each morning.
M: I see.
I: I need you to get the IT team to lift that blockage on my account. This change has to happen if you still want me to manage our customers.
M: Well, hold on a moment. Let's think about how to manage this and find a way that works for you while still ensuring you have a healthy work-life balance.
I: Well, you know I have small kids and it's important for me to have dinner with them and put them to bed every day. That's why I leave at 5 p.m. I don't mind if I then have to work from home for a few hours in the evenings.
M: OK, I understand that. But ... I can't completely lift the blockage for you. You don't need to be emailing through the night, right?
I: No, I don't, but I do need some flexibility and to be able to access my emails after 8 p.m.
M: How about if we lift the blockage until 10 p.m. Would that work?
I: Yes, I suppose I can agree to that, but it still limits me a bit. Oh, and I need access to our virtual meeting software from home in the evenings too, but I'm happy to also limit that to 10 p.m. if I have to.

4.05 B = Barbara D = Daniel

B: Hi, Daniel. You wanted to see me? What's up?
D: Hi, Barbara. Well, I'm not happy about this new policy of not being able to access our work emails after 8 p.m.
B: I see. Let me make sure I fully understand your perspective. Firstly, tell me about how this situation affects you.
D: Well, I have many clients in other continents and we often need to communicate in the evenings. Why was it introduced in the first place?
B: Well, you know this new system has been put in place for the benefit of the employees. There is an unhealthy culture of people still working

electronically long after they have left the office and sometimes into the night. It's a priority for us that our team has a good work-life balance. It's not specifically about the email block.
D: OK, I understand that, but I don't work into the night, and I'm happy with the level of flexibility I usually have in my job. I have a good work-life balance.
B: OK, well, what are your priorities?
D: Well, you know I have small kids and it's important for me to have dinner with them and put them to bed every day. That's a key priority for me. That's why I leave at 5 p.m. every day. I don't mind if I then have to work from home for another hour or so in the evenings.
B: How would you feel about having an extension on email accessibility in the evening but only for another hour or two? What do you think of that?
D: Well, the kids are in bed by 8 p.m., so it would be good to just have another hour or two in the evening to email and maybe have some virtual calls.
B: Yes, I think I can make that happen. But we should talk regularly about this. I don't want you to get snowed under or to be working too much at home in the evening.
D: It's OK, I'll let you know if I'm struggling. Thanks.

5.01 C = Carlota H = Hanna A = Antoni

C: So, as you can see from the agenda, what I want to do today is take time to think about how we are doing things. So just generally speaking, what do you think about where things have gone well and where the problems were, and how to change things going forward? Starting with Hanna: tell us, from your side, personally speaking or about the project, where have things gone well? And where do you need to improve?
H: I think, overall, it's been good. I mean, in terms of my main success, I managed to complete the first two phases of my side of the project within budget. I had to be very careful with spending but managed it; no extra resources were needed. I guess, as you all know, my big challenge was in the early phases with production. We had some real time and quality issues with our production in Poland.
C: Which aspects of the project were the most problematic exactly?
H: Well, speaking openly, the first designs which I produced were not high quality. This led to production issues. We lost some time at the beginning. I got it right in the end with a rework of the design.
C: What was the main cause of this? Why were there design mistakes?
H: Good question. Unfortunately, the designs had mistakes because I tried to do things too quickly. I had too much to do and tried to do things too fast. And then, the colleagues in Poland didn't see the problems until they produced prototypes. Yes, Antoni?
A: I think you're right.
H: They just worked with what I gave them. It got very messy. I should have planned more carefully. If I'd planned more carefully at the beginning, I could have produced a better design, and avoided time delays.
C: But I don't understand. We are all experienced. We always work under time pressure.
H: I think I just underestimated the complexity.
C: So, how do we plan to do things differently next time?
H: Yes, I've talked to my team and next time we will insist on having more time for the initial design stage and, ideally, a prototype stage too. It will pay off.
C: Yes, this has actually been useful. We now know we need to give ourselves realistic deadlines.
H: Yes, sometimes, slower is better.
C: Great! OK, Antoni, how about you?
A: Well. As far as I'm concerned ...

6.02 C = Carlota A = Antoni H = Hanna

C: OK, maybe just before we wrap up, I'd like to hear your comments on successes, things that have gone well, what we can do more of. On the whole, it turned out to be a success and I actually want to start here with a big thank you to Antoni for leading the production side so well. The production team have been amazing, so collaborative and they've produced excellent quality, and come up with quite a few design ideas.

A: Thank you, Carlota.

H: Yes, I can echo that. Your team has been so proactive, Antoni. A pleasure to work with. Please keep it up.

A: We will, we will. I'll pass on the feedback. And I'll invest the same time in positive collaboration in the future … . Same from our side, it's been great that the design team has travelled so much to see us in Poland. Having you present, face to face in meetings, that has really helped.

C: Yes, I think face to face always works better than working remotely. We have to thank our project sponsor, Gina, as she agreed quite a high travel budget. Without Gina, travel would have been very difficult in the current financial climate. So again, well done.

6.01 R = Richard K = Katrina

R: Katrina Sands is the best-selling author of *Essential Ethics*, which features on the reading list of business degree courses around the world. She's also an ethics consultant to major corporations. Many thanks for being with us today, Katrina.

K: My pleasure Richard.

R: I'd like to start by asking you to define a key concept in your book for our listeners. Can you tell us what is meant by the term, 'triple bottom line'?

K: Yes. The triple bottom line is essentially a framework, or structure, if you like, for measuring how ethical an organisation is in terms of three ideas: profits, people and planet. The problem is the TBL is difficult to measure.

R: But we can measure profits, can't we?

K: Well that's right. Financial profits are obviously the easiest to measure. Typical ways include looking at concepts such as a company's income, its costs, growth, the taxes it pays, employees' income, and so on.

R: How about measuring ethics in terms of people?

K: Social measures include, for instance, the number of hours of training employees receive, equality and diversity in the workplace, say, the percentage of female workers. Then there's health and safety, but, and this is where things get complicated, there is also the general physical and psychological well-being of staff. For example, a Human Resources manager can count the number of days taken for sick leave, but it's more difficult to measure how healthy and happy employees are. Social measures in the TBL also extend to relationships with stakeholders: suppliers and partners, the local community, and anyone else who is affected by a company's activities. And beyond that, an organisation can show its social integrity by organising philanthropic activities.

R: I see. And what about the planet?

K: Well, environmental measures in ethics include company policy on things such as its energy consumption, the use of natural resources like water, waste management, as well as carbon emissions and the impact of a company's carbon footprint, …

R: Which is?

K: Oh by carbon footprint I mean the overall impact of a business on the environment. Of course many of these different measures are connected. To give you an example of profits and planet: by reducing packaging, you can also reduce costs, so that's a measure that's good for the environment and good for profits.

6.02 R = Richard K = Katrina

R: What kind of companies can use the TBL model? Are we really talking here about the big multinationals?

K: Businesses, non-profit and government organisations can *all* use the TBL model. But we need to take into account all three categories – financial, social and environmental. *All* three areas need to be integrated.

R: So could you give us a few examples of companies that are considered 'ethical'?

K: Sure. There's Natura Cosméticos, which sells cosmetics and personal-care products, and has been in the list of the World's Most Ethical Companies since 2011. It is the only Brazilian company this year, and one of the few companies in the health and beauty industry.

R: I've read that Natura was awarded a certificate for sustainability. How exactly has it been ethical?

K: There were a variety of reasons. In financial terms, three percent of company profits at Natura were invested back into the communities. Over 75 percent of employees participated in the company's profit-sharing program. Natura also produces an annual report that is reviewed by a third party and is available to the public, so it's transparent about its profits.

R: Could you give us an example of its ethical conduct regarding people?

K: Sure, ah let me see … well, more than 50 percent of Natura's managers are women. They would have had inequality in the workplace if Natura hadn't taken on female managers. And there wouldn't have been diversity in the organisation.

R: And how can we measure what is considered ethical conduct where the planet is concerned?

K: Many of Natura's products are based on natural ingredients: indigenous, Brazilian vegetables and fruits, such as passion fruit, that are produced by farmers in small communities. In addition, Natura gives details on its energy consumption, water use and waste production. Those are just some examples.

R: It's interesting to see that some companies have appeared in the world's ethical companies list *every* year. I see these include General Electric, PepsiCo, Starbucks, UPS, Xerox and Kao Corporation. The Japanese company Kao has received recognition for being in the World's Most Ethical Companies list for well over a decade.

K: That's right.

R: I'd like to know why you think the Kao Corporation has been on the list for so long?

K: For a number of reasons. Kao specialises mainly in beauty and health care products, but the group also has two other businesses: home care products and chemicals. What's interesting is that its CEO, has said that integrity is a *core* value of the company. The Kao way is not just a philosophy: it is supported by a sustainability statement which focuses on three specific areas: conservation, community and culture. If they hadn't developed the Kao way, they might not have been listed as one of the world's most ethical companies. Kao has not only been recognised for its contribution to preserving the environment, but also for promoting diversity and for getting involved in social issues. For instance, their employees do voluntary work in local communities. You could argue Kao could have had a good relationship with local people if they had simply donated money to the community but in this case, employees got involved directly.

R: But Kao and Natura are both big multinationals, aren't they? Can you give us an example of a smaller organisation that isn't top of the list but is an ethical company?

K: Well, I'd like to mention a cooperative called La Fageda, a company that produces dairy products and is based in Catalonia, Spain. They employ staff with mental health problems. In La Fageda, at least 70 percent of positions are held by people with disabilities, so it's a good example of social integration and diversity in the workplace. What's more, they source their own milk, in contrast with the big multinationals. At first, they distributed their yoghurts through hospitals and schools.

Then they moved to the general food market and became commercially successful. But this kind of success poses a dilemma. It's the same dilemma for any responsible business: will they be able to manage growth without endangering their commitment to their users and customers? And we can also ask a similar question about a company's past. If they had grown faster, would they still have been a responsible business?

6.03 R = Richard K = Katrina

R: It's fascinating to hear about all the good stuff that companies are doing in terms of ethics. Nevertheless, isn't it extremely difficult to measure the triple bottom line?

K: It is certainly difficult to measure how an organisation affects the planet and people in the same terms as profits. The full cost of an oil disaster, for example, is huge and immeasurable in terms of money. However, Richard, to give you some more examples: if multinationals hadn't cleared huge areas of forests in the Amazon, they wouldn't have moved whole communities from their homes; and we could have slowed down the effects of climate change. If clothing manufacturers hadn't used child labour in sweatshops, those children could have continued with their education, instead of working in factories. It's totally impossible to put a price on these kinds of things.

On balance though, the TBL has fundamentally changed the way organisations measure performance and sustainability. It's in everyone's interest for companies to be ethical, transparent and socially responsible. Customers, employees, shareholders and the public expect it and, generally speaking, successful companies nowadays are looking further than just making a profit.

R: OK, many thanks Katrina. And we'll be back next week to discuss another business issue.

6.05 L = Luigi C = Caroline

L: Hello, having fun?

C: There are a lot of people, but it's interesting, yes.

L: Luigi Moretti from Romtek.

C: Caroline Macklin, Macklin Tours.

L: Macklin Tours? I know the name. You've been in business for over a year now, haven't you?

C: Very good, I'm impressed. Yes, we set up just eighteen months ago.

L: I've heard great things about you. You have a good reputation.

C: Thank you. But what do you do exactly?

L: Um, we specialise in software solutions for small and medium-sized companies. Our expertise is in providing the correct support for each client. Um, which systems are you using at the moment?

C: Oh, for now we just use the standard spreadsheet and database software we could download for free, but they're not great really.

L: I can imagine. Our solutions enable you to manage and communicate with clients more effectively. Er, so basically what we offer is better relationships and more sales, which I think everyone wants. Would you like me to talk through what we have?

C: Yes, thank you. Maybe this is something we need to look at now that we're growing.

L: Sure, shall we grab a coffee first?

C: Good idea. I think there is somewhere over there where we can go …

6.06 C = Caroline L = Luigi

C: So, tell me a bit more about this software and how it could help us.

L: OK, basically, it's software that we install on your company computers but host remotely on our server, er which helps you to organise and store customer data in a clear way. Your business will benefit when you can track sales, send out emails and mailshots to support marketing, and there's a useful finance element which you can use to track profitability per customer. Er, could that be useful for you?

C: Yes, finance tracking sounds really useful. And just what we need now we're growing and becoming more established. We need to stay on top of our numbers.

L: Well, the final price will depend on which solution you need. So we should come to that later. But I really believe it's a perfect solution for small businesses looking to become more professional.

C: How flexible is it, though?

L: It's fully customisable. With our support, you can tailor this to suit your specific needs.

C: Good. But it's not too complex, is it? Some of our people are a little older and not so confident with new systems.

L: Not a problem. We also provide intensive onsite training to make sure your people can use the software. How does that sound?

C: Sounds good. So, in principle, it sounds great, and what we've been talking about internally for some time to be honest.

L: Are there any other questions I can answer right now?

C: Well, of course, there's cost, and I think we need to see the product in more detail.

L: Absolutely. On the cost side, I think we need to see what precise solution you need, how much consulting work is needed from our side. I can't really give you a number at the moment. But it's very competitive. Is budget a major consideration for you?

C: It's an issue, of course, but we are growing, so it's more about what the software can deliver that is probably most important.

L: OK. So, what would be a useful next step?

C: I guess I need to see the product.

L: Yes, so how about if I come over, show you the product, talk to you more about what is right for you … ? I am absolutely certain that we have exactly what you need.

C: That sounds great.

L: OK … would something in the afternoon next Wednesday work for you?

C: Yes, let me just take a look at my schedule here and see what we can …

7.01 H = Haruki J = Javier

H: Hi, Javier. Thanks for coming to see me at such short notice.

J: Sure. No problem. What's up?

H: Well, it's good you asked that, but I'm also surprised that you've had to ask that. As you know, we're quite behind on this project and really need to catch up.

J: Yes, we do. We're all working flat out.

H: I know. But this also means we're all going to have to go beyond the scope of our usual roles. We're going to have to go the extra mile to support everyone on the project and get finished on time.

J: OK, so what exactly does that mean?

H: Well, what that means exactly is that I need you to go to Japan to support the local team and make sure they are able to finish their part of the project on time.

J: That's not possible. I can't go.

H: I'm sorry, Javier. I know the timing of this might not be great for you, but you have to understand the project needs your expertise and we need you in Japan to provide support. You don't have to go for two to three weeks, but you do need to be there by the end of the month. OK?

J: The end of the month?!? That's simply unreasonable. It's far too short notice. No. I can't do it.

H: But Javier, we both know that your expertise is the most relevant in this situation.

J: I'm sorry but I don't think expertise is the deciding factor here. You know everything I do. You should go instead of me. After all, you're the project leader and if the project is late, it's up to you to get it back on track.

H: OK, Javier. I'm sorry it's come to this. Let's take a break and then meet again in the café in … fifteen minutes and see what solution we can find.

J: Yeah. Whatever!

7.02 H = Haruki J = Javier

H: Hi Javier, I'm sorry about earlier. Can we talk?

J: Why, what's the point? It seems to me that the decision has already been made.

H: So what you're saying is you definitely won't go?

J: Well, I still don't think it's necessary for someone to go from here. We can just monitor the situation from here.

H: Yes, we *could* do that, but I think we can both agree that it is always better to offer real-time support in person in situations like this. And there won't be any delays due to time differences. You know we often lose a day just replying to an email.

J: OK, fine. But it doesn't have to be *me* that goes. Why can't Mia or Julio go instead?

H: Maybe, but I know we're both on the same wavelength about their experience. Yours is a lot better, both technically and also in driving local teams to hit productivity targets.

J: In other words, you don't want to send either of them, and still want me to go?

H: Yes, that would be my preference.

J: I see. But it's unreasonably short notice. I have a lot of personal plans in the next month. There are two weddings I have to attend as well as my father's sixtieth birthday.

H: Fine, I see. Well, I understand your position, and reluctance, a bit more now. You usually enjoy travelling and experiencing new countries. I thought you'd jump at this chance when I first mentioned it.

J: That may be true, but Japan? I don't speak Japanese, and being there for a few days' business trip might be OK, but for any length of time, I don't see how I could manage without Japanese.

H: Hmmm.

7.03 J = Javier H = Haruki

J: … And anyway, a business trip of this length and importance would normally be planned months in advance.

H: That may be a fair point, Javier, but the situation is what it is now, and we need to talk about it and work out a way to make sure the project gets back on track.

J: OK. So what do you want to do?

H: So, tell me your overall opinion about this issue the project is facing.

J: Well, I can see that it would help to have someone in Japan to offer support locally. And you're probably right that I'm the best person for the job. But it's just really inconvenient for me at the moment. How long do you have in mind anyway?

H: I don't know. What do you think?

J: I'm not sure. Definitely a few weeks, maybe a month.

H: OK. So from your point of view, it should take around a month of local support. Right?

J: Yes, I should think so.

H: Let's talk through these personal events you have and see what we can work out.

J: OK.

H: Well, let me first check a few of the things you've said.

J: Uh-huh.

H: So you've got two weddings and your father's sixtieth coming up, right?

J: Yes.

H: When are they?

J: Well, the first wedding is at the beginning of next month, on the 2nd, my father's sixtieth is on the 22nd. And the second wedding is a few days later, on the 25th.

H: OK, let's work together and try to find a solution.

J: How can we? You want me to go there for a month.

H: Yes, but of course you won't be there for a full month without a trip home. How about if we postpone your departure by a few days so you can go to the first wedding?

J: OK, that would be really helpful.

H: Good. And I'm open to other suggestions about how we can make the rest of it work for you.

J: Thanks. Well, if I get there by the 5th, that gives me about two and a half weeks before my father's birthday.

H: Right. So what are you suggesting?

J: Well, what if I work really fast and hard and put in some long days, and aim to have them back on track within two and a half weeks, and then I come back home.

H: OK, that works for me. But do you think it's feasible?

J: I'm not sure. I need to look into the exact problems and reasons for the delay more. But I think so. And if they're not ready, I'll go back out around the 27th for another week or so.

H: OK, so what you're saying is you're willing to go back out there after the second wedding if necessary.

J: Yes, I'm only willing to go out there if I can make all three personal events I have coming up. They're really important to me.

H: Sure. But you have to manage your time and tasks for the team in Japan so that they can manage without you there for the week in the middle.

J: OK.

H: And about the language issue. We already have an interpreter based in the local office who is always available to support. And you'll have your own office in the main department so you'll be close to everyone, and also to the General Manager there.

J: That sounds good. Thanks. But it'll be jumping in at the deep end. I really can't speak any Japanese.

H: That's great, Javier. Thanks a lot. I really appreciate your support with this.

J: And er I'll appreciate you remembering this when it comes to my performance review at the end of the year.

H: Ha! Don't worry. I will. This is a good thing that can lead to more opportunities in future. You'll have good visibility with senior management, both here and in Japan.

8.01
My trouble is I'm quite good at a lot of things. When I was studying at school, I didn't know which degree to do. My teacher advised me to follow my passion and study music, but my parents told me to study accountancy because I'm good at maths and I would have a better chance of getting a steady office job. Then my best friend, Piotr, who wanted to be an architect, suggested doing architecture with him so that we could study together. So I decided to go for architecture. The thing is, the first year was awful: it was really challenging and extremely competitive. To top it all, I found out too late that you had to study for ages before you qualified and were expected to work long hours. I was going to drop out of university altogether, but my older brother suggested I swapped subjects and studied for a degree like physics and played my music part-time. But my parents insisted that I should do accountancy.

8.02
It was a tough decision but in the end I took my brother's advice because he knows me best. It was definitely a change for the better. Now, I'm enjoying studying physics and I still get to play in my band at weekends. We're working on our first album and we'll probably have a gig at a festival this summer.

8.03 E = Ethan P = Pranali B = Boon Tek L = Leticia

E: I'm the kind of person who likes to plan everything in advance. I don't like to leave my comfort zone, so I don't like changes. They make me very anxious. So, when my boss told me she was leaving, I was upset. She was a great manager: very encouraging and very reliable. The company didn't replace her for a few months, although

...hey'd promised us that it would be a smooth transition. I hate the feeling of uncertainty, you know? Eventually, management informed us that there wouldn't be a replacement and we had to share out the work in the IT department between us! They told us that we just had to get on with it! Frankly, I'm working long hours every day. I have more responsibility but I'm not getting paid for it. I have to say I'm finding it difficult to cope. To make things worse, nobody cares if you're doing a good job. They tell us we shouldn't be so 'resistant to change'. At this rate, I'm going to have to find a new job, or ask to change departments.

P: My friends tell me I'm a very flexible person and I think I'm pretty good at adapting to change. I just get on with things and I don't mind leaving my comfort zone. However, some changes are obviously more stressful than others, like moving house, or having children. I had been working as a marketing director but suddenly a lot of us were made redundant due to restructuring in the company. That was a major change for me and it came at a bad time because we had just got a mortgage for our house. I was very low and I didn't know what to do with myself for several months. Then my best friend suggested that I reinvent myself – he advised me to get a completely new career and get out of my comfort zone. So I decided to set up my own business as a management consultant! The first year was incredibly difficult but I'm really happy because it's going so well. But I wouldn't have been able to do it if I hadn't had the support of my family and friends at the time.

B: We had to relocate university laboratories to a different city. It was a real upheaval, not well-planned at all. They had not anticipated the risks involved. It was chaotic: we had to move delicate equipment, things got lost, and we were expected to do everything overnight. There was some kind of plan for relocation but they sent it to us too late and there were loads of last minute changes. I could go on and on. Basically, management had not consulted us. I realise change is sometimes necessary, but it's extremely important to have a shared purpose and for everyone to be informed. So, it came as no surprise when students and technicians complained that the new location was in the middle of nowhere, and clients were also annoyed. I have to admit, now that we've settled into the laboratories, I'm able to appreciate we're better off than before. We've got more light and space and the equipment is all up-to-date. It takes time to adapt, doesn't it?

L: I was really looking forward to early retirement and then when it actually happened it was very disappointing. I used to enjoy my work – I was a product manager for household products. I suddenly missed my colleagues and many of my friends were still working, so they didn't have the time to be with me. My husband, Juan, suggested going back to work. He suggested going back to work because I was becoming impossible to live with! It was then that I decided to retrain, so I became a tai-chi instructor. I want to help people cope with stress. In fact, I've already promised my colleagues I'll give classes at my old company! Juan says it's given me a new purpose in life. It's great because I only work part-time and still have time to help look after our grandchildren.

8.04 **P = Presenter A = Alessia**
P: Welcome back everyone. This morning, my first guest is Alessia Russo, a team leader in a major multinational company. She's here to talk to us about brainstorming. Good morning, Alessia.
A: Hi. Thanks for having me.
P: So Alessia, what is brainstorming?
A: Well, it's a process for generating ideas collectively and spontaneously.
P: And why is it useful?
A: Brainstorming generates ideas which other methods do not, due to the freedom it gives people to think creatively.

P: OK. And can you tell our listeners how best to do it? Are there any best practice guidelines for brainstorming?
A: Well, there are no 'golden rules' as such, but these eight stages can definitely help you to have a successful brainstorming meeting.
P: Great. Let's hear them.
A: So, number 1: Define the goal, and 2: Start with a question.
P: Just the one?
A: No, it could be several questions.
P: OK.
A: Number 3: Collect as many ideas as possible, without evaluating them or commenting other than to thank each person for their ideas.
P: OK. Don't evaluate or comment on them.
A: 4: Put all of the ideas somewhere everyone can see them, for example on a board. Then you all decide how to group the ideas.
P: Uh huh.
A: 5: Ask people to give more details about their ideas before evaluating any of them.
P: That's so you don't discount them before you understand the ideas fully, right?
A: Exactly. So, 6: Only at this point should you start to discuss, evaluate and build on the ideas. You will then be able to discard ideas and this will lead to the next step, which is 7: Always end with some clear decisions.
P: Great. Clear action points.
A: And finally, 8: Thank everyone for participating. Even if some individuals didn't come up with the final idea, their presence helped to create the atmosphere that led to the outcome.
P: That's excellent. Thanks very much, Alessia.
A: It's been my pleasure.

8.05 We're here today to address the challenges presented by the fast growth in our organisation. As you know, we've grown from having fifty employees three years ago and largely having a national focus to now having around 200 employees and more and more international clients. These statements highlight the issues we're facing: we still have a very flat hierarchy and people have a lot of autonomy. But we need to introduce some structure in the way we manage our work, our teams and our reporting lines. Let me outline the structure of this brainstorming session before we begin. I'll write up a series of questions around these issues for you to think about. For example, how can we bring more structure and focus to the way we work in teams and across teams without losing flexibility and spontaneity? These opening questions will help us to think about the main challenges ahead. After a phase of collecting ideas, we'll group them on the board here, so we can bring them together. At the end of the session it would be great if we could have a clear idea of some steps we can take. Let's see what progress we can make in 45 minutes. OK? Let's get started ...
Remember, we're going for quantity of ideas here. The key is that we collect as many ideas as we can without judging or criticising them. So, feel free to introduce any idea or make any suggestion you like.

8.06 **S = Sophia M = Marco L = Lisa Sv = Sven**
S: OK, everyone. I can hear that you're all still going strong and coming up with a lot of ideas, but I need us to keep an eye on the timing so I have to stop you there. Can you please come up here with your ideas on the sticky notes and stick them to the board? Can we include them all at this point? And there's no right or wrong way to group them. Just do what you think fits best.
M: OK, thanks, Sophia. Like this here?
L: No, over here. Put that one together with my one. We can start to form groups of topics.
S: Thanks, Lisa. Just so everyone's clear. Let's think about process for a moment. How would you like to group them?

L: Well I was thinking that if we see topics that are similar, we can start to group them together.
M: Sure. That's a good idea.
S: Firstly, thank you all for your ideas. It's great to see so many all grouped like that on the board. I don't want to assume what your ideas mean, so let's discuss them to help me understand your thinking better.
All: Great. / OK. / OK.
S: Can we start with this group here? Whose idea is this one here?
Sv: That's my one.
S: Thanks, Sven. Could you expand on this point for us? What do you mean by 'Daily stand-up'?
Sv: Well, I mean that we could have a short meeting every day with all team members in a particular department. We keep the meeting quick, and do it standing up. Everyone says what they're working on, if they need support, or have capacity to support others. And then we're finished after ten to fifteen minutes. I've seen this done in other companies.
S: That's a really interesting idea, Sven. Thanks. Let's go with that ... and maybe try it out next month.
M: Great, and adding to that idea, we could also update these tasks on the team status board for those who can't make the meeting.
S: Good idea Marco. Let's have a look at some more ... How about this one? Whose is this?
L: That's mine.
S: Thanks, Lisa. So, 'Rotate team leaders'. What does everyone think about that as an option? Does it need further discussion at this point?
Sv: I'm not sure. We tried that before Lisa joined us, so she couldn't have known. It was difficult and didn't really work, though that doesn't mean it won't if we try it again.
L: OK, let's park it for now, Sophia. And Sven, let's meet and you can tell me how it went last time.
Sv: Sure Lisa.

8.07 **S = Sophia M = Marco Sv = Sven L = Lisa**
S: So, we've almost reached forty-five minutes and I'd like to finish on time, as I know you're all busy. It's been a great session. Thanks everyone for your input.
M: Thank you, Sophia. It's been useful to think about these things.
Sv: Yes, thanks.
L: From me too.
S: Great. So to review our main decision, are we all agreed that we're going to try the 'Daily stand-up' idea and also these two other ones over here. We need to research the point about rotating team leadership a bit. Lisa, can you look into this and find some examples of how it can work in practice? Let's also do some further work on this middle group of ideas as a priority. Marco, can you look into that?
M: Sure. Happy to.
S: Great. So let's meet again in two weeks and you can report back on these various actions. I'll send out a calendar invitation.

BW1.01 **J = Johannes M = Martina**
J: Hi Martina, do you have a minute? I wanted to speak to you about some problems I'm having in the Sales Department.
M: Sure, ... I wonder if they are the same problems we are having in Finance.
J: Well, my biggest worry is finding staff to fill some empty positions. I've had over ten interviews and have now contacted some of the local employment agencies but haven't found anyone who matches the job description. On top of that, I'm also concerned about keeping the people I already have. I don't know if you have heard, but Emma is leaving at the end of the month and that is a big problem for the department. I don't know how we are going to replace her and none of the people working for us already are interested in the position.

M: Johannes, I have exactly the same problem. The staff turnover has really increased in the last year – I think we must be doing something wrong. I've lost two of my key people in the last six months and when I hold interviews, candidates don't seem very enthusiastic about working for us. We've even had people leave without giving enough notice as they have found better jobs elsewhere.

J: I think we need to change the way we do things around here. I've got some ideas I would like to discuss with you, if that's OK. Then, maybe we could present them to the board together?

M: Sounds good to me. I've been thinking as well. At my last company one thing we did was to make sure the atmosphere in the departments was positive and supportive. We also did our best to be transparent about decisions when it was possible. Employees today seem to think that's really important.

J: I agree with you Martina. Everyone here works hard so I think we need to find a way to recognise that. It's important that all our employees feel respected and are told when they do a good job. We may even need to set up a proper system for doing this. I know that salaries are important too, but we just can't compete with really large multinational firms. That's why we have to stress the work-life balance that we can offer.

M: You are right. Let's fix a time to talk about this in more detail. But before we do, perhaps we could talk to some of the people in our teams to get their views. What do you think?

J: Good idea. I'll chat with some of my staff this week … you do the same … and then we can compare notes. OK?

M: Perfect!

J: Have a good day.

M: You too.

BW1.02
One
J = Johannes T = Tomasz C = Carolina

J: Hi Carolina, Hi Tomasz. Thanks for making time for this chat. I've arranged it because I'd like to get your views, informally, on a few issues that have come up recently.

T: OK sure, what can we help you with?

J: Well, I am sure you have noticed that a number of people have been leaving the company. We are trying to figure out what the problem is. Tomasz, do you have any ideas?

T: Well … I guess one thing might be the hours, um … although we have flexi-time for office staff, we don't for the field sales teams or in the production area. We try to help out when people have problems with shift work by moving them to different shifts, but it isn't always possible. Flexi-time makes a big difference to people who have to travel a long way to work or for people who have to take their kids to school before they come in. I know there are still some people who aren't happy about their hours though. Carolina, have you heard that, too?

C: Well, yes, but to be honest I hear more complaints about the fact that people feel that they don't earn enough. And then we have a few who complain about meals. The subsidised canteen is a good perk and it's cheap, but there are still a number of people who say the quality of the food isn't very good. Things have improved, though, since we started offering discounts for local restaurants and a lot of people seem willing to pay a bit more for their meals. What else? Can you think of anything else, Tomasz?

T: Yes. Some of the newer staff like me find that it can be difficult to work with other departments. I get the feeling my ideas are not always taken seriously. But it seems that people who have been here a long time don't have that problem. I'm not sure what I'm doing wrong.

J: I'm very sorry to hear that Tomasz. Anything else?

T: Ah … yes … Emma told me that one reason she was leaving was that she felt she didn't get support to help her develop her career and move to a better position.

C: Yes, I've heard this as well from a few colleagues. They said they didn't feel the courses we offer were very helpful and felt we should make sure all staff got the training and development they needed for their jobs … and for future careers too.

J: That's a really interesting point. We have a number of courses and training options but perhaps we need to see what improvements we can make. Some of our courses are very popular but maybe we need to find out why some people aren't happy with the programme. Well, thanks both of you for your input. I'll think about what you've told me and see what we can do about the issues.

C: Thanks for listening to us, Johannes. It's good to be involved.

T: Yes, absolutely.

Two
M = Martina S = Sirina A = Andy

M: Good morning, both of you. Come in, make yourselves comfortable. Now, there's nothing to worry about. I've called you in because … well, I am sure you have noticed that several people have been leaving the company …

S: Yes, we have, Martina. I think everyone has!

M: Yes, it's unfortunate, and I'd like to ask you some questions about why it might be happening … so we can address any issues. Please, you can speak freely.

S: OK, well, for one thing, I don't understand why we need to dress so formally when we're in the office and not meeting customers. Buying business clothes is expensive especially for junior staff. Andy, what do you think?

A: Well, I can see that might be a problem but I don't think it's the main issue. I have more of a problem with the other members in our department. Each person is just interested in their own job and they don't seem to want to work together, or collaborate very much. People don't socialise either, not even to get a coffee or have lunch together.

M: Thanks Andy, I have noticed that as well. We certainly need to do something about the lack of team spirit. Sirina, do you have anything to add?

S: Yes, I would also like to say that I prefer to be independent and organise my day as I think best. I find it very hard to work when someone else tells me what to do and when to do it, but that seems to be the culture here. I have been here long enough to know what needs to be done and always finish my work on time – I should be trusted by now. Do you agree, Andy?

A: That hasn't been a problem for me personally, but I have heard other people in the office say similar things. There is another thing though, I seem to spend a lot of my salary on my monthly train ticket. It would be good if the company could help me out somehow with a discounted travel card for the train or bus – I got that in my last company. And on that subject, the amount we get for fuel when we use our cars for business really isn't enough. Sorry, er one more thing! As I spend most of my day sitting, I would also really appreciate something like subsidised gym membership which would make it cheaper for us and offer discounts for activities that we could do after work or on weekends. We do get some vouchers but they're not very interesting for me.

S: And, Martina, my last company rewarded us with a bonus when we reached our goals or when the company did really well. I think that can be very motivating for staff – money isn't everything, I know, but a little extra to say 'well done' sometimes would be great. At the moment only management and some people in certain departments get bonuses, which I have heard are fairly small. But I really think we need a bonus scheme that includes everyone.

M: OK, well thank you for all of that! It sounds as if we have a lot to think about, but that's been really helpful. Perhaps a good next step would be to put together a survey for staff. I imagine we'll be asking you for more information soon!

S: Good idea.

A: Course, happy to help!

BW2.01 K = Karen A = Akito F = Frederik V = Victoria

K: Hi everyone, it's Karen here. I know for some of you it's very early or very late so thank you for making the time. How is everyone?

All: Fine. / OK. / Good, thanks.

K: Great. So first, I want to say I appreciate the feedback you've sent me over the last few months. It's been really helpful. Based on that, I'd like to discuss the difficulties we seem to be having with training and development worldwide. After reading your reports it's becoming clear that we have different problems in different regions and I'd like to talk to you about some ideas for how to solve this. Akito, I know you've had concerns about what's happening in Asia. Er, can you give us some more details?

A: Thanks for asking, Karen. We've tried several different programmes but they don't seem to be very successful. There are aspects of the business that work very well but we need more support in others in order to help our staff do their jobs well. They don't feel that the training we offered them is practical enough to help them in their day to day work. I would be very happy to get some help with this problem.

K: Thanks Akito, we definitely need to work on that. Frederik, you also mentioned that we need to find new training options in Europe, is that right?

F: Absolutely. We are having problems making training both interesting and cost-effective. Our courses cost us quite a lot of money but are not showing the results we'd hoped for. Staff also complain that they last too long which makes it difficult for them to keep up with their workload. From what we've seen the results have not been very positive so it seems to us that it's not worth spending so much on these training sessions.

K: Thanks Frederik, that's certainly something we need to look at carefully, too. Now, Victoria, would you like to add anything about South America here?

V: Well, at the moment we keep trying to interest our staff in the programmes we have but most of them just don't want to take part or drop out before they're over. They're so busy with other things and don't seem interested in spending more time at the office. Our courses have been voluntary but we often have to cancel them because so few employees sign up for them.

K: Well, thanks for the information – that's not terribly good news! Now, I have an idea about setting up global e-learning or blended-learning courses which include both online and face-to-face elements but I need your input on what exactly the staff in your area feel they need to work on. I'd say that we can teach information about the products online. However, when we teach a skill like customer service or rapport, I mean understanding another person and their point of view, we need to do this in person. Can each of you do some more research and then put together a short report for me? Then we can meet again to start working on this concept. How does that sound?

All: Good. / Great. / Good.

K: Can you get me these reports within the next two weeks? I'll then send you some ideas and we'll set up another call to discuss them.

V: Sounds like a good idea. I'll get on it right away.

F: Yes, I agree.

K: OK with you as well, Akito?

A: Of course, I'll start as soon as we finish the call.

K: Great, glad we all agree on this. And now, I'd like to go on to the second point on our agenda, our …

BW3.01 H = Hannah J = Jo A = Alex

H: Eh, morning everyone. First thing on the agenda this morning is the information sheet we need to produce for the local university business school … about what venture capital companies do and how we do it.

J: That's for the lecture they want us to do about

...C investment, right?

: Yep, and we're offering two student ...acements in our organisation next year.

: Oh right, I'd forgotten about that. We'd better ...raft something out quickly though, 'cause we ...eed to talk about new investments today.

H: Don't stress, Alex! This shouldn't take too long. Come on … do you want to start?

A: OK, well, I think we need to remind the students why we exist and not to believe all the bad press ...ve get, especially when we invest in established ...ompanies.

J: You mean the stories about asset-stripping and ...not caring about the future of employees?

A: Absolutely. We need to dispel that idea ...immediately and show that we can also be a force for good in the economy.

H: That's a good point. We should make the point that we are often the last resort for good businesses who've been turned down by traditional lenders.

A: Exactly. And also that we're giving them much more than money: that we also provide experience, advice and contacts. We should give examples to show how many successful companies today wouldn't be here if a venture capital company hadn't got involved.

J: Too right. Where would companies like Google have been without its VC backers?

H: To name but one. OK, so the next thing we need to explain is how we choose the companies we invest in. How do we know they're going to succeed?

A: Well, of course, we don't, do we?

H: Precisely but we do our best to limit the risk by checking them out as thoroughly as we can.

BW3.02 J = Jo H = Hannah A = Alex

J: It'd be a good idea to have some sort of guide about what to look for when considering how to invest – that we can hand out at the lecture.

H: Good idea. Well … I think we'd all agree that the most important thing is the management of the company.

J&A: Yeah.

J: People often think we only look at the financials. Of course the figures are really important but they're one dimensional and won't really tell us if the company is going to be successful in the future.

A: A company won't succeed without good leaders. We need to know that the management team will be capable of carrying out the business plan successfully.

H: That's right, the whole management team must have relevant experience with a good track record.

J: And if it doesn't, the company needs to recognise that and be ready to recruit managers from outside the organisation.

A: So true – do you remember that great little company last year we looked at? The CEO was also the founder and his ideas were fantastic but he flatly refused to take our advice to employ outside experienced managers. That could be an example of a situation where we decided not to invest.

H: And he went bankrupt six months later, didn't he? We could've turned that business into something remarkable.

J: But because we did our checks, we didn't waste our time fighting a losing battle with the CEO.

A: Such a shame! It was an amazing idea and shouldn't've failed.

J: And that's the next thing - the product or service itself has to have a competitive edge. It's got to have legs and not be a short-lived wonder.

H: Yes, we like the ideas that can solve real-life problems in a cost-effective way and which can generate sales before the competitors have realised what's happening.

A: That's why we've got to study the market carefully. Is the business targeting the right market and is the market big enough to generate millions so that we get the returns we need on our investment?

H: Or even billions.

A: Ideally, yes. So the business plan must have a detailed market analysis.

J: And finally don't forget the risk assessment. Obviously it's our job to take on risky businesses, that's why we need to do due diligence and evaluate potential problems, such as legal issues.

H: Yes, and it's important to ensure that there's a foreseeable exit from the business so that we can see the return on our investment.

J: And that the funding we offer must be enough to take the business to the level we expect it to reach.

H: That sounds great Jo. Can you draft out the document for the next meeting?

J: No problem.

H: Alex, can you outline our lecture?

A: Leave it to me.

H: Thanks. OK, now let's move on to the new investment opportunities …

ExtBW3.01

As you can see from this pie chart here, our biggest export market is India, where around 60% of all sales revenues are generated. Our second most important export market is North America, which generates 25% of all sales revenues for the company. This is growing and should be nearer 30% next year. The final two sections of the pie chart are 10% for Europe and 5% from Australia.

ExtBW3.02

Now let's look at the sales figures month on month compared to last year. In January total revenues were 5.6 million dollars, 6% up on the same time last year and more than we expected. Unfortunately, there were problems in February and sales fell by 1.52 million dollars to 4.08 million. This was because of supply problems and transport strikes. March saw an upturn in sales which reached 6.4 million, right on target and April was even better when sales soared to 8.75 million. This is mainly due to the launch of the new product line, which has proved to be very popular. During the next three months sales rose steadily to reach 10.8 million in July and then in August they went up to 12 million. September saw sales slow a little and in October, revenues once again returned to the August level. In November and December revenues increased by 2.1 and 2.5 million to reach 14.1 and 16.6 respectively so the year ended on a high as we surpassed our annual target.

BW4.01

1 This is Matteo Blinksmann. I want to complain about one of your robots: the security guard. I've just been pushed over by it and then it grabbed me by the arm to stop me getting up. It also shouted at me and told me to get out of the hall. This robot needs to be stopped.

2 Mr Hideaki Egami here. That's E-G-A-M-I. I've just checked in with your receptionist robot, Mayumi, and er I must tell you that her Japanese skills are terrible. I won't tell you what she said but I was extremely offended by it. I think you need to look at the programme again. I'm happy to meet you in person to discuss the problem.

3 Hi, Mark Steadman here. Er, just thought you should know that although the coffee robot, Bob, is fantastic and makes the best coffee I've ever tasted, unfortunately he managed to spill hot coffee over me and ruined my suit jacket. He said sorry but it could have been really dangerous. As it is, I'll need to have the jacket cleaned as soon as possible. As I say, he did apologise profusely for the accident, so er good speaking skills I guess!

4 Hello this is Wei Ling. I must complain about your security robot. He's completely mad. He confiscated my bag when I went in to a presentation and wouldn't let it go. He seems to be rather over-enthusiastic. He has now walked away with my bag and refused to let me have it. I don't want to miss the presentation and now I have to follow the robot because my laptop is in it.

5 Sarah Buchanan. Your robot café is a total disaster. What a stupid idea. The food was good but there were some problems with serving it. The idiot robot managed to drop my plate on the floor and the food went over my very new and expensive shoes. I demand compensation immediately and that you put real people in as waiters.

6 This is Aleksander Baron. I think you ought to know that the driver robot, Oskar, took me to the wrong destination three times. You've got some problems with him. I thought at first it was my accent that he didn't understand, but this seems to have happened to quite a few other people too, not just me.

BW5.01 C = Clara F = Felipe J = Juliana D = Diego

C: Hello everyone. I'm Clara and I'll be here for the next six months in the HR Department. I'm really pleased you could all make it here today in person. There are several issues we're dealing with at the moment and I'd very much like to get your feedback on them. Felipe, I believe you're one of the regional managers, right?

F: Yes, I manage staff in some of the northern areas of the country.

C: Uh huh and Juliana, you're also a regional manager but in the south I believe?

J: Yes, that's right.

C: Diego, great to have you with us. I really feel that a good working relationship with the union is vital when we deal with issues around performance and rewards.

D: Thanks for inviting me. I'd also like to find ways to work together on this.

C: Well, let me start with the background. As you all know, the field of renewable energy needs to stay up-to-date and innovative. In the past we always found recent university graduates to be the ones who can best help us reach these goals. However, it seems now that the grads we hire don't stay very long, which is a problem for us. On the one hand, we need people we can rely on to take ideas forward, but on the other hand, we are not happy about them taking what they have learnt about the business to our competition. That's why we need to discuss this problem and brainstorm some ideas. What do you say, Diego?

D: I agree, Clara. The problem for young staff is that they expect to be treated differently than the people we hired even ten years ago. Many of them wait longer to rent or buy their own apartments. That means that they often don't have the pressure of high living costs so if they aren't happy they go elsewhere. In many cases, the work–life balance is also more important for them than lifelong employment or spending hours at work to get ahead. Have you seen this as well?

J: Absolutely. Many of the expectations they talk about in their entry interviews never used to come up so are a bit surprising to hear. Some of them may be viable but I think we need to discuss these carefully and think about them before we start making major changes. What do you say Felipe?

F: I agree as well. I've been in the business a long time and years ago people were just happy to have a job. Today, young people see things very differently. They want time for families, friends, hobbies and seem to forget that they are just at the start of their careers. I think they need to put in a few years before they can ask for certain things. Some benefits they mention are ones we haven't even considered and others are not the ones we usually offer to employees who are just starting out. As Juliana mentioned however, some of these could be put into practice and some would be impossible to do. Clara, how would you like to take this forward?

C: I am mostly concerned about the reputation of the company, which is another reason I called this meeting. If we change things too quickly, it could have a negative effect on how we are viewed in the business community. This could really hurt us in the future. I also don't think it's fair to those employees who've been with us for many years to suddenly change the way we measure performance. Nevertheless, I also think that we need to take this situation seriously.

F: Mm hmm, what do you suggest?

C: Well, you're all going to be here at head office for a couple of days. How about if each of us thinks about this and notes down which particular changes might be necessary? I'd also like to think about how we can look at goals to make them measurable so that we can decide how and when to reward performance. Does that make sense?

D: Interesting idea. I suspect that we may have very different ideas.

J: Yes, we probably will, but it seems like a good way to approach this. What do you think, Felipe?

F: Let's give it a try.

C: Thanks everyone. So, let's meet again tomorrow morning and see what we've come up with. I'll put something in our calendars …

BW5.02 C = Clara J = Juliana D = Diego F = Felipe

C: Good morning everyone. How are you doing?

J: Fine.

D: Glad to be here.

F: Fine, thanks.

C: Great. Coffee, anyone?

J: I'd love some.

F: Yes please. Thanks Clara.

C: So, if everyone is set, let's get started. I'm really looking forward to hearing the ideas you've come up with. Juliana, do you want to begin?

J: Sure. Um, this was really an interesting exercise. I did some research and some thinking and have a couple of suggestions. First of all, as you know we have a number of projects which we assign to different groups of people. So far, we have mostly looked at whether or not they were completed on time but I think what we are missing is a quality check. We need to see if the projects meet the goals that were set and if the project teams are submitting follow-up reports that are clear and well written.

C: Good idea. Would these be checked by the bosses in the departments?

J: Yes, or even at the regional level. The goals also need to be monitored and those who manage to finish on time and deliver the quality we are looking for could be next in line for pay rises or even promotions.

D: Even if they haven't been with the company very long?

J: Er actually, the projects I'm thinking of normally take some time to complete but yes, it could include those who have recently joined us. I think it could be very motivating for staff.

C: I think it's worth trying, Juliana. Felipe, what do you think?

F: Sounds good to me. I'm curious about how it will work in practice.

C: Me too, but I like the idea. Er, and Felipe, what's your suggestion?

F: I was thinking of something like 360 degree feedback so that they get feedback from different people they work with. A survey of our business partners and clients could help us find out how staff are performing. We shouldn't forget that personal relationships are also necessary to our business and we need people who work well with others.

C: Great idea, Felipe. This is certainly something we can try. Er, Diego, any comments from you?

D: As I represent the workers here, I think anything we do has to take their needs into account. In the research I did, I found a number of articles that say it's important for employees to see a connection between their personal work goals and the overall goals of the company. I think we need to be more transparent and let everyone know what we are trying to achieve. Then we need to find ways to show staff how their jobs and tasks support our overall strategies. This might mean looking again

at the company's key performance indicators and making them clear to everyone.

C: Good idea. Thanks, Diego.

D: Glad to help.

C: Does anyone else have any comments to make?

F: Not at the moment.

J: No, it's all clear to me.

C: Then I think we can wrap this up. We've made a good start this morning, thanks everyone. I would suggest that we make sure that all staff meet regularly with their line managers to discuss what they're working on. Then they could talk about any problems they might have and any suggestions they have to improve the process. Do please send me any other ideas you have so that we can discuss them next time. Have a good day everyone.

BW5.03 C = Clara D = Diego

C: Diego, I thought it would be helpful to speak to you alone about some of the expectations that our new employees have. I understand you've been in touch with the interviewers as well as employees who've been with us only a few years so I guess you've been hearing quite a bit about what they feel they need. So, what can you tell me?

D: Well, first of all, our younger workers are frustrated by the length of time it takes to get promoted. Many of them feel that they are bringing in fresh and important ideas to drive the business and then they feel left out when promotions are announced. These always seem to go to people who have been with us a long time, no matter whether or not they are really contributing to the business.

C: I see. I've heard this as well. Is it the same problem with pay rises and bonuses?

D: Yes, if the promotion comes with an automatic pay rise. The bonuses seem to be less of a problem as we have given bonuses for ideas to younger staff. They find that to be very motivating and I would suggest we continue doing that.

C: I agree. In a business like ours, we are dependent on these new and innovative ideas and they are worth paying for. Anything else?

D: I've been hearing from younger staff that they aren't very happy that parking isn't provided if they drive to work and we don't offer any subsidised public transport tickets. They see that older staff members have their own free parking spaces and they don't understand why they are treated differently. Some of them have also mentioned the fact that they work a lot of hours and feel that discounts to a gym or even a free fitness facility on site would be greatly appreciated.

C: Mm interesting, I'll look into the gym discounts and the fitness facility although I can't promise anything. Free parking is another matter, however. As you know, we have limited space for cars in many of our locations and this is a privilege we have given to staff based on length of service. But perhaps we can do something about subsidies for those using public transport.

D: As long as we're discussing this, I'd like to just mention some of the other things I've heard from junior staff.

C: Yes, please.

D: There have been complaints about doing overtime as this means they work many hours in the week. They would either like to see overtime pay increased or get time off to make up for it. Younger staff members also feel that pay rises are not regular enough, they'd like more career skills seminars or other skills training sessions to help them with their day-to-day jobs, a limit on the number of business trips they need to take, flexible hours, and more social events to get to know their colleagues. Many of them said they are happy about the bonus system we have in place which rewards ideas and not just goals but they feel that we could do more to keep them happy.

C: Thanks, Diego. This is really helpful. I will have to think about this and get back to you when I have more information.

BW6.01 P = Presenter R = Reporter

P: One of the success stories out of Africa recently has been that of Josef Ndege, who's built a successful construction business with strong ethical principles. He's famous for his charity work and support of the underprivileged in his country. However, recent newspaper reports claim that funds destined for educational purposes have disappeared and found their way into local businessmen's pockets. This kind of corruption is something that Mr Ndege has strongly criticised all his working life. So, to understand the situation better, I've been talking to a local journalist, Precious Otieno.

R: Yes, thank you. I've now spoken to several people involved with Mr Ndege. One was Eunice Mazula, who is CEO of an educational charity here called HappyEd, which Mr Ndege has supported for many years. Ms Mazula pointed out to me that they have managed to build several schools and give thousands of children an education and that many of these children wouldn't have had an education without the funding from Mr Ndege.

P: And has everyone you've spoken to been so positive about Mr Ndege, Precious?

R: No, absolutely not. I also spoke to two of AFhomes employees about their experience working for the company, Julius and Nkomo.

Julius has worked for AFhomes for ten years. He began by saying that the company had always paid staff well and looked after their families. However, two months ago he was transferred to the Dodoma project and, since then, he hasn't been paid and is naturally becoming very worried.

Nkomo is employed as a carpenter by AFhomes working on the houses here in Dodoma. He claims that the work site isn't safe and that there have been several accidents. The company also promised to pay for his kids to go to school, but he hasn't received anything they promised so far. Like many others though, Nkomo can't leave because he needs the job and the money.

P: Aha, so a mixed picture locally. And I think you've also received a statement from the Land Conservation Agency, is that right?

R: Yes, the Land Conservation Agency has been very quick to support Mr Ndege and their joint partnership. Their statement says that despite recent negative press reports, they would like to assure the public that their involvement in the Dodoma project was agreed because they believe that this is the best way of protecting our environment and wildlife for future generations. Furthermore, they have every confidence in Mr Ndege, whose actions have always been above board and ethical and they believe that any investigation will bear this out.

P: And breaking news is just coming in. Apparently the AFhomes' Dodoma project has been closed down while the government investigates accusations of wrongdoing and unethical business practices. This is a severe blow for Josef Ndege, the flag bearer for ethical business in Africa.

BW7.01 R = Rahul D = Divya V = Varinder A = Aarav

R: Thanks everyone for joining us today on this call. As I'm out of the office for the next week, it seemed the best way for us to go over the final details for the trade fair called 'Games and toys for all' which is taking place in Hong Kong next week. Divya, I guess you have been arranging most of the details, is that right?

D: Yes, I have, with the help of my staff. As you all know, it's a four-day fair from Tuesday to Friday. Varinder and Aarav, are you clear on the arrangements for flights and hotels?

V: Yes, a staff member and I are flying on Sunday and one more from the marketing department is joining us on Monday. The centre will be open on Monday so that we can set up our stand. Those of us flying on Sunday will be working on this. Aarav, I think some of your staff from the product

...evelopment department will also be there then, is ...nat right?

...: Absolutely. Some of the toys are still in the ...evelopment phase so we wanted to make sure ...ney were displayed correctly at the stand. I have ...wo staff members coming with me on Sunday and ...nother one joining us on Monday. How many are ...oming from sales, Divya?

...): I am going myself, of course, and bringing four ...taff members with me. We are leaving here very ...arly on Monday and arriving early afternoon. We'll ...go to the hotel and then come by the centre to see ...now everything is going.

...V: Sounds good. So Rahul, just to confirm – all the ...travel plans have been approved, right?

...R: Yes, all taken care of. And you are all returning ...on Saturday when the fair is over. Some are on ...the early flight and those who need to take down ...the stand will be on the late afternoon one. We have arranged with the hotel for single rooms for five people from Sunday to Saturday and for an additional seven from Monday to Saturday. Unfortunately, I will be abroad at this time but I am sure you will all manage wonderfully. Thanks everyone for your time this morning. Could we set up another short call tomorrow morning to discuss any other last minute details that may come up? I would also like to have some time to talk about what you are hoping to get out of the trade fair. Is that OK with everyone?

D, V, A: Fine. / Sure. / Fine.

R: Great, till tomorrow then.

BW7.02 R = Rahul D = Divya V = Varinder
A = Aarav

R: Good morning everyone. Is everything still going smoothly? Has anything else come up that we need to deal with urgently?

D, V, A: No. / Everything's fine. No problems.

R: Now this is a really important event for us as it is the first time we are doing something like this. Now that you have all had time to plan the practicalities, I would like to know more about your goals in attending and how these can help us in the future to be more efficient and successful. Divya, can you fill us in on what the sales department hopes to achieve there?

D: I hope we will be able to come back from this trade fair with some sales contracts. I have heard there will be a number of buyers from large retail chains there. We need to have staff who can convince them to sell our products in all their stores. Contracts should be prepared and brought along so that buyers can sign up on the spot. This will also save us time later as we won't need to contact so many retailers.

R: That sounds very sensible. So are your staff working on the contracts?

D: Yes, they are. They are also putting together lists of some of the retail chains who will be represented there.

R: Thanks, Divya. And Varinder, what about the marketing department? What are your main goals?

V: In my opinion, we need to be looking into marketing our company and creating a network of people who know about us. We have sent out invitations to buyers to come to our stand, and we're organising a raffle, some vouchers for our visitors, and an event we can invite them to. The stand also has to have a place for us to sit and talk to visitors and where we can have some catering. Making sure we get our message out will be a time-saver in the future and help us achieve a successful image as we will have the chance to reach so many people at this fair.

R: That all sounds very positive, Varinder. Thanks. And Aarav, what about product development?

A: Mm, I would like to take the chance to talk to buyers who come to the stand and get feedback from them. I think this is an excellent opportunity to find out what is in demand in the market, informally, before we start work on our new product lines. It will help us to know what direction we should take. When we have an idea, we never know for sure if it will sell or not. This way we don't need to spend time manufacturing a product that the retailers are not interested in, giving us the chance to be successful from the beginning with product launches.

R: Excellent. It sounds like you all have this under control. I'm looking forward to reading your reports when you return. Have a good trip everyone. I'm going to be quite tied up for the next few days, but just send me an email or leave a voicemail if you have any problems or need anything from me. I'll get back to you as soon as I can.

BW7.03 R = Rahul D = Divya A = Aarav
V = Varinder

D: Rahul, this is Divya. Who's organising the kick-off meeting? Will it be here or in Hong Kong? And what about the daily meetings there? Who's in charge of them? I'm getting nervous as I really think we need a plan! Who should be doing what?

A: Rahul, this is Aarav. I really need to talk to you about the sales contracts Divya wants to prepare for the fair. They are totally different from anything we've done so far and I don't think they are appropriate for our purposes. I think we need to discuss this. And I also want to talk to you as she keeps bothering my staff. I've asked her to stop but she doesn't listen to me.

D: Rahul, it's Divya again! The contracts we agreed on aren't finished and I need to take them along for clients to sign at the fair. And Aarav is being rather difficult about all this and I don't understand the problem. Can you do something?!

V: Rahul, this is Varinder. We need to get those tickets out to our major clients. Do you have the list for me? And are we also giving them vouchers for some of our toys? Oh ... and has the website been updated? And what about the raffle we discussed? Was a decision made about that? And today I heard the stand has to be smaller, which affects our catering. Can you let me know what to do? This is really urgent!

V: Rahul, it's Varinder here again. We just got a call from the hotel and they don't have enough single rooms. We may have to find another hotel and I would need to start looking immediately! What do you think we should do? Can you let me know as soon as you can?

A: Rahul, it's Aarav. The courier service we hired to get all the samples and materials to the fair can't get into the Hong Kong Fair Centre because they don't have the correct paperwork with them. What should I do? Is there someone I need to phone who can take care of this?

D: Hi Rahul, it's Divya. I'm at the airport with the sales team and we've just found out that our flight has been cancelled. Can we rebook another flight right away? Is it OK if I do that or do I need to contact our travel department? This is really urgent! Thanks. Please call me when you get this message.

BW8.01

A: Eh, have you heard about the takeover?

B: Yeah, I read it in the newspaper. Why weren't we told? Osbruk's a terrible company to work for. I've got a friend who said that they have a ridiculous attendance policy. If he's just two minutes late for work, even if it's not his fault, he gets a warning. Can you imagine that? At least here, the managers respect us and we respect them so they trust us.

A: I know, I think our business culture is very different from Osbruk-Basri's. I also heard that they make you work overtime most days without paying you extra.

C: But that's illegal, isn't it?

B: Well apparently there's something in the contract that says they can do that.

C: I don't like the sound of this company at all. What're we going to do?

A: I can't understand why Ms Khan didn't tell us about this. She wouldn't do anything that would damage the company, would she?

C: She didn't say anything because she knows we'd be unhappy. If things get bad, I'll move back to Australia.

B: I bet we'll all lose our jobs. Every time OB takes a company over, they get rid of everyone. They're all about the bottom line. They don't care about the staff.

A: That's why I am so surprised. We've always been looked after well here. We're like a family. The company is doing well, isn't it?

C: I think so. But I know we need a bigger factory for the new export orders. Maybe this is the only way Chillhot can afford to expand.

B: What, by selling us out to Osbruk-Basri? That's not Ms Khan's style. She wouldn't do this, surely?

C: Anyway, do you always believe everything you read in the newspaper?

A: No, but why would they write it if it wasn't true? I don't want to work for a company that doesn't care about its employees at all.

C: Well I think we need to have a meeting with the boss and find out why she didn't tell us.

P6.02

1 Salvador Fidalgo | is our 'Hero of the month' | for his work on our local community programme. | He has formed and coached | a football team of local teenagers | and the youngsters have done so well | that they have just won a regional football competition. | Salvador says he has had such a rewarding time | working with these youngsters, | that he is going to start a second team.

2 Salvador Fidalgo is our 'Hero of the month' for his work on our local community programme. | He has formed and coached a football team of local teenagers | and the youngsters have done so well that they have just won a regional football competition. | Salvador says he has had such a rewarding time working with these youngsters, that he is going to start a second team.

- **adjective** (*adj.*) Headwords for adjectives followed by information in square brackets, e.g. [only before a noun] and [not before a noun], show any restrictions on where they can be used.
- **noun** (*n.*) The codes [C] and [U] show whether a noun, or a particular sense of a noun, is countable (*a customer, two customers*) or uncountable (*authority, autonomy*).
- **verb** (*v.*) The forms of irregular verbs are given after the headword. The codes [I] (intransitive) and [T] (transitive) show whether a verb, or a particular sense of a verb, has or does not have an object. Phrasal verbs (*phr. v.*) are shown after the verb they are related to.
- Some entries show information on words that are related to the headword. Adverbs (*adv.*) are often shown in this way after adjectives.
- **region labels** The codes *AmE* and *BrE* show whether a word or sense of a word is used only in American or British English.

accountability *n.* [U] the ability to be held responsible for the effects of your actions, and to explain or be criticised for them

achieve *v.* [T] to successfully do what you wanted or tried to do

achievement *n.* [C, U] something that you succeed in doing by your own efforts, or the fact of doing something you wanted or tried to do

acknowledge *v.* [T] **1** to notice and publicly say how good or important someone or something is
2 to show someone that you have noticed them or heard what they have said

active listening *n.* [U] the process of paying attention to what someone is saying, showing that you are listening, and asking questions or repeating what they have said in different words in order to make sure you understand

adapt *v.* [I, T] to gradually change your behaviour and attitudes in order to be successful in a new situation

address *v.* [T] to deal with or solve something

advance *v.* [I] to move up to a more responsible position in a company

advancement *n.* [C, U] progress or development in your job, such as moving up to a more responsible position

agile *adj.* able to change quickly and do things differently when necessary because of customer demands, changes in the market, etc.

allegation *n.* [C] a statement that someone has done something wrong or illegal, but that has not been proved

allocate *v.* [T] to use something for a particular purpose, give something to a particular person, etc., especially after an official decision has been made

analyse (*also* **analyze** *AmE*) *v.* [T] to examine or think about something carefully, in order to understand it

analysis *n.* (*plural* **analyses**) [C, U] a careful examination of something in order to understand it better

analyst *n.* [C] someone who is a specialist in a particular subject, market, industry, etc. and examines information relating to it in order to give their views about what will happen or should be done

analytical *adj.* thinking about things in a detailed and intelligent way, so that you can examine and understand things

analytics *n.* [singular or plural] **1** the practice of using computer software to carefully examine data
2 the information produced by carefully examining data, especially using computer software

announce *v.* [T] to officially tell people about something, especially about a plan or a decision

announcement *n.* [C] an important or official statement

anticipate *v.* [T] to expect that something will happen and be ready for it

appraisal *n.* [C] a meeting between a manager and an employee to discuss the quality of the employee's work and how well they do their job

appraise *v.* [T] to decide how well an employee is doing their work, usually after discussing with the employee how well they have performed during the past year

appreciate *v.* [T] to understand that something is serious or important, or to understand what someone's feelings are

apprehension *n.* [C, U] anxiety about the future, especially about dealing with something unpleasant or difficult

apprehensive *adj.* worried or nervous about something that you are going to do, or about the future

aptitude *n.* [C, U] the natural ability to do a particular activity or job

arise *v.* (*past tense* **arose**, *past participle* **arisen**) [I] if a problem or difficult situation arises, it begins to happen

artificial intelligence *n.* [U] (*abbreviation* **AI**) the ability of a computer to do intelligent things that people can do, such as think and make decisions

aspect *n.* [C] one part of a situation, idea, plan, etc. that has many parts

assessment *n.* [C, U] a process in which you make a judgment about a person or situation, or the judgment you make

asset-stripping *n.* [U] the practice of buying a company cheaply and then selling all the things or businesses it owns to make a quick profit—used to show disapproval

assure *v.* [T] to tell someone that something will definitely happen or is definitely true so that they are less worried

atmosphere *n.* [C, U] the feeling that an event or place gives you

auditor *n.* [C] someone whose job is to officially examine a company's financial records

authority *n.* [U] the power that a person or organisation has because of their official or legal position

autonomy *n.* [U] the ability or opportunity to make your own decisions without being controlled by anyone else

average *n.* [C] the amount you get when you add together several amounts and then divide by the number of amounts

awareness *n.* [U] knowledge or understanding of a particular subject or situation

backfire *v.* [I] to have the opposite effect to the one you intended

bail somebody/something ↔ **out** *phr. v.* to provide money to get a person or organisation out of financial trouble

bailout *n.* [C] money that is provided to a person or organisation to get them out of financial trouble, or the process of providing this money

bank *v.* [I always + adv./prep.] to keep your money in a particular bank

banker *n.* [C] someone who works in the management of a bank

bankrupt *adj.* **go bankrupt** to no longer have enough money to pay what you owe

bankruptcy *n.* (*plural* **bankruptcies**) [C, U] the state of being unable to pay your debts

benchmarking *n.* [U] the process of comparing one thing or action to another or to a standard, so that you can judge or measure it

benefit¹ *n.* **1** [C usually plural] something, especially money, that you get in addition to your pay
2 [C] a good effect or advantage that something has, for example a product or service

benefit² *v.* [I, T] if you benefit from something, or it benefits you, it gives you an advantage, improves your life or helps you in some way

blended learning *n.* [U] a way of teaching students that uses both online lessons and lessons taught by a teacher

bonus *n.* [C] an extra amount of money added to an employee's wages, usually as a reward for doing difficult or good work

boom *v.* [I] to be very successful and grow very quickly

boost *v.* [T] to increase or improve something and make it more successful

bottom line *n.* [C usually singular] **1** the figure showing a company's total profit or loss
2 the end result of something or the most important point about something

bottom-line *adj.* relating to the total profits or losses that a business makes

brainstorm *v.* [I, T] to suggest a lot of ideas for an activity or for solving a problem, especially during a discussion or meeting with other people

brainstorming *n.* [U] the process of suggesting a lot of ideas for an activity or for solving a problem, especially during a meeting or discussion with other people

brave new world a situation or a way of doing something that is new and exciting and meant to improve people's lives

budget¹ *n.* [C] the money that is available to an organization or person, or a plan of how it will be spent
be over budget spend more than you have planned to spend on a particular project or activity in a set period of time

budget² *v.* [I, T] to carefully plan and control how much you spend

business casual *n.* [U] clothes that are not formal but that are suitable for wearing while working in an office

call (something) into question to make people uncertain about whether something is right, good or true

campaign *v.* [I] to lead or take part in a series of actions intended to achieve a particular social or political result

campaign *n.* [C] a series of actions intended to achieve something or persuade people to do something

capability *n.* (*plural* **capabilities**) [C] the ability or power that makes someone or something able to do something

capital expenditure *n.* [C, U] the money a company spends on buildings, machinery, equipment, etc., or the process of spending the money

carbon emissions *n.* [C usually plural] the gases that are sent into the air when petrol, oil, coal, etc. are burned for fuel

cash flow *n.* [singular, U] the movement of money coming into a business as income and going out as wages, materials, etc.

cater *v.* [I, T] to provide and serve food and drinks at a party, meeting etc, usually as a business

centred, -centred *adj.* (*also* **centered** *AmE*) [only after noun] having a particular person or group as the most important part or focus of something

charity *n.* (*plural* **charities**) [C] an organisation that gives money, goods or help to people who are poor, sick, etc.

circumstances *n.* [plural] events or facts that affect a situation

clarification *n.* [C, U] the act of making something clearer or easier to understand, or an explanation that makes something clearer

clarify *v.* (**clarified, clarifying, clarifies**) [T] to make something clearer or easier to understand

climb *v.* [I] to increase in number, amount or level

close a deal/sale to reach the point in a deal or sale where everyone involved agrees to it

cloud *n.* [singular] **the cloud** the internet used as something that provides software or space for storing information, rather than having it on your own computer

coach *v.* [T] to help someone find ways of improving their skills and abilities

collaboration *n.* [C, U] the activity of working together with another person, company, etc. in order to achieve something

collective *adj.* shared or made by every member of a group

come into place to start being used in an official way

come to light if new information comes to light, it becomes known

commitment *n.* [U] the hard work and loyalty that someone gives to an organisation or activity

commuting *n.* [U] the process of regularly travelling a long distance to get to work

company car *n.* [C] a car that your employer gives you while you work for them

compensation *n.* [U] money that someone is paid, especially when they have worked more hours than is usual, worked on something particularly difficult, etc.

competency *n.* [C, U] the fact of having enough skill or knowledge to do something to a satisfactory standard, or the skill and knowledge someone has

competent *adj.* having enough skill, knowledge or ability to do something to a satisfactory standard

competitive edge *n.* [singular] something that makes a person or business able to compete successfully against other people or businesses

competitiveness *n.* [U] the ability of a company, country or product to compete with others

completion *n.* [U] the act of finishing something

complex *adj.* consisting of many different parts and often difficult to understand

compulsory *adj.* something that is compulsory must be done because it is the law or because someone in authority orders you to

concept *n.* [C] **1** an idea for a product
2 an idea of how something is or should be done

concern *n.* [singular, U] a feeling that something or someone is important and that you want them to be happy

conduct *n.* [U] the way someone behaves, especially in public, in their job, etc.

confident *adj.* [not before noun] sure that something will happen in the way that you want or expect

confirmation *n.* [C, U] a statement, document, etc. that says that something is correct or true

connectivity *n.* [U] the ability of computers and other electronic equipment to connect with the internet or with other computers or programs

consensus *n.* [singular, U] agreement among a group of people

conservation *n.* [U] the protection of natural things such as animals, plants, forests, etc., to prevent them from being spoiled or destroyed

consider *v.* [I, T] to think about something carefully, especially before making a choice or decision

consistent *adj.* always behaving in the same way or having the same attitudes, standards, etc.—**consistently** *adv.*

constructive *adj.* useful and helpful, or likely to produce good results

consult *v.* [I, T] to discuss something with someone or ask for information, especially so that you can make a decision together

consultant *n.* [C] someone whose job is to give people or businesses advice or training in a particular area

consultative *adj.* [usually before noun] providing advice and suggesting solutions to problems

consulting firm *n.* [C] a company that gives advice and training in a particular area to people in other companies

consumption *n.* [U] the amount of energy, oil, electricity, etc. that is used

conversion *n.* [C, U] the number of sales that a website makes in relation to the number of people who look at the website

convert *v.* [I, T] to change or make something change from one thing to another

convince *n.* [T] to persuade someone to do something

cope *v.* [I] to succeed in dealing with a difficult problem or situation

corporate *adj.* [only before noun] belonging to or relating to a corporation

corporate culture *n.* [C, U] the way that people in a corporation think and behave

corruption *n.* [U] dishonest, illegal or immoral behaviour, especially by someone with power

cost-efficient *adj.* saving money by making a product or doing an activity in a better way

crash *n.* [C] an occasion on which the stocks and shares in a stock market suddenly lose a lot of value

credit crunch *n.* [C] a time when borrowing money becomes difficult because banks reduce the amount they lend and charge high interest rates

crisis *n.* (*plural* **crises**) [C] a situation in which there are a lot of problems that must be dealt with quickly so that the situation does not get worse or more dangerous

criteria *n.* [plural] the standards that you use to judge something or make a decision about something

criticism *n.* [C, U] remarks that say what you think is bad about someone or something

cross-functional *adj.* relating to doing different jobs or activities, or involving people from different areas of a company who do different jobs or activities

culture *n.* [C, U] the attitudes or beliefs that are shared and accepted by a particular group of people or in a particular organisation

data *n.* [plural, U] information or facts about a particular subject, especially in a form that can be stored and used on a computer
data dump *n.* [C] an act of copying information from one computer to another, especially a very large amount of information
data mining *n.* [U] the process of using a computer to examine large amounts of information, for example about customers, in order to find out information that is not easily noticed

deadline *n.* [C] a date or time by which you have to do or to complete something

decline *v.* [I] if sales, profits, production, etc. decline, they become less

define *v.* [T] to describe something correctly and thoroughly, and to say what standards, limits, qualities, etc. it has that make it different from other things

delegate *v.* [I, T] to give part of your power or work to someone else, usually someone in a lower position than you

demonstrate *v.* [T] to show that you have a particular ability, quality or feeling

demotivate *v.* [T] to make people less willing to do their job

depression *n.* [C, U] a long period during which there is very little business activity and many people do not have jobs

develop *v.* [I, T] to become stronger or more advanced, or to make someone or something do this

development *n.* [U] the teaching or learning of a range of skills that someone can use in many different positions and in their future careers

devil's advocate *n.* [C] someone who pretends to disagree with you in order to have a good discussion about something

digital *adj.* relating to computers or other devices that store or send information electronically in the form of numbers, usually ones and zeros
digital immigrant *n.* [C] someone who is not very good at using digital equipment such as computers or mobile phones, because they have only recently started using them
digital native *n.* [C] someone who is very good at using digital equipment such as computers and mobile phones because they have used them since they were young
digital nomad *n.* [C] someone who uses digital equipment such as computers and mobile phones to do their work or run their business from anywhere that has a connection to the internet

digitalise (*also* **digitalize**) *v.* [T] to change to using computers or other digital devices in order to do something

digital personal assistant *n.* [C] a small digital device, for example a smartphone, that you can speak to in order to ask it to do tasks

dimension *n.* [C] a part of a situation

disrupt *v.* [T] to start doing something in a new and more effective way that changes the way an industry does things

disruption *n.* [U] the process of beginning to do something in a new and more effective way that changes the way an industry does things

disruptive *adj.* **1** causing problems and preventing something from continuing in its usual way
2 changing the way an industry does things by doing something in a new and more effective way

disruptor *n.* [C] a person or company that changes the way an industry does things, by doing something in a new and effective way

distraction *n.* [C, U] something that stops you paying attention to what you are doing

distrust n. [U] a feeling that you cannot trust someone

diverse adj. very different from each other

diversity n. [U] the fact of including many different types of people or things

dividend n. [C] a part of a company's profit that is divided among the people with shares in the company

donate v. [I, T] to give something, especially money, to a person or an organisation in order to help them

downturn n. [C usually singular] a period in which business activity is reduced and conditions become worse

dress code n. [C] the way that you are expected to dress in a particular situation, especially as an employee of a particular company

drop¹ n. [singular] a fall in the amount, level or number of something, especially a large or sudden one

drop² v. [I] to fall to a lower level or amount, especially a much lower level or amount

earn v. [T] to do something or have qualities that make you deserve something

earnings n. [plural] the profit that a company makes in a particular period of time

ease v. [T] to make a process happen more easily

EBIT n. [C usually singular] the abbreviation for **earnings before interest and tax** – the amount of profit a company makes after its costs have been taken away but before any tax has been paid and before any money earned from interest payments has been added

eco-friendly adj. not harmful to the environment

effective adj. working well and producing the result or effect that was wanted or intended

effectiveness n. [U] the fact of working well and producing the result or effect that was wanted or intended

efficiency n. [U] the quality of doing something well and effectively, without wasting time, money or energy

efficient adj. working well without wasting time, money or energy

elaborate v. [I, T] to give more details or new information about something

embrace v. [T] to eagerly accept a new idea, opinion, way of doing something, etc.

emotional intelligence n. [U] the ability to understand and control your own emotions, and to understand and deal with other people in a caring way

empathy n. [U] the ability to understand other people's feelings and problems

employment n. [U] the condition of having a paid job

empower v. [T] to give someone more control over their own life or situation

enable v [T] to make it possible for someone to do something, or for something to happen

encourage v. [I, T] to persuade someone to do something

end of play n. [U] (abbreviation **EOP**) the end of the working day

engage v. [I, T] to communicate well with someone and involve them in a process or activity

ensure BrE, **insure** AmE v. [T] to make certain that something will happen properly

entrepreneurial adj. having the qualities that are needed to start a company and arrange business deals, such as the ability to take risks

equity n. [U] the money that a company has available to use that comes from shares rather than from loans

establish v. [T] to start a company, organisation, system, etc. that is intended to exist or continue for a long time

estimate v.[T] to try to judge the value, size, speed, cost, etc. of something, without calculating it exactly

ethical adj. **1** connected with principles of what is right and wrong **2** morally good or correct —**ethically** adv.

ethics n. [plural] moral rules or principles of behaviour for deciding what is right and wrong

evaluate v. [T] to carefully consider something to see how useful or valuable it is

excessive adj. much more than is reasonable or necessary

execute v. [T] to do something that has been carefully planned

executive n. [C] someone who has an important job as a manager in a company or business

executive summary n. [C] a short statement or piece of writing that gives the most important points of a business report or proposal

exhibit v. [T] to clearly show a particular quality, emotion or ability

expand on/upon phr. v. to add more details or information to something that you have already said, so that it is more complete

expectation n. [C usually plural] a feeling or belief about the way something should be or how someone should behave

expertise n. [U] special skills or knowledge in an area of work or study

extend v. [T] to make something include more people or things

external adj. coming from or happening outside a particular place or organisation (opposite **internal**)

face v. [T] to have a difficult problem or situation that you must deal with

facilitate v. [I, T] to make a discussion, meeting, etc. run well, so that everyone has a chance to speak and give their ideas and the group can make any decisions together

facilitation n. [U] the process of making a discussion, meeting, etc. run well, so that everyone has a chance to speak and give their ideas and the group can make any decisions together

facilitator n. [C] someone who makes a discussion, meeting, etc. run well, so that everyone has a chance to speak and give their ideas and the group can make any decisions together

fair adj. a fair situation, system, way of treating people, or judgment seems reasonable, acceptable, and right —**fairly** adv.

fairness n. [U] the quality of being fair

fair trade n. [U] the activity of making, buying and selling goods in a way that is morally right, for example by making sure that the people who grow or make a product have been paid a fair price for it

fast fashion n. [U] inexpensive clothes that are designed and made quickly and that are very fashionable, but that are not in shops for a long time

feedback n. [U] advice, criticism, etc. about how successful or useful something is

field n. [C] a subject that people study or are involved in as part of their work

financial institution n. [C] a business organisation that lends and borrows money, for example a bank

financial services n. [plural] the business activity of giving advice about investments and selling investments to people and organisations

flexibility n. [U] the ability to change or be changed easily to suit a different situation

flexible hours a situation in which an employer allows people to choose the times that they work so that they can do other things

follow v. [I, T] to understand something such as an explanation or story

forecast v. [T] to make a statement saying what is likely to happen in the future, based on information that is available now

form v. [T] to start an organisation, committee, government, etc.

forum n. [C] a web page where people can discuss something by writing and replying to messages

framework n. [C] a set of ideas, rules or beliefs from which something is developed, or on which decisions are based

freelance n. [C] someone who works independently for different companies rather than being employed by one particular company

fulfil (also **fulfill** AmE) v. [T] to do or provide what is necessary or needed

functional adj. relating to doing one job or activity, or relating to the people who do that job or activity

garment n. [C] a piece of clothing

gather v. [T] to get things or information from different places and put them together in one place

globalisation (also **globalization**) n. [U] the fact of companies doing business in many countries all around the world

go forward phr. v. [I] if something that is planned to happen goes forward, it starts to happen or starts to make progress

go over phr. v. [T] to repeat something, especially in order to explain it

go the extra mile to try a little harder in order to achieve something, after you have already used a lot of effort

goal n. [C] something that you hope to achieve in the future

gross adj. relating to a total amount before any tax or costs have been taken away (opposite **net**)

group n. [C] a large business organisation that consists of several companies that all have the same owner

guarantee n. [C] a formal promise that something will be done

hierarchy n. (plural **hierarchies**) [C, U] an organisation or structure in which the staff are organised in levels and the people at one level have authority over those below them

high-growth adj. relating to companies whose earnings are increasing much faster than the rate at which the economy is growing

highlight v. [T] to make a problem or subject easy to notice so that people pay attention to it

hit a problem/snag etc. to experience trouble, problems, etc.

housing market n. [C usually singular] the number and type of houses that are available in a particular area, how much they cost, etc.

humanoid adj. having a human shape and human qualities.

identify v. [T] to recognise something and understand its qualities

image n. [C] the general opinion that most people have of a person, organisation, product, etc.

impact n. [C] the effect or influence that an event, situation, etc. has on someone or something

implement v. [T] to take action or make changes that you have officially decided should happen

implementation *n.* [U] the process of taking action and making changes that you have officially decided should happen

incentive *n.* [C] something which is used to encourage people to do something, especially to make them work harder, produce more or spend more money

increase *n.* [C] a rise in amount, number or degree

induction *n.* [C, U] the introduction and training of someone into a new job

industry *n.* [C] businesses that produce a particular type of thing or provide a particular service

infrastructure *n.* [C, U] the basic systems and structures that a country or organisation needs in order to work properly, for example roads, railways, banks, etc.

initiative *n.* [C] **1** an important new plan or process, done to achieve a particular aim or to solve a particular problem
2 take the initiative to take responsibility for doing or controlling something, and make decisions without waiting for someone to tell you what to do

innovate *v.* [I] to design and develop new and original products

innovation *n.* [U] the introduction of new ideas or methods

innovative *adj.* an innovative idea or way of doing something is new, different, and better than those that existed before

insolvent *adj.* not having enough money to pay what you owe

insufficient *adj.* not enough, or not large enough

integrity *n.* [U] the quality of being honest and strong about what you believe to be right

interconnected *adj.* joined together either physically or electronically

interest rate *n.* [C] the amount charged by a bank, etc. when you borrow money, or paid to you by a bank when you keep money in an account there

internal *adj.* within a company or organisation, rather than outside it (*opposite* **external**)

internationalisation (*also* **internationalization**) *n.* [U] the process of making something international or bringing it under international control

interpersonal skills *n.* [C usually plural] the ability to communicate and work well with other people and understand their feelings and needs

intranet *n.* [C] a computer network used for exchanging or seeing information within a company

invest *v.* [I, T] to buy shares, property or goods because you hope that the value will increase and you can make a profit

investment *n.* [C] something that you buy, such as shares (=one of the equal parts a company's ownership is divided into), bonds (=official documents that say a government will pay you back more than the money you used to buy the document) or property (=land or buildings), in order to make a profit later

irregular *adj.* not happening or done at the normal time for doing something

irritation *n.* [C] something that makes you annoyed

issue *n.* [C] a subject or problem that is often discussed or argued about

junior *adj.* having a low or lower rank in an organisation or a profession

key *adj.* very important or necessary

kick off *phr. v.* [I, T] to start something such as a project, meeting or event

label *n.* [C] a company that makes something such as clothes, or music recordings

labour-intensive (*also* **labor-intensive** *AmE*) *adj.* needing a lot of workers in order to do or produce something

law-abiding *adj.* respectful of the law and obeying it

lending *n.* [U] the process or activity of allowing someone to borrow money from a bank or other financial institution

lengthy *adj.* (**lengthier**, **lengthiest**) continuing for a long time, often too long

limited partner *n.* [C] someone who invests in a new business but does not have control of the business, and is responsible for the business's debts only up to the amount they invested in it

line *n.* [C] a type of product that a company makes or sells, often with several different sizes, models, etc.

line manager *n.* [C] someone who is one level higher in rank than you in a company and is in charge of your work

loan *n.* [C] an amount of money that you borrow from a bank, financial institution, etc.

long-term *adj.* relating to a long period of time into the future (*opposite* **short-term**)

loss *n.* [C] the fact of no longer having something that you used to have, or the fact of a business having less money than it did before, especially because of spending more than it earns

loyalty *n.* [U] the quality of always supporting your friends, company, country, etc.

mainstream *adj.* accepted by or suitable for most ordinary people

make up ground to make progress towards becoming successful again after a period of having difficulties

make your mark to have an important or permanent effect on something

make your mind up/make up your mind to decide which of two or more choices you want, especially after thinking for a long time

manage *v.* [T] **1** to direct or control a business or department and the people, equipment, and money involved in it
2 to succeed in doing something difficult, especially after trying very hard
management *n.* [U] **1** the activity of controlling and organising the work that a company or organisation does
2 the people who are in charge of a company or organisation
3 the process of dealing with something difficult and controlling the effects that it has
change management *n.* [U] the process of organising and introducing new methods of working in a business or other organisation.
conflict management *n.* [U] the ability to deal with arguments or disagreements in a sensible, fair way
time management *n.* [U] the activity or skill of controlling the way you spend your time in order to work as effectively as possible
waste management *n.* [U] the activity of controlling or organising how a company or area gets rid of unwanted materials or substances

margin (*also* **profit margin**) *n.* [C, U] the amount of profit a business makes when selling something, after taking away what it costs to produce it

market *n.* [C] **1** a particular country, area or group of people to which a company sells or hopes to sell its goods or services
2 the business of buying and selling shares, the place where this is done, or the companies that are involved in it (=**stock market**)
market research *n.* [U] a business activity that involves collecting information about what goods people in a particular area buy, why they buy them, etc.
market share *n.* [C, U] the percentage of sales in a particular market that a company or product has

maximise (*also* **maximize**) *v.* [T] to increase something or use it in a way that gives you the best value or result (*opposite* **minimise**)

measure *v.* [T] to judge the importance, value, or true nature of something

menial *adj.* menial work needs little skill and is usually badly paid

mentee *n.* [C] someone who is getting help and advice from a mentor, to help them in their work

mentor¹ *n.* [C] an experienced person who gives advice to less experienced people to help them in their work.

mentor² *v.* [T] to be someone's mentor

mentoring *n.* [U] a process in which people with a lot of experience give advice and help other people at work, or young people preparing for work

merge *v.* [I, T] if two or more companies, organisations, etc. merge, or if they are merged, they join together

millennial *n.* [C] someone who was born in the 1980s or 1990s and became an adult during or after the year 2000

minimise (*also* **minimize**) *v.* [T] to make something seem less important or difficult (*opposite* **maximise**)

minimum *adj.* the smallest or least that is possible, allowed or needed

minimum wage *n.* [singular] the lowest amount of money that an employer can legally pay to a worker

mixed *adj.* having some good and some bad parts or features

moral *adj.* relating to ideas about what is right and wrong behaviour

morale *n.* [U] the level of confidence and positive feelings among a group of people who work together

motivate *v.* [T] to encourage someone and make them want to work hard

motivated *adj.* eager to do something or achieve something, especially because you find it interesting or exciting

motivation *n.* [U] eagerness and willingness to do something without needing to be told or forced to do it

movement *n.* [C] a group of people who share the same ideas or beliefs and who work together to achieve a particular aim

mutually *adv.* relating to feelings or help that two people give each other

needs analysis *n.* [C] the process of finding out what a person or group needs to learn or know in order to improve their skills, knowledge, etc.

negative *n.* [C] something bad or harmful (*opposite* **positive**)

negotiate *v.* [I, T] to discuss something in order to reach an agreement

negotiation *n.* [C usually plural, U] official discussions between groups who are trying to reach an agreement

net *adj.* a net amount of money is one that remains after things such as costs and tax have been taken away

objective *n.* [C] something that you are trying to achieve

obstacle *n.* [C] something that makes it difficult to achieve something

online training *n.* [U] the process of using computers and the internet to teach the skills or knowledge needed for a particular job

on-the-job *adj.* while working, or at work

open *adj.* willing to consider something new or to accept something new

openness *n.* [U] the quality of being honest and willing to talk about things and accept new ideas and people

open-plan *adj.* an open-plan office, school, etc. does not have walls dividing it into separate rooms

operating cost *n.* [C usually plural] a cost involved in the general running of a business or organisation

opportunity *n.* [C, U] a chance to do something, especially something interesting or something that will improve your situation

optimistic *adj.* believing that good things will happen in the future (*opposite* **pessimistic**)

option *n.* [C] a choice you can make in a particular situation

organic *adj.* relating to methods of growing plants without using artificial chemicals, or produced or grown by these methods

organisational behaviour (*also* **organizational behavior** *AmE*) *n.* [C, U] the way in which the people in an organisation work together, and how this affects the organisation as a whole

outside the scope of something to not be included in the range of things that a subject, activity, book, etc. deals with

overloaded *adj.* having more work, information, etc. than you can deal with

oversee *v.* (*past tense* **oversaw**, *past participle* **overseen**) [T] to be in charge of a group of workers and check that a piece of work is done satisfactorily

oversight *n.* [C, U] a mistake in which you forget something or do not notice something

overtime *n.* [U] time that you spend working in your job in addition to your normal working hours

overview *n.* [C] a short description of a subject or situation that gives the main ideas without explaining all the details

overwhelmed *adj.* having too much work and feeling like it is too difficult to deal with it

paraphrase *v.* [T] to express in a shorter, clearer or different way what someone has said or written

partnership *n.* [C, U] a relationship between two people, organisations or countries that work together, or the situation of working together
  joint partnership *n.* [U] a business relationship in which two companies or organisations work together on a particular project and share the costs and profits

partner up *phr. v.* [I] to work with someone on a business project

passion *n.* [C] a very strong liking for something

pay *n.* [U] money that you are given for doing your job
  pay rate *n.* [C] a payment for a job that is set according to a standard scale
  pay rise (*also* **pay raise** *AmE*) *n.* [C] an increase in the amount of money you are paid for doing your job
  pay structure *n.* [C] the way in which different amounts of pay are connected with different jobs and levels of responsibility

performance *n.* [U] the way that someone does their job, and how well they do it
  performance-related pay *n.* [U] money that you earn for your work, which is increased if you do your work very well
  performance review *n.* [C] a meeting between a manager and a worker to discuss the quality of someone's work and how well they do their job (=**appraisal**).

personalisation (*also* **personalization**) *n.* [U] the process of designing or changing something so that it is suitable for a particular person —**personalised** *adj.*

personalise (*also* **personalize**) *v.* [T] to design or change something so that it is suitable for a particular person

perspective *n.* [C] a way of thinking about something, especially one which is influenced by the type of person you are or by your experiences

persuade *v.* [T] to make someone decide to do something, believe something or feel sure about something

pessimistic *adj.* expecting that bad things will happen in the future or that something will have a bad result (*opposite* **optimistic**)

petition *n.* [C] a written request signed by a lot of people, asking someone in authority to do something or change something

pick up on *phr. v.* to return to a point or an idea that has been mentioned and discuss it more

picture *n.* [C] the general situation in a place, organisation, etc.
  the big picture the general situation, considered as a whole

piece rate *n.* [C] an amount of money that is paid for each item a worker produces, rather than for the time taken to make it

platform *n.* [C] a particular type of computer system or software that can be used to create applications

policy *n.* [C] a course of action that has been officially agreed and chosen by a political party, business or other organisation

position *n.* [C] *formal* a job

positive *n.* [C] a quality or feature that is good or useful (*opposite* **negative**).

postpone *v.* [T] to change the date or time of a planned event or action to a later one

potential *adj.* likely to develop into a particular type of person or thing in the future

practice *n.* [C] something that people do often, especially a particular way of doing something

predict *v.* [T] to say what you think will happen

prediction *n.* [C, U] a statement about what you think is going to happen, or the act of making this statement

predictive *adj.* relating to a system's ability to use information to say what is likely to happen next

present *v.* [T] to show or describe someone or something

presentation *n.* [C, U] an event at which you describe or explain a new product or idea, or the way in which you show or explain something

press release *n.* [C] an official statement giving information to the newspapers, radio or television

prioritise (*also* **prioritize**) *v.* [I, T] to put several tasks, problems, etc. in order of importance, so that the most important ones are done first

priority *n.* [C] the thing that is more important than anything else, and that needs attention first
  high priority important and needing to be done or dealt with quickly
  low priority not important and not needing to be done or dealt with quickly
  top priority the thing that you think is most important

proactive *adj.* making things happen or change

problematic *adj.* involving problems and difficult to deal with

process *n.* [C] a series of actions taken to perform a particular task or achieve a particular result

productivity *n.* [U] the rate at which goods are produced, and the amount produced in relation to the work, time and money needed to produce them

profile *n.* [C] **1** a short description of someone or something, giving the most important details about them
  2 raise/increase your profile if a person or an organisation raises their profile, they get more attention from people

profit *n.* [C, U] money that you gain from selling something, or from doing business in a particular period of time, after taking away costs

profitability *n.* [U] the amount of profit a company makes

promote *v.* [T] **1** to give someone a better-paid, more responsible job in a company or organisation
  2 to try hard to sell a product or service, especially by advertising it widely, reducing its price, etc.

promotion *n.* [C, U] **1** the fact of getting a better paid and more responsible job or position in a company or organisation
  2 an activity such as special advertisements or free gifts intended to sell a product or service

proposal *n.* [C, U] a plan or idea which is suggested formally to an official person, or the process of suggesting a plan or idea

propose *v.* [T] to suggest something such as a plan or course of action

public *n.* [singular] **the public** ordinary people who do not work for the government or have any special position in society

publicity *n.* [U] the attention that someone or something gets from newspapers, television, etc.

put something ⟷ **off** *phr. v.* to delay doing something or to arrange to do something at a later time or date, especially because there is a problem or you do not want to do it now

qualification *n.* [C usually plural] an examination that you have passed at school, university or in your profession

quarter *n.* [C] a period of three months

questionable *adj.* not likely to be good, honest or true

rapport *n.* [singular, U] friendly agreement, communication and understanding between people

real economy *n.* [U] **the real economy** the part of the economy that is concerned with actually producing goods and services, as opposed to the part of the economy that is concerned with buying and selling on the financial markets

real time *n.* [U] a system in which a computer deals with information as it receives it, and is able to use this information to change how it is doing a task

re-assess, reassess *v.* [T] to think about something again carefully in order to decide whether to change your opinion or judgment about it

recap *v.* [I, T] to repeat the main points of has just been said

recede *v.* [I] if prices, interest rates, etc. recede, they decrease

recession *n.* [C, U] a difficult time when there is less trade, business activity, etc. in a country than usual

recognise (also **recognize**) v. [T] **1** to say publicly that someone has done a good job or achieved something good
2 to notice something and know what it is or what it means

recognition n. [singular, U] public respect and thanks for someone's work or achievements

recommend v. [T] to advise someone to do something, especially because you have special knowledge of a situation or subject

recover v. **1** [I] to return to a normal condition after a period of trouble or difficulty
2 [T] to get back money that you have spent or lost

recovery n. (plural **recoveries**) [C, U] when prices, sales, etc. increase or the economy grows again after a difficult period of time

recruit n. [C] someone who has recently joined a company or organisation

recruitment n. [U] the process or the business of finding new people to work for your company

redundancy n. (plural **redundancies**) [C, U] BrE a situation in which someone has to leave their job, because they are no longer needed (=**lay-off** AmE)

redundant adj. BrE if you are redundant, your employer no longer has a job for you (=**laid off** AmE)

re-entry n. [C, U] the act of starting to be involved in something again

refine v. [T] to improve a method, plan, system, etc. by gradually making slight changes to it

reflect v. [I, T] to think carefully about something that has happened, or to say something that you have been thinking about

regret v. [T not in progressive] to feel sorry and sad that something bad has happened, especially when you caused the problem

reinvent v. **reinvent yourself** to do something differently from before, especially in order to improve or change your career

relocate v. [I, T] if a company or worker relocates or is relocated, they move to a different place

relocation n. [U] the process of moving to a different place for your job, or of a company moving to a different place

rely on phr. v. [T] to trust or depend on someone or something, especially to do what you need

remotely adv. from far away

reputation n. [C] the opinion that people have about someone or something because of what has happened in the past

request v. [T] to ask for something in a polite or formal way

resist v. [T] to refuse to accept or agree to a change or to something someone wants you to do

resistance n. [singular, U] a refusal to accept or agree to something

resources n. [C usually plural] something such as money, property, skill, labour, etc. that a company has available

respect n. [U] the belief that something or someone is important and should not be harmed, treated rudely, etc.

responsible adj. able to be trusted, because you accept you have a duty to look after something or someone and behave in a moral way
socially responsible adj. behaving in a moral way towards society, for example by being fair, taking care of the environment, being involved in your community, etc.

responsive adj. ready to react in a useful or helpful way to problems, complaints, market changes, etc.

restructure v. [I, T] if a company restructures, or someone restructures it, it changes the way it is organised or financed

retain v. [T] if a company retains workers, the workers stay with the company rather than taking jobs with other employers

retention n. [U] when workers stay with a company rather than taking a job with another employer

retire v. [I] to stop working, usually because you have reached a certain age

retirement n. [C, U] when you stop working, usually because of your age

return (also **return on investment**, abbreviation **ROI**) n. [singular, U] the amount of profit that a company gets from something in a particular period of time, in relation to the amount it has invested in it

revenue (also **revenues** plural) n. [C] money that a business or organisation receives over a period of time, especially from selling goods or services

review¹ v. [T] to examine a situation or process carefully in order to see if changes are needed or if it can be improved

review² n. [C, U] a careful examination of a situation or process, especially to see if it can be improved

revise v. [T] to change something by adding new information, making improvements or correcting mistakes

reward¹ n. [C] something that you receive because you have done something good or helpful

reward² v. [T] to give someone something, such as money, because they have done something good or helpful

reward system n. [C] a system in which employees receive extra money or other advantages from their employer, especially for achieving particular results

rewarding adj. making you feel happy and satisfied because you feel you are doing something useful or important

rise through the ranks to make progress in your job, moving from a low position to a high position with more responsibility

risk n. [C, U] the possibility that something may be lost, harmed or damaged, or that something bad, unpleasant or dangerous may happen
risk assessment n. [C] an examination of the possible risks involved in doing something, so that organisations can decide whether something is worth doing and how they can reduce the risks

role n. [C] the way in which someone or something is involved in an activity or situation, and how much influence they have on it

room n. **there is room for improvement** used to say that something is not perfect and can be improved

routine n. [C, U] the usual order in which you do things, or the things you regularly do

sabbatical n. [C] a period of time when someone takes an agreed break from their work in order to study or travel

salary n. (plural **salaries**) [C] money that you receive as payment from the organization you work for, usually paid to you every month

savings n. [plural] all the money that you have saved, especially in a bank or financial institution

schedule n. [C] a plan of what someone is going to do and when they are going to do it
behind schedule when events are happening later than the time that was planned

scheme n. [C] an official plan or system for doing something or providing something (=**program** AmE)

sector n. [C] all the organisations or companies in a particular area of activity, industry, etc.

seminar n. [C] a class on a particular subject, usually given as a form of training and often a few hours or days long

senior adj. having a high position in an organisation, company, etc.

session n. [C] a period of time used for a particular activity, especially by a group of people

set v. [T] to decide that something should happen or be achieved

setback n. [C] a problem that delays or prevents progress, or makes things worse than they were

settle v. [I] to feel comfortable, calm and relaxed in a new situation, place, job, etc.

severity n. [U] the quality of being very bad or very serious

shadow v. [T] to watch someone very closely or work with them in order to learn how they do their job

shame n. [U] the feeling you have when you feel guilty and embarrassed because you, or someone who is close to you, have done something wrong

share n. [C] one of the equal parts into which the ownership of a company is divided

shareholder n. [C] someone who owns shares in a company or business

short-term adj. continuing for only a short time, or concerned only with the period of time that is not very far into the future (opposite **long-term**)

significant adj. large enough to be noticeable or have noticeable effects

six-figure adj. [only before noun] used to describe a number that is 100,000 or more, especially an amount of money

skill n. [C] an ability to do something well, especially because you have learned and practised it
skills set n. [C] all the different skills that are needed to do a particular job
soft skill n. [C usually plural] an ability to get along with and talk to other people, understand and deal with your own emotions and tasks, and behave properly in many different situations

slowdown n. [C usually singular] a time when there is less activity

social integration n. [U] the process of including people from different countries, races, religions, abilities, etc. into a group, organisation or society so that everyone feels that they belong there

source v. [T] if a company sources materials, parts, etc. from a particular place, it gets them from there

specialised (also **specialized**) adj. designed or trained for a particular purpose or type of work

specialist n. [C] a person or business that has a lot of skill or knowledge in a particular subject

spidergram n. [C] a way of organising information, in which you put the subject in the middle and draw lines to other information about the subject (=**spider diagram**)

stable adj. not likely to move or change

stakeholder n. [C] someone who has good reasons to be interested in a company, organisation or society and what it does or what happens to it, often someone who has invested money in it

standard *n.* [C] a size, shape, quality, etc. that is usual or accepted, and that can be used to measure or judge something similar

status *n.* [U] your social or professional rank or position, considered in relation to other people

steady *adj.* (**steadier**, **steadiest**) continuing or developing gradually or without stopping

stock market *n.* [singular] the business of buying and selling shares, the place where this is done or the companies that are involved in it

straight answer *n.* [C] an answer that is honest and direct and does not hide any facts

strategy *n.* [C] a plan or series of plans for achieving an aim

stressful *adj.* a job, experience or situation that is stressful makes you worry a lot

structure¹ *n.* [C] the way in which the parts of something are connected with each other and form a whole

structure² *v.* [T] to arrange or organise the different parts of something into a useful order

structured *adj.* carefully organised, planned or arranged

style *n.* [C] the particular way that someone does something or deals with other people

subsidised (*also* **subsidized**) *adj.* if an activity, food, housing, etc. is subsidised, the government or an organisation has paid for part of the costs so that people do not have to pay as much

sufficient *adj.* as much as is needed for a particular purpose

sum (something ↔) **up** *phr. v.* [I, T] to use only a few words to describe something or give the main information from a report, speech, etc.

summarise (*also* **summarize**) *v.* [I, T] to write or say a short statement giving only the main information and not the details of a plan, event, report, etc.

summary *n.* (*plural* **summaries**) [C] a short statement or piece of writing that gives the main information about something, without giving all the details

supplier *n.* [C] a company that provides a particular type of product

supply chain *n.* [C] the series of companies that are involved in making parts of a product and getting the product from the manufacturers to the public

support *n.* [U] approval, encouragement and often help for a person, idea, plan, etc.

sustainability *n.* [U] the ability to continue doing something or making something without causing damage to the environment

sweatshop *n.* [C] a small business, factory, etc. where people work hard in bad conditions for very little money—used to show disapproval

symptom *n.* [C] a sign that a serious problem exists

system *n.* [C] an arrangement or organisation of ideas, methods or ways of working

takeover *n.* [C] the act of getting control of a company by buying over 50 percent of its shares

take something on board to listen to and accept a suggestion, idea, etc.

talented *adj.* having a natural ability to do something well

target¹ *n.* [C] a result such as a total, an amount or a time which you aim to achieve

target² *adj.* **target market/audience** the group of people that a product, service, idea, etc. is aimed at

team-building *n.* [U] the process of getting employees to work together well and communicate effectively

team up *phr. v.* [I] to join with someone in order to work on something

tension *n.* [U] the feeling that exists when people do not trust each other and may suddenly start arguing

think out loud to say what you are thinking, without talking to anyone in particular and sometimes in order to give an idea that is not fully developed

time *n.*
  ahead of time done earlier than the time when something should be done
  by the time after something else has already happened
  in time done or finished before the time when something must be done or finished
  make time for something to plan so that you have time available for something
  out of time not having any more time available for something
  spend time to use time doing a particular thing, or pass time in a particular place
  time is money used to say that wasting time or delaying something costs money

timeline *n.* [C] a plan for when things will happen

to-do list *n.* [C] a list of all the tasks you need to do

tool *n.* [C] a piece of software, a piece of equipment, a device or a skill that you use to do a particular task

track *n.* **on track** continuing to work in a way that makes you likely to achieve the result you want

trade fair *n.* [C] a large event when several companies show their goods or services in one place, to try to sell them

trainer *n.* [C] someone whose job is to teach people skills for a particular job or activity

training *n.* [U] the process of teaching or being taught the skills for a particular job or activity

transformation *n.* [C, U] a complete change in someone or something

transition *n.* [C, U] the act or process of changing from one state or form to another

transparency *n.* [U] the quality of doing things in a way that is easily understood or can easily be seen

transparent *adj.* doing things in a way that is easily understood or seen

transport *v.* [T] to take goods, people, etc. from one place to another in a vehicle

triple bottom line *n.* [singular] a way of examining or measuring how a company's actions have affected its profits, the people who work for it or live in the area, and the environment

troubleshoot *v.* [I, T] to examine problems and find ways to solve them

trust¹ *n.* [U] a strong belief in the honesty, goodness, etc. of someone or something

trust² *v.* [T] to believe that someone is honest or will not do anything bad or wrong

trustworthiness *n.* [C] the quality of being honest and being able to be trusted or depended on

turn (something) ↔ **around** *phr. v.* [I, T] to do something in order to be successful again after a period of being unsuccessful, or to begin to be successful again

turnover *n.* [singular] the rate at which workers leave an organisation and are replaced by others

underestimate *v.* [I, T] to think or guess that something is smaller, cheaper, easier, etc. than it really is

under pressure having a lot of things that must be done

unethical *adj.* morally wrong

unforeseen *adj.* not expected to happen and not planned for

union *n.* [C] an organisation formed by workers to protect their rights

urgency *n.* [U] the quality of being very important and needing to be dealt with immediately

urgent *adj.* very important and needing to be dealt with immediately

valid *adj.* accepted as reasonable, sensible or useful

value¹ *n.* [C often plural] a principle that a business or organisation thinks is important and which it tries to follow

value² *v.* [T] to think that someone or something is important

venture capital *n.* [U] money lent to someone so that they can start a new business

vintage *adj.* old, but high quality

viral *adj.* **go viral** if a picture, video, joke, etc. goes viral, many people see it and share it on social media

virtual reality *n.* [U] images produced by a computer that give you the experience of seeing or being inside a real place or physical object

vision *n.* [C] an idea of what you think something should be like

visualisation (*also* **visualization**) *n.* [U] the practice of using pictures, tables, graphs, etc. to show data, so that it is easier to understand

visualise (*also* **visualize**) *v.* [T] to use pictures, tables, graphs, etc. to show data, so that it is easier to understand

voice recognition *n.* [U] a system in which a computer understands and obeys instructions spoken by a person

volume *n.* [C, U] the total amount of something

volunteer *n.* [C] someone who does a job willingly without being paid

water *n.* **be in deep water** to be in trouble or in a difficult or serious situation

wavelength *n.* **be on the same/a different wavelength** to have the same or different ideas, opinions and feelings as someone else

webinar *n.* [C] a lesson or training that is done using the internet, so that people in different places can all take part using their computers

weigh something ↔ **up** *phr. v.* to consider something carefully so that you can make a decision about it

wiki *n.* [C, U] a website with information that users can change or add things to

workforce *n.* [singular] all the people who work in a particular country, industry or factory.

work-life balance *n.* [U] a situation in which you are able to give the right amount of time and effort to your work and to your personal life outside work, for example to your family or to other interests

workload *n.* [C] the amount of work that a person or organisation has to do

workshop *n.* [C] a meeting at which people discuss a subject and do practical exercises, especially in order to find solutions to problems

work your way up to work hard and make progress in your job, moving from a low position to a high position with more responsibility

yield *v.* [T] to produce profits